CLUBS AND ASSOCIATIONS

An Industry Accounting and
Auditing Guide

CLUBS AND ASSOCIATIONS

An Industry Accounting and Auditing Guide

Valerie Steward BSc, ACA

Accountancy Books
Gloucester House
399 Silbury Boulevard
Central Milton Keynes
MK9 2HL
Tel: 01908 248000

ISBN 1 85355 653 X

SAS 410 *Analytical Procedures* is reproduced with permission of the Auditing Practices Board.

British Library Cataloguing-in-Publication Data.

A catalogue record for this book is available from the British Library.

Throughout this book the male pronoun has been used to cover references to both the male and female.

Typeset by J&L Composition Ltd, Filey, North Yorkshire
Printed in Great Britain by Bell & Bain, Glasgow

Contents

Contents

Preface

I have always had an interest in Industrial and Provident and Friendly Societies. This interest started even before I began my training as a chartered accountant, through my father who worked for the co-operative movement. When I started my training I worked for a practice which acted, almost exclusively, for these societies, thus my first exposure to the audit of working men's clubs. I was fascinated by these audits. The clubs and associations were full of personalities and the work was never boring. A little way into my training contract the practice I worked for was taken over by Thomson McLintock, but, because of my interest, every time an Industrial and Provident or Friendly Society audit came up I was the one who did it. This has continued throughout my career. I was, therefore, very pleased when I was asked to write this book. It has been an interesting experience and I hope that you, as a reader, will find it interesting and informative.

Although I always found these audits interesting they had a number of complications, particularly as they were cash businesses and were governed by different legislation, which although very similar to company legislation has its own peculiarities which can cause complications. Within this publication I have highlighted these differences as well as giving detailed information on the laws and regulations governing these bodies. I have paid particular attention to the new Deregulation Order which could have a significant impact on a number of these organisations, and have also provided background information on some of the more significant non-accounting laws and regulations which have a bearing on clubs and associations. Through my experience I have tried to highlight the best way to audit these organisations and have provided some tailored audit documentation which I trust accountants in practice will find useful.

I would like to thank my colleagues at SWAT for their help with the research and also for providing useful input into some of the chapters, particularly those relating to tax. I would also like to thank Howard Roe and Howard Thomas, partners in practices who deal with large working men's clubs, for their input, and the staff at the Registry of Friendly Societies for dealing with numerous queries, particularly when the Deregulation Order was still in draft form.

Valerie Steward
June 1996

Foreword

Clubs and associations have been with us for many years but have always been a specialised field. The majority are registered with the Registrar of Friendly Societies either under the Industrial and Provident Societies Acts or, less commonly now, the Friendly Societies Acts. There are subtle and important differences between them.

This book by Valerie Steward is a very welcome addition on the subject, and comes at an appropriate time in connection with audit exemption.

It is well laid out and deals in the necessary detail with the regulations already mentioned governing Industrial and Provident Societies and Friendly Societies. It is most important for the reader to appreciate the differences there are between them. The reader is also guided through the intricacies of accounts and accounting records together with comprehensive consideration of audit regulations. This is followed by necessary references to the various taxes and their impact.

Valerie Steward has had a long and practical experience with clubs and associations. Her book therefore reflects this and, whilst it necessarily has to deal in depth with legislation, it is also comprehensive on accountancy and other matters specifically relating to these bodies.

P. Howard Roe FCA
Partner, Broomfield & Alexander Chartered Accountants
President, South Wales District Society
August 1996

Chapter 1 – Types of clubs and associations

1.1 Definition

There is no precise legal definition to pigeonhole a club or association, as there is no legal obligation for them to incorporate.

A club or association can, however, be described as a group of persons joined to promote a common purpose or object.

1.2 Types of clubs and associations

Clubs and associations can take many forms and may be either registered or unregistered. In this context, 'registered' means incorporated as a limited company, or more usually as an Industrial and Provident or Friendly Society. The following is a summary of the most 'common' types.

1.3 Proprietary club

Some clubs are run as a commercial enterprise owned by the proprietor. These could be either incorporated or unincorporated businesses. Examples of these could be nightclubs or gaming clubs.

Clubs run as commercial enterprises, if incorporated, would have to register under the Companies Act 1985. They would be unable to meet the criteria for registration as an Industrial and Provident or Friendly Society.

Although the audit section of this publication may well be relevant to this type of operation, much of the rest of the book would not.

1.4 Members' clubs

Up until the late nineteenth century, members' clubs were really the province of the wealthy. Working men had nowhere to go to socialise with their peers, nor to read newspapers or books.

During the period of great social reform that occurred during the late nineteenth century, the Working Men's Club and Institute Union was formed. The movement was first formed to provide working men and their families with an alternative to the gin houses and the like that prevailed in most large cities. At the start of the movement, these clubs did not serve drinks, they merely provided a place where working men could go to meet with their peers. Over time, it became clear that many people enjoyed a drink whilst carrying on such social activities and thus the movement, as it stands today, was formed. From this start, the Working Men's Club and Institute Union has grown and there are a large number of these types of social clubs in both town and rural areas. Over time various other associations to which clubs could affiliate, such as the Royal British Legion and the Association of Conservative Clubs, have also been founded with slightly different objects. However, the Working Men's Club and Institute Union is still the dominant mover in the field.

Although many of these clubs are still called working men's clubs, they do hold appeal for all strata of the population. They provide entertainment and a social atmosphere which is not available elsewhere. Many of them have extensive facilities available to their members, such as games rooms, etc., and they provide regular entertainment in the form of live entertainment, bingo, etc. for members, their families and their guests.

Although a members' club does not need to be affiliated to the Working Men's Club and Institute Union or one of the other bodies, they do tend to be. There are many advantages of doing so, including the ability for the members to enter any other club that their club is affiliated to, without having to become a member.

Although such organisations may encourage clubs to register as an Industrial and Provident Society or Friendly Society, they will also receive unregistered bodies as members.

1.5 Unregistered members' club

The club would have to satisfy the rules of 'mutuality' to be exempt from tax (see **11.2**). It would need to be registered under the Licensing Act 1964 (see **4.2**) to be able to sell alcohol.

The club would need to produce its own sets of rules. It would not be recognised as a separate legal entity and, therefore, any liabilities incurred would be the responsibility of all the members in equal shares. Although the majority of clubs will be registered as Industrial and Provident or Friendly Societies, there are a significant minority who are not; these may include trades or works clubs, sports clubs, political clubs, etc. Many of these clubs have not seen the need to incorporate in the past due to the level of their activities, i.e., they are too small. Many will not incorporate until they inherit or purchase property. In addition, many clubs are very proud of their history and some fairly large operations may remain as private members' clubs in spite of their size, as they do not wish to change.

Accountants dealing with this type of club or association may need to undertake an audit if the rules require, although such an audit, even if it must be undertaken by a registered auditor, would not be governed by the new audit regulations.

The accountant also needs to ensure that the members of the club or association are aware of their obligations in the event of a winding-up. The accountant should advise the client if, and when, it would be more appropriate for them to incorporate. The ongoing costs of incorporation are not as significant now due to audit deregulation (see **2.25** and **3.17**).

1.6 Registered members' clubs

Up until the introduction of the Friendly Societies Act 1992, clubs which wished to incorporate could do so as Industrial and Provident or Friendly Societies. Since the Friendly Societies Act 1992 they have only been able to register as Industrial and Provident Societies.

Prior to this change it was still fair to say that the majority of registered clubs were Industrial and Provident Societies. However, many of the older clubs will have been registered as Friendly Societies and were reluctant to re-register as Industrial and Provident Societies (see **1.14**).

In the context of the remainder of this chapter, the term 'registered' has been used to describe a society incorporated under the Industrial and Provident Societies Act 1965 or the Friendly Societies Act 1974.

Clubs registered as Industrial and Provident or Friendly Societies will have to deal with the Registrar of Friendly Societies, the equivalent of the Registrar of Companies. The Registry of Friendly Societies is the equivalent of Companies House.

1.7 Clubs registered/incorporated under the Industrial and Provident Societies Act 1965

The vast majority of registered clubs, apart from those being run strictly as a commercial enterprise, will be registered under this Act. The registration process is relatively straightforward and is set out below.

A society can register under the Act if it meets the following requirements:

(a) it is a society for carrying on an industry, business or trade; and
(b) it satisfies the Registrar of Friendly Societies that either:
    (i) it is a bona fide co-operative society (see **1.8**); or
    (ii) in view of the fact that its business is being, or is intended to be, conducted for the benefit of the community, there are special reasons why it should be registered under the Act, rather than as a company under the Companies Act (see **1.9**).

The Act goes on to describe what are bona fide co-operative societies and societies for the benefit of the community. These are defined below.

In the context of the legislation, the term 'society' is used to classify an organisation incorporated under the Act – akin to the term 'company' for an organisation incorporated under the Companies Act 1985. The term 'society' has been used along with 'club' and 'association' throughout this publication to describe a working men's club or similar body. However, it should also be noted that many of the provisions dealt with in Chapters **1–3** wil be equally relevant to all societies which are registered as Industrial and Provident or Friendly Societies.

1.8 Bona fide co-operative society

Although there is no statutory definition, such a society will normally be expected to satisfy the following conditions.

1.8.1 Conduct of business

The business of the society will be conducted for the mutual benefit of its members in such a way that the benefit which members obtain will, in the main, stem from their participation in its business. An example of this could be purchasing from or selling to the society, e.g., in the case of a farmers' co-operative. In addition, the members of a registered club benefit from cheaper alcohol, etc. as a result of their participation in the business. No one person or group of persons should derive benefit at the expense of other members.

1.8.2 Control

Under the rules of the society, the control will be invested in the members equally and not in accordance with their financial interest in the society, i.e., one member, one vote. This serves to protect, for example, the smaller farmer in a farmers' co-operative who will have an equal say in its running.

1.8.3 Interest on share and loan capital

The rules will state that the interest payable on share and loan capital will not exceed a rate necessary to obtain and retain the capital required to carry out the objects of the society, i.e., it must not exceed a normal commercial rate (often if interest is paid it will be lower).

1.8.4 Profits

Any profits made by the society after payment of interest on share capital, if these are distributed among the members, will in accordance with its rules be distributed in relation to the extent to which they have traded with or taken part in the business of the society. Where the profits are not distributed among the members, they should be ploughed back into the society to cheapen and improve the amenities available to members. A farmers' co-operative may distribute profits by paying a dividend on the basis that the biggest member is paid the highest amount. In comparison, a working men's club will use its profit to improve the facilities available to its members and to decrease the cost of drinks, or for some charitable purpose allowed by the rules. This provision also serves to protect. Hence, all members will have an equal say in the running of the society but those who put the most in will derive the greatest financial benefit.

1.8.5 Restriction on membership

There should be no artificial restriction on membership with the object of increasing the value of proprietary rights and interest. Therefore, although it would be acceptable to stipulate that only farmers could join a farmers' co-operative, any further restriction may be difficult to justify.

1.9 Societies for the benefit of the community

To qualify for registration under the Industrial and Provident Societies Act 1965, other than as a bona fide co-operative society, a society must satisfy two principal conditions:

(a) that its business will be conducted for the benefit of the community; and
(b) that there are special reasons why it should be registered under the Act, rather than as a company under the Companies Act.

For a society to claim that it will be conducted for the benefit of the community, the society must be able to show that it will benefit persons other than its own members and that its business will be in the interest of the community. An example of a society which will qualify for registration in this category would be a housing association.

1.10 Other conditions of registration

When registering either as a co-operative or otherwise, the society must also meet a number of conditions.

Unless the society consists of two or more registered societies, it must have at least three members – until the Deregulation Order came into force a society was required to have seven members.

The proposed name of the society must, in the opinion of the Registrar, not be undesirable. The Registrar of Friendly Societies may refuse to register a society which is proposing a name which is obscene, misleading and/or offensive.

The rules of the society must contain all the matters required by Schedule I of the Industrial and Provident Societies Act 1965. These are described in detail below.

1.10.1 The name of the society

Most clubs and associations will have a name which is associated to their geographical location. The rules will also usually contain a section on the use of the name. It will stipulate that the registered name of the club needs to be painted or attached in some form to the outside of the registered office or any other place of business of the club. This notice should be in a conspicuous place and be in easily readable letters. The name should also be printed legibly on a club seal and printed on any business letters, notices, advertisements or any other official documents of the club.

1.10.2 The objects of the society

The objects of the society are similar to those of a company contained in its memorandum and articles of association. Most clubs will have objects which state that they have been set up to carry on business as a social club by creating an environment which enables social activity, encourages mutual helpfulness, mental and moral improvement, recreation and other advantages. In addition, where a club is also affiliated to a charity such as the Royal British Legion or one of the political parties their object clause may contain specific objects relating to this. Guidance on this would be given by the relevant organisation.

1.10.3 The registered office of the society

The situation of the registered office, to which all communications and notices of the society should be addressed, will be given in the rules. It will generally be a place of business of the club or association, i.e., the club premises. The rules will normally contain, additionally, a statement with regard to any change in the situation of the registered office. This will stipulate that notice of any change needs to be sent to the Registrar of Friendly Societies within 14 days of its occurrence.

1.10.4 Terms of admission of members

The terms of admission of members must be included. These should include details of the terms relating to any society or company investing funds in the society under the provisions of the Act. Although statute allows members to join at 16, working men's clubs will usually have a requirement that an individual must attain at least 18 years of age to be able to apply for membership. Most clubs will have an application form which must be signed by prospective members and they will generally be required to have the form signed by at least two existing members of the club. This application form would then need to be submitted along with payment for one share (which should be returnable if membership was denied) for consideration by the club. Generally the form will be posted in a prominent position within the club for a number of days (this will usually be somewhere between two and seven days) for consideration by existing club members. However, although the views of existing members will be taken into consideration, the rules will stipulate that the ultimate decision to admit an individual to membership will lie with the committee.

On admission to membership each new member will be provided with a copy of the rules for a nominal charge, which by statute must not exceed 10 pence. There was a recent proposal to increase this statutory maximum, but it was decided that no increase should be allowed as it would be punitive to the members of the club. The rules will have a provision with regard to the payment of subscriptions and joining fees and potentially allowing for different categories of membership.

Where the club is affiliated to one of the promoting bodies (see **1.15**), it may well have a provision within its rules regarding the admission of associate members onto the club's premises (associate members being members of other clubs which are affiliated to the same promoting body).

The rules will also contain a provision with regard to the register of members stipulating that such a register will be kept by the secretary of the club at the registered office. This register should contain details of the names and addresses of all the members along with a statement of the number of shares they hold, any other property in the club held by each member, the date at which the person became a member and, where appropriate, ceased to be a member, and the names and addresses of all the officers of the club together with the offices held and the dates on which they assumed office.

The rules will stipulate that this register should be maintained in such a way that the details, excluding the details of the shares and other property held, should be available for inspection by all members.

As well as giving details of admission to membership, the rules will also give details of cessation of membership. Not only will this cover resignation of members but also other circumstances such as misconduct where members have been excluded from the club.

1.10.5 Meetings

The rules must contain details of the mode of holding meetings, the scale and right of voting and the mode of making, altering or rescinding rules.

The rules relating to meetings will deal with aspects including the type of meeting to be held, the notice to be given and the quorum. General provisions that may be included are as follows:

Holding an annual general meeting at a specific time each year
The order of business and notice of this meeting should be posted in the club at least 14 days before the meeting is held. Members normally have a right to add additional items to the agenda but would generally have to do this in writing within a certain amount of time before the meeting is due to be held. During the annual/ordinary meeting the accounts will be received and approved. The auditor or independent accountant will have the right to be notified of, attend and be heard at the meeting.

Special meeting
A special meeting can be called in a number of circumstances, usually either at the direction of the committee or at the request of a certain proportion of the members of the society. For the members to call a special meeting, normally one-fifth of the total number of members entitled to attend and vote at a meeting or 30 members, whichever is

the least, will have to elect to have such a meeting. Where such a special meeting is requested by the members then this must take place within a certain time period from the officers receiving notice of the meeting.

Notice of any special meeting will need to be posted within the club and the time period for such notice will be stipulated in the rules.

Quorum
The issue of what is quorum will differ from rules to rules. However, they will always stipulate that where a quorum is not achieved the meeting should be dissolved. If the meeting is convened by order of the members, it will not be reconvened. However, if the meeting is a special or general/ annual meeting convened by order of the committee then the meeting will be held again one week later. If quorum is still not achieved at this meeting it should still go ahead and resolutions can be passed even though no quorum has been achieved. The rules will stipulate that everyone present at the meeting being entitled to vote shall have one vote.

1.10.6 The committee

The rules must contain provisions relating to the appointment and removal of a committee of management, and of managers and other officers and their respective powers and remuneration.

Make-up and duties of committees
Rules of the club or association will generally have some specific guidance on the make-up of the committee of management and the responsibilities of the officers. They will also contain specific provisions in relation to the nomination and election of members of the committee. The rules may also stipulate that the club should set up one or more sub-committees to deal with specific aspects of the management of the club. In particular they are likely to have a rule stipulating that a finance sub-committee should be set up to deal with specific aspects of running the club.

The rules would normally require the club to have a management committee consisting of a president, vice president, chairman, treasurer and a number of committee members. The treasurer and secretary of the club would normally be appointed by the committee, although the secretary may be elected in general meeting, and his election may be for a fixed term.

The committee will be responsible for controlling the management of the club and will have the exclusive power to appoint and dismiss a steward and other members of staff. The rules will generally stipulate that neither the steward nor any other member of staff may be a member of the club, and if someone is appointed who is already a member of the club then they should be asked to resign as a member of the club. The rules will also give the committee the power to make purchases on behalf of the club and to make any decisions in order to run the club in accordance with its objectives. The committee will not be able to act outside of the objects of the club. In addition, no committee member will be able to carry out business on his own behalf with the club or alternatively receive any remuneration from the club without being authorised by a general meeting.

The committee with which the accountant will have the most involvement will be the finance committee. It is the finance committee's responsibility to ensure that the financial aspects of the club are dealt with properly. It has a responsibility to monitor the performance of the club, to arrange for stocktaking, to check all bills to ensure that they are correct, to report to the full committee on the performance of the club, to see that vouchers are produced by the secretary or treasurer for all payments made by him, to ensure that all cash records have been made up and that an adequate reconciliation has been made to the bank and to present up-to-date records to the full committee on a regular basis. The proceedings of this committee need to be recorded in a minute book.

Election of officers
In order for somebody to be eligible for election as a member of a committee most rules will require them to have been a member of the club or association for a specific period of time first. Any person eligible who wants to become a member of the committee must be proposed and seconded by two members of the club. Nominations for any vacant positions would have to be posted within the club for a certain period of time before the meeting at which the ballot is going to be held. The rules will normally provide that a ballot can either be held at an annual general meeting or within a certain period of time after such a meeting.

The rules will stipulate the procedures for ensuring that the votes are properly collated and counted.

Specific duties
The rules will generally lay out specific duties of the president (where applicable), chairman, treasurer and secretary of the club or association. Although they may also contain details of the responsibilities of other designated officers, only the duties of the first four have been set out below.

The president will chair general meetings of the club, and possibly those of the managing committee. The rules may contain a provision allowing the president an additional or casting vote in the event of a tied vote. The president will not usually have any involvement in the day-to-day running of the club, i.e., he is often just a figurehead and may well be an 'important' individual in the local community, or in the case of the Royal British Legion, for example, a retired senior officer from the armed services.

The chairman will usually preside over all meetings of the committee. He will also have overall responsibility for the conduct of club affairs, as directed by the committee. The chairman's role is similar to that of the managing director of a limited company.

A club may have both a president and a chairman, however, where only one of the positions is filled, it is likely to be that of the chairman.

The treasurer will be responsible for banking all monies received by the club. Standard rules usually stipulate that such banking should be gross and therefore if any deductions are made for the payment of wages, etc. then the club will have breached its rules. The treasurer will also be responsible for paying all the bills of the society and for being present at all meetings of the society and committee as required to render an account of his activities. The treasurer will usually be elected by the committee and may not vote at any meeting of the committee.

The secretary must keep a register of members as required by the rules and the provisions of the Industrial and Provident Societies Act 1965. He will be required to be present at any general meeting of the club and any committee meeting in order to take minutes. He will usually be required to collect money to pay to the treasurer and to keep books of account as required by the committee. He will also usually be responsible for ensuring that the accounts are produced and presented for audit. In reality, this will usually mean that he will arrange with the accountant/auditor to have the accounts prepared and audited.

Other issues

The rules may require the club to maintain fidelity insurance in respect of any officer or servant of the society who has responsibility for handling cash. Even if the rules do not contain such a provision, insurance cover of this kind should be encouraged as good practice.

1.10.7 Members' shareholdings

The maximum amount of interest in the shares of the society which may be held by any member should be stipulated in the rules, otherwise and

11

by virtue of section 6(1)(a), (b) or (c) of the Act. In working men's clubs each member is normally entitled to one share only.

1.10.8 Loans

The rules should stipulate whether the society may contract loans or receive money on deposit, subject to the provisions of the Act, from members or others, and under what conditions and security and to what limits of amount. Standard rules will usually contain a facility to enable the club to issue more stock but it is unusual for them to do so.

1.10.9 Transfer of shares

The rules must state whether the shares shall be transferable, the form of transfer and registration of the shares, and the consent of the committee thereto; whether the shares or any of them shall be withdrawable, and the mode of withdrawal, and the payment of the balance due thereon on withdrawing from the society.

The provision in most standard rules regarding shares will state that they are neither withdrawable or transferable. There will generally be a standard nominal value (often £1). In addition, there will usually be a stipulation to say that no dividend will be payable and that the share will be forfeited on a member leaving the club irrespective of the reason for leaving.

1.10.10 Audit of accounts

The audit of accounts by one or more auditors appointed by the society is necessary, in accordance with the requirements of the Friendly and Industrial and Provident Societies Act 1968.

Standard rules will generally give very detailed guidance on auditors and the audit. The rules will contain details of who is eligible to be an auditor (see **2.19–2.24**) and their rights and duties. It is important to remember that an old set of rules may well stipulate that a body corporate cannot undertake the audit of the club. If this is the case and the auditor is a limited company then the rules would need to be changed in order for them to be able to continue their appointment. Where a club is eligible to take advantage of audit exemption, the rules should be amended to allow for the appointment of an independent accountant (see **2.25**).

1.10.11 Ending membership

The rules must contain provisions as to whether and, if so, how members may withdraw from the society, and provision for the claims of the representatives of deceased members or the trustees of the property of bankrupt members, or, in Scotland, members whose estate has been sequestrated, and for the payment of nominees.

As already stipulated, members can cease to be members by a number of means, either by being removed, by resigning or by failing to pay their subscription. When this happens the rules will usually stipulate that their shares are forfeited. However, most standard rules will have a provision allowing the transfer of other property held for the member in the club to their personal representative in the event of death or bankruptcy.

1.10.12 Application of profits

Most club rules stipulate that the application of profit should be for the improvement of facilities for the club. However, they may have other specific provisions that allow them to apply profits to promoting educational activities and/or certain other charitable activities of affiliated bodies. In addition, there is normally a catch-all provision allowing profits to be applied to any other lawful purpose determined by the committee or at any general or special meeting of the members. However, there will also be a provision stipulating that unless the club is dissolved no profit will be distributed amongst the members.

1.10.13 Custody and use of the society's seal

The club's seal should be kept in the custody of the secretary or other elected committee member and should only be used with the permission of the committee.

1.10.14 Investments

The rules should stipulate whether and, if so, by what authority, and in what manner, any part of the society's funds may be invested.

Some clubs have very specific restrictions on investments. They may allow money just to be invested in building societies and other such bodies whereas other clubs have fairly far-reaching allowances. It is always worth knowing what is allowed to ensure that the rules are not breached.

1.11 Other provisions contained in the rules

The rules of the society can include issues over and above those set out in the Act. Typically, additional rules may be drafted covering the following issues.

1.11.1 Admission of associates and visitors

The rules relating to the admission of associates and visitors are very important in terms of ensuring that the club actually maintains its position as a mutual trading organisation. If it does not adhere to the rules with regard to the admission of visitors then it could find itself in a position where via revenue investigation, the mutual trading status is revoked. Generally speaking the rules will be as follows:

(a) Clubs that are affiliated will generally have a provision to enable members of other similar clubs to enter their premises as members. They will have to produce not only their membership card to the club to which they belong but also their affiliate card to show that they are entitled to do this. There may additionally be a provision for the committee to make special arrangements where a special event is organised by the club.

(b) The name and address of the visitor and the name of the club to which they belong has to be entered in a book kept by the club.

(c) Any affiliated member will be able to enjoy the facilities as if they were a full member but will not be able to vote at any meeting.

(d) The rules will normally stipulate that any member or associate member may introduce friends as their guests. However, no one person will be able to introduce more than two people at a time. The visitor and the person introducing them must sign their name in the book kept for this purpose. Most clubs will have some sort of provision in their rules excluding certain people from being introduced as a guest, this will include people who were formerly members but who have been expelled.

Generally speaking, the rules will stipulate that no visitor may purchase alcohol. However, there may be provisions within the rules for alcohol to be sold to visitors on specific occasions, for example, where a family party has been arranged on the premises.

1.11.2 Levels of subscription

The rules will have a provision with regard to the level of subscription to be paid and the period it covers. Some clubs will have annual subscriptions, others will have one paid on a quarterly basis and in some cases it will be a choice of the two.

In addition, they will have a provision which allows for the exclusion of the member on non-payment of their subscription within a certain period of time. This is normally 28 days after it is due to be paid.

14

1.11.3 Exclusion of members

The rules will generally allow for the committee to order a person from the premises and exclude them as a member for poor conduct or for breach of any other rules.

1.11.4 Opening hours

It is a requirement of the Licensing Act for the club to have a provision in its rules regarding opening hours. Although the hours may not be detailed within the rules, they will stipulate that they have been set in accordance with the Licensing Act (see **4.2**).

1.11.5 Disputes

The Industrial and Provident Societies Act 1965 also requires a club or association to contain a provision within its rules setting out the details of how disputes are dealt with. The specific provisions will usually vary from club to club.

The rules of a society are akin to the Memorandum and Articles of Association of a limited company, and bind the actions of the society in the same way. It is important that they are suitably tailored for the needs of the individual club or association. Pro-forma rules can be obtained from a number of promoting bodies, and details of the purpose of these bodies can be found at **1.15** and a list of such bodies has been produced within Appendix 6.

If the accountant is involved in the setting-up of a club or association it is always useful to approach one of the promoting bodies. Not only are there financial benefits to the club in terms of the cost of the initial set-up, but it also gives the club the ability to attract members who will be able to visit other clubs and associations which are also affiliated to the relevant body.

1.12 The registration process

Registration of an Industrial and Provident Society is a reasonably straightforward process. The procedure is set out below.

Firstly, form A should be obtained from the Registry of Friendly Societies (15–17 Great Marlborough Street, London W1V 2AX). Then a set of model rules should be devised, which provide for all the matters required by the Act (as detailed in **1.10** and **1.11** above). Model rules can be obtained from a number of promoting bodies, and if this has been the case then the Registrar of Friendly Societies should be told. If model rules are obtained from one of the promoting bodies, then the registration process is a lot quicker and considerably cheaper. If the society wishes to draw up its own rules or wishes to amend model rules then they should be submitted to the Registrar of Friendly Societies in draft form for preliminary examination, before being printed.

Once model rules have been obtained from one of the promoting bodies or alternatively the draft rules have been approved by the Registrar of Friendly Societies, then the final rules, along with the completed form A should be submitted to the Registrar of Friendly Societies. These should be submitted together with the necessary registration fee. In due course, acknowledgement of registration will be received from the Registrar of Friendly Societies.

1.13 Types of societies registered under the Industrial and Provident Societies Act 1965

There are a number of different types of society which may be registered under the Industrial and Provident Societies Act 1965 and these include the following:

- working men's clubs;
- retail, distributive, wholesale or productive societies;
- agricultural societies;
- smallholding or allotment societies;
- agricultural pest control societies;
- co-ownership societies;
- housing societies or associations.

Although part of this publication will be equally applicable to all of these types of societies, the chapters dealing with audit and accounting issues concentrate on working men's clubs.

1.14 Clubs registered under the Friendly Societies Act 1974

Although it is possible for a club or association, as outlined above, to be registered under the Friendly Societies Act 1974, its registration cannot be transferred to the Friendly Societies Act 1992 and no further registrations as Friendly Societies will be allowed.

The provisions of the Friendly Societies Act 1992 are, therefore, outside the scope of this publication and have not been considered here.

As the Registrar of Friendly Societies feels that clubs and similar orga-nisations should not be registered under the Friendly Societies Act, provision has been made in the 1992 Act to allow certain societies, including clubs, to deregister and re-register under the Industrial and Provident Societies Act 1965.

There are advantages to doing this, namely that:

(a) the club no longer needs to have trustees, these are replaced by a management committee;

(b) under the Friendly Societies Act, most clubs pay an annual fee, which is quite high but covers the filing of accounts, rule changes, etc., whereas under the Industrial and Provident Societies Act administration charges are only made when documents are filed with the Registrar, i.e., when changes are made and since 31 August 1995 when the accounts and annual return are filed. It is, therefore, likely to be cheaper to be registered as an Industrial and Provident Society, unless regular (i.e., annual) changes are likely to be made to the rules.

The procedure for re-registration is relatively straightforward, and is detailed below. There are five stages which need to be followed.

Stage 1: members must consent to the proposal. This consent must be obtained in the same way that the society would amend its registered rules. This will involve a general meeting of the society. An officer of the society must then make a statutory declaration before a Commissioner for Oaths or a Notary Public or a Justice of the Peace that the procedure as laid down in the rules has been followed. Evidence of that declaration on a standard form R/FS/REG 6 must be submitted with the applica-tion form to register as an Industrial and Provident Society.

Stage 2: drawing-up of rules under the 1965 Act. The easiest way of doing this is to obtain a copy of model rules from one of the promoting bodies (see **1.15** and also Appendix 6).

Once the rules have been drafted or obtained, a copy of the proposed rules should be put to the members for their approval.

Three members and the secretary of the society should sign two copies of the rules to say that they have been approved.

If model rules have not been obtained from one of the promoting bodies, draft rules will need to be submitted for examination to the Registrar of Friendly Societies.

Stage 3: completion of the application form. The application form A should be obtained from the Registrar of Friendly Societies and this should be signed by the same three members who signed the rules and also the secretary.

Stage 4: registration of the application. Once stages 1 to 3 have been completed, the following need to be lodged with the Registrar of Friendly Societies:

(a)   completed form A;
(b)   two identical signed copies of the rules; and
(c)   the statutory declaration on form R/FS/REG 6.

Once the forms and rules have been received and found to be acceptable, the application will be registered and an acknowledgement, bearing the seal of the central office will be sent to the society. Registration of the society under the 1965 Act causes the registration of that society under the Friendly Societies Act 1974 to be void and, without need for further action by the society, the latter is cancelled. The effect of this is that any appointment as trustee of the society will cease, all officers of the society other than its trustees shall, upon its registration under the 1965 Act, become officers of the Industrial and Provident Society, holding corresponding offices in that society, and any agreement made, transaction effected or other things done by, to or in relation to the society which is in force or effective immediately before its registration under the 1965 Act, shall have effect as if made, effected or done by, to or in relation to the Industrial and Provident Society in all respects.

Stage 5: transfer of all property and documents. Not later than the end of the period of 90 days beginning with the day on which the registered society is registered under the 1965 Act:

(a)   the former trustees of the society shall deliver to the registered office of the Industrial and Provident Society any property of the registered society held by them and any documents relating to the property, rights and liabilities of the registered society or its financial affairs; and
(b)   if the public trustee holds property on trust for this society, he shall deliver to the registered office the property held by him and any documents relating to it.

The trustees of the registered society will still be liable for any liability arising from acts or omissions which occurred before that registration.

1.15 Promoting bodies

A number of promoting bodies have been set up over the years. A full list of these can be obtained from the Registry of Friendly Societies. The purpose of most of these bodies is to assist societies which have a common purpose. A list of some of these organisations, along with a few background details can be found in Appendix 6. It should be noted that this is not an exhaustive list.

Chapter 2 – The regulatory framework governing Industrial and Provident Societies

2.1 The Industrial and Provident Societies Act 1965

This Act deals with the main rules and regulations applying to clubs and associations registered as Industrial and Provident Societies. Most of the provisions are still in effect although the provisions relating to accountancy and audit have been superseded in the main by the 1968 Act.

Some relevant parts of the legislation have been summarised below.

2.2 Registration

The detailed conditions and procedures for registration can be found in Chapter **1**. They are contained in section 2 of the Industrial and Provident Societies Act 1965.

2.3 Society rules

The provisions relating to the society's rules can be found in sections 9 to 16 of the Act. The rules of a society are akin to the Memorandum and Articles of Association of a limited company.

A copy of the rules of each society must be lodged with the Registry of Friendly Societies. The Act contains specific provisions which must be included in the rules of the society. Details of these requirements can be found in **1.10** and **1.11** and Schedule 1 to the Industrial and Provident Societies Act 1965. It is important to remember that the rules will not only contain requirements of this Act, but also certain specific requirements of the Licensing Act. Details of these can be found in **4.2**. The rules must be lodged with the Registrar of Friendly Societies as part of the registration process. Where the society wishes to amend its rules, such a change must be agreed by the members in general meeting, and the proposed changes must be registered with the Registrar of Friendly Societies. The amendments must be signed by three members and the secretary of the society. No amendment will be valid until acknowledgement has been received by the society of its registration with the Registrar of Friendly Societies. On registering the rule change, a fee will be payable. The fees are amended on a regular (usually annual) basis by statutory instrument; the current (1996) fee for a rule change is £90 for a complete amendment using unamended model rules, increasing to £290 where model rules are used with up to six minor amendments. In these circumstances, the Registrar of Friendly Societies must be consulted first. A partial amendment of the rules would cost £200.

2.3.1 Rule changes

When the rule change has been notified to the Registrar of Friendly Societies, once he is satisfied that it is not contrary to the provisions of the Act, an acknowledgement of registration of the amendment will be issued to the society. This acknowledgement is conclusive evidence that the change has been registered and is valid.

2.3.2 Supplementary provisions relating to rules

With one or two exceptions, the Act stipulates that the register of rules of the society will bind the society and all its members to the same extent, as if each one of them had subscribed their name to the rules.

The society may put a provision in its rules imposing reasonable fines on members who break or who fail to comply with any of the rules. Any fine so imposed by the rules will be recoverable on the summary conviction of the individual. Although this provision is possible it is not a normal provision in the rules of clubs and associations.

Any person has the right to demand a copy of the rules of the society and these can be received by them on payment of a nominal fee. The Act stipulates, and the rules of the society will usually contain, a provision as to the maximum amount that can be charged. This currently must not exceed 10 pence.

Any person who gives someone else a copy of the rules of a society which suggest it is an Industrial and Provident Society where it is not, or gives a copy of rules for a registered society which are not the existing rules, will be liable to a fine. The amount of the fine is included in the Act and may, from time to time, be changed.

2.4 Cancellation of registration

The Registrar of Friendly Societies may, where certain conditions apply, by writing to the society cancel the registration of any registered society. For such action to be taken one of the following conditions would need to apply:

(a) The registration will be cancelled if the Registrar of Friendly Societies is satisfied that one of the following conditions or situations has occurred:

    (i) the number of members has fallen below the minimum level, i.e., three; or

    (ii) the initial registration was obtained by fraud or mistake, for example, the club or association was not entitled to register, maybe as a result of it being a commercial enterprise; or

    (iii) the society, for whatever reason, has ceased to exist.

(b) Registration may be cancelled in certain circumstances at the request of the society. This request must be evidenced in a manner which will be prescribed. Should the society wish to cancel its registration then the Registrar of Friendly Societies should be approached to obtain details of how such a request should be made.

(c) Registration may be cancelled with the approval of the Treasury for one of the following reasons:

    (i) if the Treasury has proof that the society exists for an illegal purpose or alternatively has wilfully, and after notice from the Registrar of Friendly Societies, failed to adhere to any of the provisions of the Act;

    (ii) if the Registrar of Friendly Societies feels that the society is neither a bona fide co-operative society or that the business is neither at present nor intends to be conducted for the benefit of the community;

    (iii) where the society has been registered as an agricultural, horticultural or forestry society, but it appears to the Registrar of Friendly Societies that the society no longer consists mainly of such members.

If the Registrar of Friendly Societies or the Treasury is looking to cancel the registration of the society, then notice of this must be given in writing, giving brief details of the grounds for the proposed cancellation to the society. In this circumstance, the society has a right to appeal against the cancellation of registration.

Where the registration is going to be cancelled, the society can either be dissolved or alternatively transfer its engagements to those of a limited company. The Act actually stipulates that where a transfer is made to a limited company then the rights of any creditors will not be prejudiced. A society would be likely to transfer its engagements to a limited company where the registration is being cancelled on the basis that the operation is not a bona fide co-operative society, i.e., it is being run strictly as a commercial operation.

If the cancellation of registration is at the behest of the Registrar of Friendly Societies, then, if the society has not taken steps to either convert to a limited company or dissolve the society in accordance with the Act, the Registrar of Friendly Societies may give such directions as he thinks fit to ensure that the affairs of the society are wound up properly before the cancellation of the registration takes effect. Where the Registrar of Friendly Societies gives such direction, any person failing to comply with those directions will be liable on summary conviction to a fine or imprisonment or both.

Notice of any cancellation of registration will be published in the *London Gazette* and in a local newspaper circulated in the area in which the club or association is situated. The provisions relating to cancellation of registration can be found in section 16 of the Act.

2.5 Suspension of registration

As well as having the right to cancel the registration of a society, the Registrar of Friendly Societies also has the right to suspend the registration of a society for a term not exceeding three months or, with the approval of the Treasury, to renew any suspension for the same period. This right is contained in section 17 of the Act, and is likely to be invoked in a situation where the Registrar of Friendly Societies is threatening to cancel the registration and the club or association has lodged an appeal against the proposed cancellation of registration of the society by the Registrar of Friendly Societies (see **2.4**).

2.6 Members

Shares of an Industrial and Provident Society can be held by individuals or by any other body corporate. If a society holds shares in another society, where any document or application, etc. has to be signed, then the society which holds the shares will need two members of the committee and the secretary to sign any such document. For this purpose these two members and the secretary are deemed to be a member of the society.

A person who is over the age of 16 but under the age of 18 may be a member of a society and enjoy all of the benefits of membership but may not be a member of the committee, a trustee, manager or treasurer of the society. This can however be overridden by the individual rules of the society, i.e., most clubs will not allow anyone under 18 to be a member. In addition, most working men's clubs' rules will require a member to have been a member for at least six months before they are eligible to become members of the committee.

2.7 Loans

In certain circumstances a society may (provided it is allowed by the rules) make advances of money to members.

If any money is outstanding from a member to the society then this money can be recovered through the County Court. In addition, section 22 of the Act provides that the society will have a lien on the shares of any member for any debt due to the society.

2.8 Annual return

The provisions relating to the annual return of a society can be found in section 39 of the Act. All societies are required to lodge with the Registrar of Friendly Societies an annual return. The annual return can be filed on one of two forms.

If the accounts presented to the members and prepared by the accountant comply with all of the disclosure requirements set out in Chapter **5**, then the Registrar will accept an abbreviated annual return setting out the following details:

(a) the number of members at the end of the year;
(b) the turnover for the year;
(c) the net surplus or deficit for the year;
(d) the value of the fixed assets;
(e) the value of the current assets;
(f) the total value of fixed and current assets ((d) and (e));
(g) the value of the current liabilities;
(h) the amount of the share capital;
(i) the value of loans and reserves;
(j) the total value of the liabilities and members' funds ((g) to (i)) inclusive).

The return must also set out the details of the committee of management, the name of any organisation to which the club is affiliated and the date of the AGM. This form should be signed by the secretary. If this return alone is to be filed with the Registrar of Friendly Societies, then it must be filed accompanied by a set of accounts which have been signed by the secretary, two committee members and the auditor or accountant. The Registrar of Friendly Societies requires the accounts to contain original signatures.

This form must be filed with the Registrar of Friendly Societies within seven months of the period end. This is an extended time period which was introduced in the Deregulation (Industrial and Provident Societies) Order 1996. It will serve to ease the time pressure which is currently on this type of organisation at the end of the year. However, there may need to be a change to the rules of the society if they specify a date by which the annual general meeting must take place which was set to enable them to meet the old filing deadline. Although the filing deadline has been relaxed, the Registrar of Friendly Societies is not proposing to relax the requirement for a club to have a year end between August and January. An alternative year end may be achieved with the specific permission of the Registrar of Friendly Societies, and on payment of a fee.

If the accounts do not contain all of the disclosure requirements set out in the guidance notes issued by the Registrar of Friendly Societies (see Chapter **5**), then a supplementary return will need to be filled out – this is like a full set of statutory accounts. Obviously, it is much more cost-effective and time-efficient to ensure that the accounts prepared for the club contain all the information in the first place.

Section 39(5) stipulates that a copy of the latest return should be provided, free of charge, to any member or person interested in the funds of the society who requests it.

2.9 Officers

There are a number of specific provisions which relate to the situation where officers are required to handle cash. They will, in this instance, be required to account for any cash that has been held. There was a suggestion when the Deregulation (Industrial and Provident Societies) Order 1996 was being drafted that this provision should be removed, however, a large percentage of those making representations felt that it offered a measure of protection and therefore it will remain.

There is also a provision which enables the society, within its rules, to require any officer handling cash to give security for any cash held. Most clubs and associations will at least require the steward of the society to provide a bond. The value of the bond will vary from club to club, but will usually at least equal the float maintained. This bond will be placed in a specific building society or bank account in the name of the steward, and the book maintained by the secretary. In the accounts of the society it will be treated as an asset and a liability and, should the steward leave, the capital sum plus any interest accrued will be due to him, provided no defalcation has occurred.

Where officers are required to provide a bond, Schedule 4 of the Act contains a pro-forma bond which may be used. This has been reproduced below.

2.9.1 Pro-forma bond agreement

Know all men by these presents, that we, *A.B.*, of ....
one of the officers of the .... Limited, hereinafter referred to as
'the Society' whose registered office is at ....
in the county of ...., and *C.D.*, of .... (as
surety on behalf of the said *A.B.*), are jointly and severally held and
firmly bound to the said society in the sum of £........ to be paid to the
said society, or its certain attorney, for which payment well and truly to
be made we jointly and severally bind ourselves, and each of us by
himself, our and each of our heirs, executors and administrators, firmly
by these presents. Sealed with our seals. Dated the .... day of
....

Whereas the above-bounden *A.B.* has been duly appointed to the office
of .... of the .... Society, and he, together with the
above-bounden *C.D.* as his surety, have entered into the above-written
bond, subject to the condition hereinafter contained. Now therefore the
condition of the above-written bond is such, that if the said *A.B.* do
render a just and true account of all moneys received and paid by him on
account of the society, at such times as the rules thereof appoint, and do
pay over all the moneys remaining in his hands, and assign and transfer
or deliver all property (including books and papers) belonging to the
society in his hands or custody to such person or persons as the society
or the committee thereof appoint, according to the rules of the society,
together with the proper and legal receipts or vouchers for such
payments, then the above-written bond shall be void, but otherwise
shall remain in full force. Sealed and delivered in the presence of
....

There are no specific provisions relating to the duties of individual
officials of the society, however, both the 1965 and the 1968 Acts give
circumstances (for example, the failure to produce true and fair view
accounts) where individual members of the committee, and also potentially members of the club, could commit offences.

Most clubs will have provisions in their rules setting out the content of
the committee of management and the responsibilities of the specific
members of the committee. There may also be provisions to set up sub-
committees, such as a finance committee. Details of the specific requirements likely to be included in the rules, along with the specific duties of
individual officers have been included in **1.10.6**.

2.9.2 Other responsibilities of officers

Officers will have duties above and beyond those laid out in the 1965 and 1968 Acts. Those duties can be classified into two distinct types; those where the officers will owe a fiduciary duty and those of skill and care.

Fiduciary duties

Equity imposes similar duties on an officer of a club to those of trustees, often referred to as fiduciary duties. These primarily fall into three main areas:

(a) not to allow the interests of the club to conflict with his personal interests or his duty to a third party;
(b) not to profit out of his position as an officer, unless the club allows him to do so; and
(c) to act in good faith in the interests of the club.

The club's governing document must therefore specifically provide for remuneration and reimbursement of officers in order to allow any officer to be paid for working on the club's behalf.

As fiduciaries, officers would be liable to compensate any person to whom they owe these duties for any loss arising from default.

Duty of skill and care

The duty of an officer to act with skill and care is likely to be very similar to that of directors of a company. The main case law on this subject states that directors are expected to act with a degree of skill as might be 'reasonably expected from a person of his knowledge and experience' (*Re City Equitable Fire Insurance Co. 1925*). This is further split into the following criteria:

(a) to display such skill as their personal qualifications warrant. Hence more would be expected of experienced businessmen than the amateur, unless other specific statutory duties were imposed;
(b) to exhibit such care as an ordinary person might be expected to take on his own behalf. Again, a professional person would be expected to be more diligent generally; and
(c) not to participate in the wrongful actions of any of his co-officers. Participation could be very easy to establish; for example, merely signing minutes approving a misapplication of property was held to attract liability for a company director.

2.10 Registered office

The registered rules of the society must dictate where the registered office, where any legal documents can be lodged, will be situated. This will generally be the main place of business of the society.

2.11 Registers and books

2.11.1 Books to be maintained

Every registered society is required to keep at its registered office a register of members. Section 44 of the Act details the items which must be included in the register, i.e.:

(a)   the names and addresses of the members;
(b)   the number of shares they hold;
(c)   a statement of other property held in the society (for example, loans or deposits);
(d)   the date the person became a member;
(e)   the date, where relevant, the person ceased to be a member; and
(f)   the names and addresses of the officers of the society with the offices held by them and the dates on which they assumed office.

There is a requirement for a duplicate register to be held, which is open for inspection, containing all the details set out above with the exception of the shareholding and other property held.

This latter register can be inspected by any members of the society. The individual members are also entitled to see their own entry in the full register. In addition to the member being entitled to inspect their own account, the rules of the society may authorise inspection of all accounts in special circumstances. However, the rules may not allow any person who is not an officer of the society, or specifically authorised by resolution of the society, to inspect the loan or deposit account of any other person without that other person's written consent.

In reality, the society is likely to maintain only one register, but in such a way that the items which only the individual member is entitled to view are arranged in such a way that these would not be seen on examination by another member.

The register of members can be kept in a bound book or by some other means, but if it is maintained by some other means then the society must ensure that adequate precautions are taken to guard against falsification of the entries. As well as being open to inspection by the members, section 44(4) of the 1965 Act allows for the Registrar of Friendly Societies or any person acting on his behalf to have access to the register at all reasonable hours.

Section 44(5) stipulates that this register shall provide prima facie evidence of any of the following particulars which are entered in it:

(a) the names, addresses and occupations of the members;
(b) the number of shares respectively held by the members;
(c) the date at which the name of any person, company or society was entered in that register or list as a member;
(d) the date at which any such person, company or society ceased to be a member, where applicable.

2.11.2 Members' right to request an inspection

Under section 47 of the Act, if 10 members of the society, each of whom has been a member for at least 12 months immediately preceding the date of the application, apply to the Registrar of Friendly Societies, then the Registrar of Friendly Societies may, if he feels there is a reason, appoint an accountant or actuary to inspect the books of the society and to report on this. If the members make such an application they will have to place a deposit with the Registrar of Friendly Societies as security for the costs. The Registrar of Friendly Societies has the right to decide how the costs of such an inspection will be met once the examination has been completed.

The Registrar of Friendly Societies may also at any time, by notice in writing to the registered society or any person who holds office with the society, request the society to produce to him any books, accounts and other documents relating to the business of the society that he requires. If the society or officer fails to comply with this requirement then they may be liable on summary conviction to a fine or imprisonment, or both. Where the Registrar of Friendly Societies exercises this right, which is conferred by section 48 of the Act, then he can decide who will meet the cost of the exercise.

2.12 Appointment of inspectors and calling of special meetings

Section 49 of the Act provides that where 10 per cent of the members apply to the Registrar of Friendly Societies, then the Registrar of Friendly Societies may, with consent of the Treasury, appoint an inspector or inspectors to examine into and report on the affairs of the society, or call a special meeting of the society.

Where such an application is being made, then it must be supported by evidence showing that the applicants have good reason for requiring the examination or meeting and are not motivated by malicious intent.

As with **2.11**, the Registrar of Friendly Societies may require the applicants to give security for costs and will ultimately decide who should meet the costs and, where appropriate, in what proportion.

2.13 The society's name

The society must not have a name which is considered undesirable.

Where it is considered that the objects of a society are wholly charitable or benevolent the Registrar of Friendly Societies may give it permission to use a name that does not contain the word 'limited'. In all other cases the last word of a society's name shall always be 'limited'.

Should a society wish to change its name it needs to pass a resolution at a general meeting, in accordance with its rules, and obtain approval in writing from the Chief Registrar of Friendly Societies.

The registered name of the society must be displayed in a conspicuous position, in easily legible letters on the outside of its registered office.

The name must also be shown in legible characters on all of the following:

(a) the society seal;
(b) any notices, advertisements and other official publications;
(c) business letters;
(d) bills of exchange, promissory notes, endorsements, cheques, and orders for money or goods, purporting to be signed by or on behalf of the society; and
(e) bills, invoices, receipts, and letters of credit of the society.

2.14 Display of balance sheet

Section 40 of the Act requires the society to keep a copy of the latest balance sheet and audit report or accountant's report in a conspicuous place at the registered office at all times.

2.15 General offences by societies

If any of the following conditions apply in respect of any registered society, officer, member, or any other person, then that society, officer, member or other person shall be liable on summary conviction to a fine:

(a) the individual or society fails to give notice, send any return or other document, do anything or allow anything to be done which that society, officer, member or other person is required by the Act to give, send, do or allow to be done, as the case may be; or

(b) the individual wilfully neglects or refuses to carry out any act or to furnish any information required for the purposes of the Act by the Chief Registrar of Friendly Societies or any other person authorised under the Act, or does anything forbidden by the Act; or

(c) the individual makes a return required by this Act, or wilfully furnishes information so required, which is in any respect false or insufficient.

This provision is contained in section 61 of the Act and is an all-encompassing provision which covers offences relating to any other requirement of the Act.

Section 62 of the Act states that any such act committed by the society will be deemed to be an offence of each officer of the society who is bound by the society's rules to fulfil the duty of which that offence is a breach, or in a situation where there is no such officer, by every member of the society's committee, who is not proved to have been ignorant of, or to have attempted to prevent, the commission of that offence.

Section 63 states that any act or default committed under the Act shall be deemed to be a new offence in every week during which it continues. Therefore, the longer it goes on, the larger the fine.

Section 64 of the Act deals with punishment for fraud or misappropriation of funds and stipulates that any person found to have committed such an offence will be liable to a fine and/or imprisonment, and will be required to repay any sums misappropriated. As stated in **1.10.6**, the society's rules may require it to have fidelity insurance to cover this situation.

Section 65 stipulates that any person making a false entry or omitting an item from the accounting records of the society will be liable on summary conviction to a fine.

31

2.16 The Friendly and Industrial and Provident Societies Act 1968

The main purpose of this Act was to modernise the law governing audit and accounts of registered societies. The relevant provisions of this Act have been summarised below.

2.17 The requirement to maintain proper books and records

Section 1 of the Friendly and Industrial and Provident Societies Act 1968 requires every society to keep proper books of account with respect to its transactions and its assets and liabilities, and establish and maintain a satisfactory system of control of its books of account, its cash holding and all its receipts and remittances.

The society also needs to operate a system of control over its books of account, cash held and all receipts and payments.

The Act goes on to say that if it is not possible for true and fair accounts to be prepared from the accounting records, then proper books of account have not been kept.

This legislation is not as specific as the Companies Act in its requirements for maintaining proper books and records but the Registrar of Friendly Societies is likely to approach societies for an explanation where there has been a qualification in the audit report stating that proper books and records have not been maintained.

Obviously, as clubs and associations tend to be cash businesses, this can cause great concern in relation to completeness of income. Guidance on the maintenance of books and records can be found in Chapter **5**. Books and records maintained by the society may be kept either in bound books or by recording the matters in any other manner. Therefore, they could be maintained on computer if necessary. The Act then goes on to say that where bound books are not maintained, the society must take adequate precautions to guard against falsification. It must also take precautions to ensure that where falsification has occurred it is discovered.

2.18 The accounting requirements

The Act requires that each revenue account prepared by the society should give a true and fair view. If there are separate statements for different businesses conducted by the society, then each individual income and expenditure statement must also show a true and fair view. There is also a requirement to produce a balance sheet of the society which gives a true and fair view of the state of affairs, as at the balance sheet date.

The Act states that the income and expenditure account and the balance sheet cannot be published until an audit or independent examination has been conducted where one of these is necessary and that the accounts should be accompanied by an audit report, unless the society has taken advantage of the exemptions available to it. The accounts must also be signed by the secretary of the society, two other members of the committee and the auditor or independent accountant, where appropriate. The committee signatures will usually be on the balance sheet.

If the above requirements are not complied with, then certain members of the committee may be guilty of an offence under the Industrial and Provident Societies Act 1965.

Although the Act is not specific regarding the provisions to be included in the accounts of societies, the Registry of Friendly Societies produces guidance notes detailing the disclosure that they feel is appropriate for clubs and for various other types of registered society. If accounts do not comply with the guidance given in this leaflet then the full annual return document has to be produced.

There are further guidance notes on the form and content of club accounts in Chapter 5 and also Appendices 1 and 2.

2.19 Appointment of auditors

Every society shall annually appoint a qualified auditor or qualified auditors to audit its accounts and balance sheet for that year unless they are eligible to take advantage of the exemptions conferred by the Deregulation (Industrial and Provident Societies) Order 1996, in which case an independent accountant should be appointed where the society has a turnover between £90,000 and £350,000. Within section 7 of the 1968 Act, there are details of what constitutes a qualified auditor. It is now easier to say, since the introduction of audit regulation, that in order to be a qualified auditor, the report under the Friendly and Industrial and Provident Societies Act 1968 needs to be signed by a registered auditor. The provisions relating to the appointment of an auditor can be found in section 4 of the Act.

2.20 Re-appointment and removal of auditors

The auditor will automatically be re-appointed as auditor of the society unless:

(a) a resolution has been passed at a general meeting of the society appointing somebody instead of him or providing expressly that he shall not be re-appointed; or

(b) he has given to the society notice in writing of his unwillingness to be re-appointed; or

(c) he is ineligible for appointment as auditor of the society for the current year of account; or

(d) he has ceased to act as auditor of the society by reason of incapacity.

This is a subtle difference from the provisions relating to companies, as the auditor will remain in office unless steps are taken to remove him.

A resolution to be proposed at a general meeting of a society, either appointing another person as auditor in place of a retiring qualified auditor, or providing expressly that a retiring qualified auditor shall not be re-appointed, is not effective unless notice of the resolution is given to the society not less than 28 days before the meeting. As soon as the society receives the notice, the resolution must be notified to the retiring auditor.

Where the society is required by its rules to notify its members of the meeting at which the resolution is to be moved, the society should give the auditor notice of the resolution at the same time. Where there is no such requirement, the society should give notice of the resolution to its members not less than 14 days before the meeting where the resolution is to be moved.

It is likely that most clubs and associations will have provisions relating to the re-appointment of auditors in their rules.

When the retiring auditor receives notice from the society that either another person will be appointed as auditor, or a resolution be proposed at the general meeting that he shall not be re-appointed, he may at any time before the date of the general meeting make representations in writing to the society.

Where this is the case, the auditor should notify the society that such representations will be made and he may request that either his intention to make such representations or any such representations made by him are received by the society before notice of the intended resolution is given to members.

If the society receives notification of the intended representations or the representations themselves before they tell the members that a resolution not to re-appoint the auditors has been proposed at the general meeting, any notice of the resolution to the members should state that either those representations have been received or will be received (whatever the situation is). Any member can then demand a copy of the representations once they have been received by the society.

The retiring auditor can then either be heard orally at the general meeting, or require that the representations are read out at the general meeting. If the society does not wish for the auditor's representations to be sent out or read at the meeting, then an application must be made to the courts.

2.21 Restrictions on appointment of auditors

The provisions relating to the restriction on appointment of auditors can be found in section 8 of the Act. The auditor of a society cannot be:

- an officer or servant of that society;
- a partner of an officer or servant of the society;
- in the employment of, nor employ, an officer or servant of the society.

Under section 8(2) this concept of independence is extended to any subsidiary or holding society.

Up until audit regulation, where a consequential amendment order changed the Act, a body corporate could not be appointed as auditor of an Industrial and Provident Society. Although this has now been removed from the legislation, most clubs and associations will not have amended their rules to enable them to appoint a body corporate as auditor.

Therefore, if a practice is a limited company and undertakes the audit of any Industrial and Provident Society it will be appropriate to ensure that the rules allow the practice to be appointed.

It is also worth noting that the Act provides that not only should the auditor himself not be in the employment of the society but he must also not employ an officer or a servant of the society. Therefore, if a member of staff in the practice holds a position at the club or association the practice would be precluded from accepting appointment as auditor. This would be the case even if the post were an honorary position.

2.22 Duties of the auditor

The auditor is required to report to the society on the income and expenditure and the state of affairs of the society at the period end for the year that he is appointed. The audit report should contain an opinion as to whether or not the accounts give a true and fair view of the income and expenditure and the state of affairs of the society at the period end. The report also needs to consider whether or not the accounts comply with the requirements of the Act.

The auditor also has to carry out sufficient work for him to be able to form an opinion as to whether or not the following have been complied with:

(a) the requirement for the society to keep proper books of account in accordance with the Act;
(b) the requirement for the society to maintain a satisfactory system of control over its transactions in accordance with the Act; and
(c) the requirement for the accounts to be in agreement with the books and records of the society.

These matters should only be referred to in the audit report on an exception basis. If the requirements have not been complied with, then this should be specifically stated in the audit report. If these requirements have been complied with, then no mention is made.

2.23 Rights of the auditor

The auditor has a right of access at all times to the books, deeds and accounts of the society and to all other documents relating to its affairs. The auditor is also entitled to require from the officers of the society such information and explanations as he thinks necessary for the performance of his duties. If the information and explanations that the auditor requires are not obtained from the officers of the society, this should be stated in his report.

The auditor is entitled to attend any general meeting of the society. The auditor should also receive all notices of and other notices relating to any general meeting which any member of the society is entitled to receive. The auditor may also be heard at any meeting which he attends on any part of the business of the meeting which concerns him as auditor.

2.24 Remuneration

There is a provision in the Act which enables the Chief Registrar of Friendly Societies, with the consent of the Treasury, to prescribe the maximum rates of remuneration to be paid by societies for the audit or independent examination of their accounts and balance sheet by qualified auditors or independent accountants. When the Deregulation (Industrial and Provident Societies) Order 1996 was in draft form and up for consultation, there was a proposal put in place to remove this provision from the Act. However, although this did receive general support, it was decided that with the introduction of the independent accountant's report it was a useful provision to protect societies from over-burdensome fees. It is, however, unlikely that the Chief Registrar of Friendly Societies will exercise this power.

2.25 Power to opt out of audit

The Deregulation (Industrial and Provident Societies) Order 1996 came into force on 1 September 1996. This brought in some minor changes to the Industrial and Provident Societies Act 1965, the Friendly and Industrial and Provident Societies Act 1968 and the Friendly Societies Act 1974. However, it also brought in the more significant changes extending the ability of societies registered under the Industrial and Provident Societies Act 1965 and Friendly Societies Act 1974 to opt out of an audit should certain conditions be met. A summary of the conditions has been set out below. It should be noted that the Deregulation Order changes sections in the existing Acts and, therefore, the accountant should refer in any report to existing Acts and not to the Deregulation Order.

For accounting periods commencing on or after 1 September 1996, a society is able to disapply section 4 (which requires it to have an audit) where the following conditions are met:

(a)   the value of its assets at the end of the preceding year of account did not in the aggregate exceed £1,400,000; and
(b)   its turnover for that year did not exceed £350,000.

This is a significant difference from limited companies as the society qualifies on the basis of the previous year's figures. Therefore, even in the situation where it has exceeded the limits in the year on which an independent accountant's report is being prepared, if it qualified for exemption in the previous year, an audit is not required. In actual fact, this is quite a sensible provision, as it enables the society to table a motion at the annual general meeting to opt out of an audit when the accounts used to calculate whether the exemption applies are to be adopted.

This provision is also, potentially, why the order applies for accounting periods commencing after 1 September 1996. In practice, the first time a club with a 31 December 1996 year end will be able to take advantage of the exemption will be for the year ended 31 December 1997. However, it will qualify on the basis of the accounts for the year ended 31 December 1996, so a resolution to take advantage of the exemption should be put to the annual general meeting held in early 1997 at which the 1996 accounts are to be approved.

Where the society is drawing up its accounts for a period other than a year then the turnover figure should be pro-rated.

When calculating the turnover all amounts derived from the society's activities should be included, having made any necessary deductions for VAT, discounts and any other relevant taxes. The turnover calculation will, therefore, include income from all activities of the club, not just bar income.

In addition, the following conditions must be met:

(a) a resolution must be passed at a general meeting electing not to have an audit, and at this meeting:
(i) less than 20 per cent of the total votes cast must be cast against the resolution; and
(ii) less than 10 per cent of the members of the society at the time being entitled under the society's rules to vote must cast their votes against the resolution;
This vote must take place on an annual basis. It was proposed, at one time, that the society would only need to pass a resolution once. However, when the provisions of the draft order were being tabled, clear representations were made that an annual vote should take place.
(b) the society will not be able to take advantage of the exemption if it is, or has been at any time during the period, any of the following:
(i) a credit union within the meaning of the Credit Unions Act 1979;
(ii) registered in the register of housing associations maintained by the Housing Corporation, Housing for Wales or Scottish Homes;
(iii) a subsidiary;
(iv) prepares accounts under the Insurance Accounts Directive

(Miscellaneous Insurance Undertakings) Regulations 1993 (a); or

(v)   holds, or has held, at any time since the end of the preceding year of account, a deposit within the meaning of the Banking Act 1987 (b), other than a deposit in form of withdrawable share capital, i.e., have operated as a bank.

In addition, unlike companies registered under the Companies Act 1985, the Registrar of Friendly Societies may, by notice to a society, force the society to have an audit should he so wish. This right can also be applied for accounting periods where an annual return has already been submitted.

In the case of a society which is a charity, the turnover parameter decreases to £250,000.

Where the society has fulfilled all the aforementioned conditions but has turnover in excess of £90,000 then it must appoint a reporting accountant within 28 days of its period end.

The person who is appointed as reporting accountant must be a qualified auditor for the purpose of the Act (i.e., a registered auditor) and must also be independent within the meaning of section 8(1) of the Act, i.e., must not be ineligible by reason of not being independent. This is another difference from the requirements for limited companies.

The reporting accountant must make a report stating:

(a)   whether, in his opinion, the revenue accounts or account, the other accounts (if any) to which the report relates, and the balance sheet are in agreement with the books of account kept by the society under section 1 of the Act; and

(b)   whether, in his opinion, on the basis of the information contained in those books of account, the revenue account or accounts and the balance sheet comply with the requirements of the Act and the appropriate registration Act.

He also needs to report whether in his opinion the financial criteria for the exercise of the power to forego an audit were met in relation to that year. On the face of it, this provision seems more onerous than the provisions in the Companies Act. This section requires the reporting accountant to form an opinion on the society's ability to forgo an audit, i.e., to stipulate that it has met the financial criteria. In companies legislation, the equivalent provision only requires the accountant to form the opinion on the basis of the information contained within the accounting records. For accountants of societies, this provision may require them to carry out a limited amount of audit-type work where a society is approaching the exemption limits.

In order to be able to perform these duties a reporting accountant has a number of rights, namely:

(a) rights of access at all time to the books, deeds and accounts of the society and to all of the documents relating to its affairs; and
(b) entitlement to require from the officers of the society such information and explanations as he thinks necessary.

If the reporting accountant fails to obtain all the information and explanations which he feels necessary for the purposes of doing his job then this should be stated in his report.

The reporting accountant is also entitled to receive notice of, and attend, any general meetings of the society at which any relevant matter is discussed and to be heard at any such general meeting on any matter which is relevant.

Unlike with limited companies, there is no requirement for a statement to be placed on the balance sheet by a secretary and a member of the committee. In addition, there is no requirement for any report or statement to be made by a society whose turnover is less than £90,000, and which meets all the other criteria.

Chapter 3 – The Friendly Societies Act 1974

A number of societies may be registered under the Friendly Societies Act 1974. However, when the Friendly Societies Act 1992 came into force, registration under the 1974 Act was suspended. Clubs and associations such as working men's clubs would not be able to qualify for registration under the Friendly Societies Act 1992 so no new registrations will occur. Details of how to re-register a Friendly Society as an Industrial and Provident Society can be found in **1.14**. The relevant provisions of the Friendly Societies Act 1974 have been summarised below.

3.1 Annual returns

The provisions relating to annual returns can be found in s43 of the Friendly Societies Act 1974. An annual return should be lodged with the Registrar of Friendly Societies each year. The annual return should be accompanied by a copy of the auditors' report or independent accountant's report on the accounts and balance sheet contained in the report. As with Industrial and Provident Societies the club or association will have the choice of filing a full annual return or an abbreviated annual return. The full annual return will need to be filed in the situation where the details required by the full annual return are not contained in the financial statements of the club or association. Where such details are contained in the financial statements then an abbreviated return can be filed. The following details need to be included in the abbreviated return:

(a) the number of members at the end of the year;
(b) the turnover for the year;
(c) the net surplus or deficit for the year;
(d) the value of the fixed assets;
(e) the value of the current assets;
(f) the total of the society's fixed and current assets;
(g) the value of the current liabilities;
(h) the value of the society's loans and reserves (shown separately); and
(i) the total of the last three items.

In addition, details of the trustees; members of the committee; secretary; date of the annual general meeting and the name of any organisation, such as the Working Men's Club and Institute Union Limited, to whom the club is affiliated should be recorded on the form.

This form must be signed by the secretary of the society. The financial statements filed with the return must be signed by the secretary, two members of the committee and the auditor or independent accountant.

Obviously, the completion of the abbreviated return is easier and more cost-effective for most societies.

The 1974 Act stipulates that the annual return should be lodged with the Registrar by 31 July. Effectively, this will give all Friendly Societies at least seven months to file their annual return after their year end. This time period was extended from 31 May in the Deregulation (Industrial and Provident Societies) Order 1996.

Every society will provide to any member or person interested in its funds, free of charge, a copy of the last annual return of the society or a balance sheet or other document duly audited or examined, where appropriate, containing the same particulars relating to the affairs of the society as are contained in the annual return.

Any such return provided to a member or person interested in the affairs of the society will be supplied with a copy of the audit report or independent accountant's report, where appropriate.

3.2 The requirement to maintain proper books and records

The provisions relating to the maintenance of books and records are contained within s29 of the Act. This section requires that every society and branch must maintain proper books of account in respect of its transactions and its assets and liabilities and that the officers must establish and maintain a satisfactory system of control over its books of account, its cash holdings and all its receipts and remittances.

As with Industrial and Provident Societies, the requirements are not as prescriptive as those within the Companies Act and rather than give guidance on what types of books and records must be maintained, the Act purely states that societies must maintain 'such books as are necessary to give a true and fair view of the state of affairs of the society or branch and to explain its transactions'.

The books and records maintained can be kept either in bound books or by recording the information in another manner, such as by a computer. The Act goes on to say that if the books are kept in a form other than a bound form, then precautions must be taken to guard against falsification and the society must ensure that any such falsification would be discovered.

3.3 Accounts

Section 30 of the Friendly Societies Act 1974 deals with the issue of accounts. Again, the Act is not as prescriptive in its requirements as the Companies Act, but detailed guidance notes are provided by the Registrar of Friendly Societies and specific guidance on the accounting requirements have been included in Chapter **5** of this publication. There is also additional help within Appendix 1 and 2 in the form of some model accounts and a disclosure checklist.

In summary, section 30 stipulates that every revenue account of the society should give a true and fair view of the income and expenditure of the society or branch as a whole for the period in question or, if it deals with a particular business conducted by the society or branch in respect of that business, for the period to which the account relates. In addition, every registered society must in respect of each year of account prepare or have prepared a revenue account which deals with the affairs of the society or branch as a whole for the year, or two or more revenue accounts for that year which deal separately with the particular business conducted by the society or branch.

Where two or more revenue accounts have been produced then when taken together they should give a true and fair view of the income and expenditure of the society or branch as a whole for the year of account to which they relate.

Every balance sheet produced by the society or branch must give a true and fair view as at the date of the balance sheet of the state of affairs of the society or branch.

A society is not able to publish any revenue account or balance sheet unless the following conditions apply:

(a) it must have been previously audited by the auditor or auditors last appointed to audit the accounts and balance sheet of the society or branch (or an independent examination must have been undertaken unless the turnover of the society is less than £90,000); and

(b) it must incorporate a report by the auditor or independent accountant stating whether in their opinion it complies with the accounting requirements of the Act; and

(c) it must be signed by the secretary of the society or branch and by two members of the committee acting on behalf of the committee.

If in relation to any revenue account, revenue accounts or balance sheet of the society, any member of the committee who fails to take all reasonable steps to secure compliance with the accounting requirements, shall be liable, on summary conviction, to a fine unless he proves that he had reasonable grounds to believe, and did believe, that a competent and reliable person was charged with the duty of seeing that the relevant provision was complied with and was in a position to discharge that duty.

This may be the case where you have a member of the main committee who is not involved in the finance committee.

3.4 Audit

3.4.1 Appointment and removal of auditors

Section 31 of the Friendly Societies Act 1974 requires that any society which is not eligible to take advantage of exemption from audit (detailed later in this section) must appoint a qualified auditor or qualified auditors to audit its accounts and balance sheet for the year.

As with Industrial and Provident Societies, a qualified auditor who has been appointed to audit the accounts and balance sheet of a registered society for the preceding year of account will be re-appointed as auditor of the society for the current year of account unless one of the following conditions apply:

(a) a resolution has been passed at a general meeting of the society or branch appointing somebody instead of him or, alternatively, providing expressly that he shall not be re-appointed; or

(b) he has given notice in writing of his unwillingness to be re-appointed to the branch or society; or

(c) he is ineligible for appointment as auditor of the society or branch for the current year of account (potentially because he is no longer independent); or

(d) he has ceased to act as auditor of the society or branch by reason of death or incapacity.

A resolution put to a general meeting of the society appointing another person as auditor in place of a retiring qualified auditor, or providing expressly that a retiring qualified auditor shall not be re-appointed, will not be effective unless notice of the intention to put the resolution to the meeting has been given to the society or branch at least 28 days before the meeting at which it is placed.

Where the rules of the society prescribe how such notice should be given then notice of the proposed removal of the auditors should be given in the same way. For most clubs and associations this will mean that it has to be posted in a conspicuous place within the club.

Notice of any meeting at which an auditor is not to be re-appointed shall also be sent to the retiring auditor of the society.

Having received such notice, the retiring auditor may at any time before the date of the general meeting make representations in writing to the society (provided this is a reasonable length) with respect to the intended resolution and may also:

(a) notify the society that he intends to make such representations; and
(b) request that such notice or representation made by him is given to the members.

Where the society receives such representations prior to notification being given to the members of the meeting then they have several options:

(a) they can mention in the notice that representations have been received or that notification that representations are to be made has been given;
(b) they can state in the notice that any member may receive on demand a copy of the representations made; and
(c) they may send a copy of any representations received to any member on demand.

Without prejudicing any right he has to be heard at the general meeting, the retiring auditor may require representations made to be read out at the general meeting.

If the society does not want the representations to be sent out or read at the meeting then, if on application the High Court is satisfied that the rights conferred on the auditor to make representations are being abused to secure needless publicity for defamatory reasons, then the Court may order that the representations may not be made.

3.4.2 Qualification as auditor

In order to be qualified to undertake the audit of a society, the person appointed must be a member of one of the qualifying bodies for limited companies, i.e., must be a registered auditor.

The Act, in section 37, gives details of specific people who are unable to act as auditors of the society. These are as follows:

(a)   an officer or a servant of the society or branch; or
(b)   a person who is a partner of or in the employment of or who employs an officer or a servant of the society or branch.

This latter provision is a departure from the Companies Act requirements in that a practice employing somebody who works, even in an honorary post, for any club or association for whom they act will be unable to accept appointment as auditor.

Any appointment made under this section of somebody who is ineligible will not be deemed to be an effective appointment.

3.4.3 Auditors' rights and duties

The auditors of the society are required to make a report to the society or branch on the accounts examined by them and on a revenue account or accounts and balance sheet for the year of account in respect of which they are appointed.

The report must state whether the revenue account or accounts and the balance sheet for the year comply with the requirements of the Friendly Societies Act 1974 and whether, in the opinion of the auditors:

(a)   the revenue account or accounts give a true and fair view of the income and expenditure of the society or branch as a whole for that year of account; and
(b)   the balance sheet gives a true and fair view, either of the state of the affairs of the society or branch or of the assets and current liabilities of the society or branch and the resulting balances of its funds as at the end of that year of account.

In addition to the report on the truth and fairness of the accounts, when preparing the report the auditors are required to carry out such investigations as are necessary for them to form an opinion on the additional following matters:

(a) whether the society or branch has kept proper books of account in accordance with the requirements of s29(1)(a); and

(b) whether the society or branch has maintained a satisfactory system of control over its transactions in accordance with the requirements of s29(1)(b); and

(c) whether the revenue account or accounts, the other accounts (if any) to which the report relates, and the balance sheet are in agreement with the books of account of the society or branch.

If any of these situations do not apply then the auditors must state this in their report. Failure to do so will, by default, imply that the conditions have been met.

The auditors must also state in their report if they fail to obtain all the information and explanations which they believe are necessary for the purposes of their audit.

The auditors have certain rights conferred on them by the Act, which are as follows:

(a) they have the right of access at all times to the books, deeds and accounts of the society or branch and to any other documents relating to its affairs; and

(b) they are entitled to require from the officers of the society or branch any information and explanations as they think necessary for the performance of their duties as auditors.

They are also entitled to attend any general meeting of the society and to receive all notices and other communications relating to any general meeting which any member of the society or branch is entitled to receive and to be heard at any meeting which they attend on any part of the business of the meeting which concerns them as auditors.

3.5 Fees

The Chief Registrar of Friendly Societies has the right, on application to the Treasury, to set a maximum level of fee to be charged for the audit of the society or for an independent examination of the society's accounts.

3.6 Trustees

The Act requires every registered society to have one or more trustee.

The trustee(s) should be appointed at a meeting of the society and by resolution of the majority of the members present and entitled to vote at the meeting.

The society is required to send to the Registrar a copy of every resolution appointing a trustee, signed by the trustee and the secretary of the society.

The Act prohibits an individual from being the secretary or treasurer of the society if he is also a trustee.

The Act also prohibits a minor from being either a member of the committee, a trustee, a manager or treasurer of the society.

The Act provides that all property belonging to the society, whether it is acquired before or after the society is registered, shall vest in the trustees for the use and benefit of the society and its members.

The trustees of the society shall not be liable to make good any deficiencies in the funds of the society or branch but each trustee shall be liable for sums of money actually received by him on the account of the society or branch.

In the event of the death, resignation or removal of a trustee, all property vested in him shall, without conveyance, assignment or assignation, be transferred to the succeeding trustees of the society.

3.7 Officers

Every officer of a society who has receipt or charge of money shall, if it is required by the rules, or on demand or on notice in writing, render an account of any monies held by him and pay over all sums of money and deliver any property he holds to any person the committee or trustees may appoint.

If he refuses to do this, then the trustees or officers may sue on any bond held in relation to any money. To this effect, every officer of the society who has receipt of or charge of any money can be asked to give security for the money held. Schedule 3 to the Act provides a standard form of bond which can be used. This has been reproduced below.

3.7.1 Officers' bond

Know all men by these presents, that we, A.B. of _____
_____, one of the officers of the _____
Society [or of the _____ branch of the

_____ Society] having its registered office at _____, in the county of _____ and C.D of _____ (as surety on behalf of the said A.B.), are jointly and severally held and firmly bound to E.F. of _____ , G.H. of _____, and I.K. of _____ the trustees of the said society [or branch], in the sum of _____ to be paid to the said E.F., G.H. and I.K., as such trustees or their successors, trustees for the time being, or their certain attorney; for which payment well and truly to be made we jointly and severally bind ourselves, and each of us by himself our and each of our heirs, executors, and administrators, firmly by these presents. Sealed with our seals. Dated the _____ day of _____ in the year of our Lord _____.

Whereas the above-bounden A.B. has been duly appointed to the office of _____ of the _____ Society [or of _____ the _____ branch of the _____ Society] having its registered office situated as aforesaid, and he, together with the above-bounden C.D. as his surety, has entered into the above-written bond, subject to the condition herein-after contained: Now therefore the condition of the above-written bond is such, that if the said A.B. do render a just and true account of all moneys received and paid by him on account of the said society [or branch], at such times as the rules thereof appoint, and do pay over all the moneys remaining in his hands, and assign and transfer or deliver all property (including books and papers) belonging to the said society [or branch] in his hands or custody to such person or persons as the said society [or branch], or the trustees or committee of management thereof, shall appoint, according to the rules of the said society [or branch], together with the proper and legal receipts or vouchers for such pay-ments, then the above-written bond shall be void, otherwise shall remain in full force.

Sealed and delivered in the presence of

[two witnesses]

3.7.2 Additional duties of officers and trustees

The officers and trustees will have duties under common and other law in addition to those laid down in the 1974 Act. The officers' responsi-bilities will be the same as those for officers of Industrial and Provident Societies (see **2.9.2**), however, a number of the officers are also likely to be trustees, and so will have additional duties. It is also possible that there will be trustees who are not officers.

A detailed discussion of trustees' duties is outside the scope of this publication, but trustees of clubs and associations will have the following general duties and responsibilities:

(a) Duty to establish the trust. This means being aware of what their exact duties are, and what property, if any, is involved.

(b) Duty to comply with the terms of the trust. This may be augmented by provisions in the governing document.

(c) Duty not to delegate the trust. Individuals may delegate specific responsibilities to more experienced people, for example, appoint an accountant, but the overall responsibility can never be delegated.

(d) Duty to act prudently. This is similar to the general duty of skill and care, in that the trustees should exert the same degree of prudence as an ordinary businessperson would take in similar affairs of his own, but an extra degree of skill might be expected from a professionally qualified trustee, such as a chartered accountant.

(e) Duty only to invest in those investments which are authorised. Express powers, although rather limited, are given in the Trustee Investment Act 1961, but again the governing document may add to the types of investment that the club can hold. Trustees are also expected to act prudently with regard to investments, but need to balance this with the requirement to act in the best interests of the trust and hence obtain the best possible return on investments. So trustees would be expected to:
   (i)   obtain the best return with economic prudence;
   (ii)   diversify investments as far as possible;
   (iii) consider the suitability of investments; and
   (iv)   not allow any personal, moral or social views to affect investment policy.

(f) Duty not to profit from the trust, beyond the reimbursement of reasonable and proper expenses. Again, the governing document should include specific provisions if trustees are to be paid for their services. Such provisions would usually only be considered reasonable if they related to remuneration for special skills and not for the day-to-day duties of a trustee, such as attending meetings.

3.8 Displaying accounts

Section 45 of the Act requires that every registered society should keep hung up in a conspicuous place at the registered office of the society a copy of the last annual balance sheet together with a copy of the audit report or independent accountant's report.

3.9 Membership and rights of members

The Act stipulates that the rules of a registered society may provide for the admission of minors as members. However, in practice most working men's clubs will require the minimum age to be 18.

Any member or person who has an interest in the funds may inspect the books at all reasonable hours at the registered office of the society or at any place where the books are kept.

However, unless he is an officer of the society, or especially authorised by resolution of the society to do so, a member or person having an interest in the funds of a registered society shall not have the right to inspect the loan accounts of any other member without the written consent of that member.

3.10 Rules

Schedule 2 Part 1 of the Act contains details of the provisions which must be included in the rules of a society. These are as follows:

(i)   The name of the society.
(ii)   The place which is to be the registered office of the society, to which all communications and notices may be addressed.
(iii)   The objects for which the society is to be established, the purposes for which the funds thereof shall be applied.
(iv)   The terms of admission of members, the conditions under which any member may become entitled to any benefit assured by the society, and the fines and forfeitures to be imposed on any member and the consequences of non-payment of any subscription or fine.
(v)   The mode of holding meetings and right of voting, and the manner of making, altering or rescinding rules.
(vi)   The appointment and removal of a committee of management (by whatever name), of a treasurer and other officers and of trustees and, in the case of a society with branches, the composition and powers of the central body and the conditions under which a branch may secede from the society.
(vii)   The investment of the funds.
(viii) The keeping of the accounts and the audit of the accounts at least once a year or under the new regulations the conditions under which an audit or independent investigation needs to be undertaken.
(ix)   The completion of an annual return and its submission to the

Registrar of Friendly Societies relating to the affairs and numbers of members of the society.

(x) The inspection of the books of the society by every person having an interest in the funds of the society.

(xi) The manner in which disputes shall be settled.

(xii) In the case of dividing societies, a provision for meeting all claims upon the society existing at the time of division before any such division takes place.

The above provisions are the minimum requirements of the Act. In addition to the above it is likely that the society will have provisions covering the following issues, many of which will be required by the Licensing Act:

(a) the opening hours;

(b) details on the admission of visitors and affiliate members to the club premises.

More details on how some of the provisions above may be dealt with in the rules of clubs and associations can be found in Chapter **1**.

Any amendment to the rules must be carried out in accordance with the rules of the society. Any such change in the rules must be submitted to the Registrar of Friendly Societies, signed by three members and the secretary. The amendment is not valid until the Registrar of Friendly Societies has acknowledged receipt of the change. This will only be given when the Registrar of Friendly Societies is satisfied that any amendment is not contrary to the provisions of the Act.

The amendment of the situation of the registered office of the society is treated in the same way as a change in the rules and must be lodged with the Registrar of Friendly Societies.

A copy of the rules shall be delivered to any person on demand, on payment of a nominal sum which must not exceed 10 pence. During the consultation prior to the introduction of the Deregulation (Industrial and Provident Societies) Order 1996 there was a proposal to remove this maximum level that could be charged for the rules but it was felt that this would place an unfair burden on the individual members of the society.

In addition to the prescribed provisions for the rules, the rules may provide for the admission of minors as members. However, this is unlikely for most clubs and associations.

3.11 Society name

On first registering as a society the name would have to be approved by the Registrar of Friendly Societies. The society would not have been able to be registered under a name if it was the same as that under which any other existing society was registered, or so closely resembled it that it could cause confusion. It could also not be registered under a name that was otherwise deemed to be undesirable. The society may at a later date change its name by amending its rules. It cannot be changed in any other manner.

As with any other change of rule the amendment will not be valid until it has been lodged with the Registrar of Friendly Societies and approval has been obtained in writing.

Where a name is changed the change of name will not affect any right or obligation to the society or any member and, where appropriate, any pending legal action can be continued via the trustees of the society or any other officer who may still be sued or sue on behalf of the society, in respect of the name.

3.12 Meetings/special resolutions

The rules will provide details of how and when societies should hold meetings. However, there are specific provisions within the Act with regard to special resolutions. Special resolutions shall only be passed at a general meeting due notice of which has been given to the members. The resolution must be passed by not less than three-quarters of those members of the society who are entitled to vote and do vote either in person, or by proxy, at the meeting.

A copy of every special resolution must be sent to the Registrar of Friendly Societies. This resolution should be signed by the chairman of the meeting and countersigned by the secretary. Until the copy is registered the special resolution will not take effect. When the resolution has been lodged with the Registrar of Friendly Societies a period of six weeks commencing on the date it is received must pass before it becomes effective.

3.13 Registrar's power to inspect

If the Registrar of Friendly Societies feels that there is due cause to do so and it is in the interest of the members of the society or of the public at large then he can appoint an inspector to examine and report on the affairs of the society.

Such an inspector may require whatever books and records from the society he deems necessary and whatever information he requires from its officers, members, agents and servants.

If, once he has received the report, the Chief Registrar of Friendly Societies feels that it would be appropriate for the society to be wound up then he can apply to the High Court for permission to do so.

Where such an examination has taken place the Registrar of Friendly Societies can decide who should pay for the cost of the investigation. He can elect that this should come out of the society's funds or be paid by the members or officers or former members or officers of the society in such proportion as he sees fit.

The Registrar of Friendly Societies, if he feels that there is good reason to do so, may also ask the society to produce such books or papers as he requires or alternatively authorise an officer of the central office on producing evidence of this authority to require a society to produce to him any books or papers which the officer may specify.

Where these books and papers have been produced then the power conferred enables the Registrar of Friendly Societies or his officer to take copies of anything given. He also has the power to make any reasonable request for information from any officer or former officer of the society.

Failure to provide the Registrar of Friendly Societies or his representative with any information will be an offence.

In addition to the Registrar's own right to demand an inspection, if an application is made to him by one-fifth of the members of the society to appoint an inspector to examine and report on the affairs of the society or to call a special meeting of the society, then on consideration he may order an inspection to take place.

If an application is made for this to happen under s90 of the Act then it must be supported by whatever evidence the applicants have to show there is good reason for requiring an inspection or meeting. There must be proof that such a request has not arisen out of malicious intent.

If such an application is made then the Registrar of Friendly Societies may ask the applicants to provide security for the costs. Such expenses will ultimately be payable by the members and/or the society in such proportion as the Registrar of Friendly Societies directs.

The appointed inspector may have access to all books and records of the society and to all officers and former officers.

3.14 Registrar's power to suspend business

Provided he has due cause and is acting in the interest of the members of the society or the public, the Registrar of Friendly Societies may make an order forbidding a society to accept any new members or to enter into a new contract with any member of the society.

Where this is likely to happen, not less than a month before such an order is made, the Registrar of Friendly Societies must send notice to the society. This notice will give an explanation of why the action is being taken.

Once the society has received such notice it will have the right to make representations to the Registrar of Friendly Societies on its own behalf.

Where a society's business is suspended notice of this will be placed in the *London Gazette* and in any other manner that the Registrar of Friendly Societies feels is necessary for informing the public, which will usually involve some sort of advertisement in the local press.

If such an order is made and the society chooses to ignore this then it will be liable on conviction or indictment to a fine. In addition, every officer of the society who knowingly and wilfully authorises or permits the contravention shall be liable to a fine or imprisonment or both.

3.15 Cancellation and suspension of registration

Section 91 states that the registration of a society can be cancelled by the Registrar of Friendly Societies if one or more of the following conditions applies:

(a)   if he feels it is a reasonable request by the society, and that such a request has been sent in a manner which is acceptable. Where a society wishes to cancel its registration the Registrar of Friendly Societies should be approached for guidance on the form such an application should take;

(b)   on proof that the registration was obtained by fraud; or

(c)   on proof that the society exists for an unlawful purpose or has wilfully, and after notice from the Chief Registrar of Friendly Societies or any assistant Registrar, violated any provisions of the Act or has ceased to exist.

In addition, should either condition (b) or condition (c) apply then the Registrar of Friendly Societies may, by writing, suspend the registration of the society for a period not exceeding three months.

This suspension can be renewed from time to time for the same period.

Where the cancellation of registration is being made at the behest of the Registrar of Friendly Societies then notice must be given to the society at least two months before the cancellation of registration rule takes place. The society will have a right to appeal against this.

Where a registration has been suspended or cancelled then notice has to be published in the *London Gazette* and in a local newspaper.

3.16 Offences, penalties and legal proceedings

Section 98 of the Friendly Societies Act 1974 recognises a number of situations where an offence will have occurred by the society or alternatively the officers or trustees of the society. The relevant provisions have been summarised below.

(a) It is an offence if a society or officer or member fails to make any return or give due notice or do anything else which is required of him by the Act. This is a fairly all-encompassing provision which basically means that an offence has occurred if there is a breach of any of the requirements of the Act.
(b) An offence has occurred if the society, officer or member wilfully neglects or refuses to do any act or to provide any information required for the purposes of the Act by the Registrar of Friendly Societies or any other person authorised to request such information under the Act.
(c) It is an offence if a society or branch or officer or member makes a return or furnishes information which is in any respect false or insufficient.

Anyone who commits an offence as detailed above will be liable on summary conviction to a fine. A maximum level of fine will be set by the Act. Where a society has been guilty of an offence under the Act then every officer of the society who is bound by the rules to fulfil any duty relating to the offence or if there is no such officer then every member of the committee other than someone who is proved ignorant of, or who can prove that they have attempted to prevent the commission of, the offence will be liable to the same penalty as if he had personally committed the offence.

As with the Industrial and Provident Societies Act every default under the Act which constitutes an offence will, if it continues, constitute a new offence in every week during which the default continues. This allows a substantial increase in the level of fine that can be incurred.

If any person, with an intention to mislead or defraud, gives somebody a copy of any rules, laws or regulations or other documents other than the valid rules of the society on the pretence that they are the existing rules or gives a copy of rules on the pretence that they are rules of a registered society when they are not, then he shall, on summary conviction, be liable to a fine or on indictment to a fine and/or imprisonment.

Where someone has obtained property from the society by fraudulent means not only will he be liable on conviction to a fine but he may also be required to repay the money.

Section 100 of the Act stipulates that anyone who wilfully and with intent to falsify the document in question makes, orders or allows to be made any entry or erasure in or omission from a balance sheet or internal document required to be sent, returned or delivered for the purpose of the Act should be liable on summary conviction to a fine.

3.17 Power to opt out of audit

The Deregulation (Industrial and Provident Societies) Order 1996, which came into force for accounting periods commencing on or after 1 September 1996 extended the power of Friendly Societies registered under the 1974 Act to opt out of audit. As with Industrial and Provident Societies, the Deregulation Order does not stand in its own right – it amends and adds to the existing legislation, namely the Friendly Societies Act 1974. The section references that follow, therefore, are to the 1974 Act.

In order for them to take advantage of this exemption, the conditions set out in s32A must apply. Effectively the way this works is that if the conditions apply then they disapply s31 which is the section requiring the society to have an audit. In order to qualify for the exemption the following conditions need to be met:

(a) the value of the society's assets at the end of the preceding year of account must not in aggregate exceed £1,400,000; and
(b) the turnover for that year must not exceed £350,000.

As with Industrial and Provident Societies, for a society to qualify it must meet the requirements for the preceding period. There is no requirement for it to have to meet the criteria in the current year (see **2.25**).

Once the financial criteria have been met then the society must go to its members to obtain their permission to take advantage of the exemption. A power to opt out will be:

(a) exercisable by resolution passed at a general meeting of the society at which less than 20 per cent of the total votes cast are cast against the resolution; and

(b) less than 10 per cent of the members of the society or branch who for the time being are entitled under the body's rules to vote cast their votes against the resolution.

This resolution would need to be passed on an annual basis. As the exemption is based on the previous year's figures, the club will be able to table a resolution at the meeting to adopt those accounts not to have an audit in the current year.

A society which holds or has at any time during the preceding year of account held a deposit within the meaning of the Banking Act 1987 may not take advantage of the exemption.

In addition, the Registrar of Friendly Societies may by giving notice to a society require it to have an audit. The Order does not consider in what circumstances this power may be exercised, but in common with many provisions in the Act it may just be a protective measure.

Where the society or branch is a charity within the meaning of the Charities Act 1993 then the gross income parameter will be decreased to £250,000.

Where the society's accounts have been drawn up for a period other than a year then the figures can be pro-rated.

The section gives some guidance in relation to turnover and says that it means the amounts derived from provision of goods and services falling within the society's or branch's activities after the deduction of:

● trade discounts;
● value added tax; and
● any other taxes based on the amounts so derived.

As, for example, fruit machine income actually falls within the normal activities of a society then this should be incorporated when deciding whether the society is eligible to take advantage of the exemption.

The following section, which is s39A of the Friendly Societies Act 1974, requires the society to obtain an independent accountant's report where the society meets the criteria set out in s32A and has turnover above £90,000. For societies with a turnover below £90,000 there is no requirement for anything to be done, not even for there to be a statement by the committee on the balance sheet. Neither is there a requirement for the committee to place a statement on the balance sheet where an independent examination is being undertaken.

Where an independent accountant's report is required then the society must appoint an individual within 28 days of the year end. The report by this independent accountant must contain the following information:

(a) Whether in the opinion of the person making the report the revenue account or accounts, the other accounts (if any) to which the report relates, and the balance sheet are in agreement with the books of account maintained by the society or branch under section 29 of the Friendly Societies Act 1974.
(b) Whether, in that person's opinion, on the basis of the information contained in those books of account, the revenue account or accounts and the balance sheet comply with the requirements of the Act.

In addition, the report must state whether in the opinion of the person making the report the financial criteria for the exercise of the power were met in relation to the year. It should be noted that, unlike for companies, this opinion is not merely on the basis of the information contained in the accounting records (see **2.25**).

The person appointed to be an independent accountant must be a qualified auditor for the purposes of the Act and must also be independent within the terms of the Act.

This again is a departure from the requirements of the Companies Act where an independent accountant must be someone who is qualified to undertake the audit of a company but does not have to be a registered auditor.

In order to enable the individual to undertake the work, s39B of the Friendly Societies Act 1974 sets out details of their rights. These can be summarised as follows:

(a) they have a right of access at all times to the books, deeds and accounts of the society and to all other documents relating to its affairs; and

(b) they are entitled to require from the officers of the society or branch any information and explanation that they feel necessary.

Where the independent accountant has been unable to obtain all the information and explanations which to the best of his knowledge and belief he feels necessary for the purposes of doing the work then this must be stated in the report.

In addition to the above rights, the person who has been appointed an independent accountant shall be entitled:

(a) to receive notice of and attend any general meeting of the society at which any relevant matter is discussed; and

(b) to be heard at any such general meeting on any business which is relevant to him.

Section 39C of the Act also confers the right on the Registrar of Friendly Societies to require a previous year's accounts to be audited even if the annual return has been sent to him with an independent accountant's report before he has decided such an audit is required.

It is highly unlikely that the Registrar of Friendly Societies will take advantage of this right but the provision is within the Act as a measure of protection.

Chapter 4 – Other relevant legislation and regulations

This chapter contains some background details on other legislation and regulations which could be relevant to a number of clubs and associations. Although it contains extracts from the Acts and a run-down of most of the salient points, it is not a substitute for having copies of the said Acts available should any problems occur.

4.1 Charities Act 1993

Under the second Schedule to the Charities Act 1993, Industrial and Provident Societies and Friendly Societies fall under the definition of exempt charities, where they carry out charitable activities. However, this exemption does not extend to a charity administered by an Industrial and Provident or Friendly Society, nor to a charity simply because it has a subsidiary which is exempt.

As from 1 January 1992 exempt charities were not permitted to register as charities, and if they were already registered charities, registration ceased to have effect. The implication of this is that exempt charities are not able to refer to themselves as registered charities nor to quote a registered charity number. They can however still carry out charitable activities and there would appear to be no reason why they could not put a statement on their letterhead that they are an exempt charity under Schedule 2 to the Charities Act 1993. Their activities are largely outside of the jurisdiction of the Commissioners. They are also excluded from many of the provisions of the Charities Act 1992, however they are covered by the following provisions:

(a) the public have a right to request (in writing) accounts direct from the charity;
(b) the rules over disqualification and who may not act as trustees are the same; broadly speaking, this means that no-one under the age of 18 can be a trustee nor some classifications of people who are disqualified by law. This will include anyone described in s72(1) of the Charities Act 1993, which includes, for example, anyone who has been convicted of an offence involving deception or dishonesty,

an undischarged bankrupt, anyone who is disqualified from being a director, etc.;
(c) the rules over public collections;
(d) the rules governing the activities of professional fundraisers; and
(e) the rules governing *ex gratia* payments.

A firm acting for a club or association that carries out charitable activities needs to ensure that if they were previously a registered charity they are no longer quoting their charity number or suggesting that they are a registered charity and should be familiar with the above provisions.

4.2 The Licensing Act 1964

In order to be able to sell intoxicating liquor a club must apply to the local magistrates' court for a registration certificate. (In the context of this section, 'registered' means registered or licensed to sell alcohol.) This certificate will usually require renewal on an annual basis. However, in certain circumstances a longer period of time may elapse before a renewal is required. The registration certificate will only be issued for a period exceeding one year when the club has been in existence for at least two years. In addition, the maximum length of issue of the registration certificate is ten years.

For a club incorporated under the Industrial and Provident Societies Act or Friendly Societies Act to qualify for a liquor licence it must satisfy certain conditions in addition to those which the relevant Acts require it to have in its rules. These provisions are covered by s41 of the Licensing Act 1964. The following conditions will apply:

(a) the rules must stipulate that no person can be admitted to membership unless at least two days have expired between their nomination or application for membership and their admission as a member; and
(b) anyone who is admitted to membership without prior nomination or application must not be admitted to the privileges of membership without an interval of at least two days between them becoming members and their admission.

Where the club has adopted standard rules prepared by any of the promoting bodies, there will be a provision requiring the name of any prospective new member to be posted on the noticeboard for at least two days before being considered for admission. They may be able to enter the club as a visitor but will not be able to purchase alcohol.

In addition, the club will only qualify to receive the registration certificate to sell alcohol for any premises if:

(a) the club is established and conducted in good faith as a club and has at least 25 members; and
(b) intoxicating liquor is not supplied, or intended to be supplied, to members on the premises otherwise than by or on behalf of the club; and
(c) the purchase for the club and supply by the club of intoxicating liquor is managed by an elective committee (this condition is treated as satisfied for Industrial and Provident Societies and Friendly Societies and will, anyway, be included in any standard rules); and
(d) no-one receives, at the expense of the club, any commission or similar payment in relation to the purchase of liquor and no person should derive any benefit individually from the supply of liquor.

In seeking to determine whether a club is established and conducted in good faith, any magistrates' court will take into consideration the following:

(a) any arrangement restricting the freedom of the club to purchase intoxicating liquor;
(b) any provisions in the rules or other arrangement which will enable profit to be applied elsewhere than for the benefit of the members or for charitable, benevolent or political purposes;
(c) the arrangements made by the club for giving members proper information on the club's finances and also on the type of books and records maintained to ensure that information is recorded accurately; and
(d) the nature of the premises occupied.

For clubs that are registered under the Industrial and Provident Societies Act or the Friendly Societies Act, there would be no problem in demonstrating that they are established and conducted in good faith. The reason for this being that in order to qualify for registration under either of those Acts they would need to meet the above criteria.

4.2.1 The registration process

To apply for a licence an application has to be made to the magistrates' court for the area in which the premises are situated. For the application to be made there are certain requirements to be complied with by the club. These are contained in Schedule 5 to the Licensing Act 1964. The requirements can be summarised as follows:

(a) The application must contain the name, objects and address of the club and must stipulate that a list of the names and addresses of members is actually held on the premises – this is a requirement of both the Industrial and Provident Societies Act 1965 and the Friendly Societies Act 1974.

(b) The application must state that the club fulfils the requirements of s41(1) and (2) and is qualified under those sections to receive a registration certificate. These sections deal with the admission of new members and the other items summarised in (a) to (d) above.

(c) The application needs to contain details of the committee members, i.e., their names and addresses. This will include details of members of any committees of the club who have an involvement in the general management of the club and/or purchase decisions.

(d) The application must include details of the rules, or a copy of the rules should be attached. Where a new application is being made, changes in the rules since the previous application should be put into the application or, if no changes have been made, the application should contain a statement saying that this is the case.

(e) The application needs to contain details of the premises for which the renewal is sought.

(f) The application needs to state that the premises are or are about to be occupied by and will be used for the purposes of the club.

(g) Details of the times that the club will be or is open to members and the hours fixed under the rules of the club as its permitted hours must be included (within most working men's clubs this will be within their rules although the specific hours may not be stated).

(h) The application needs to state whether the club owns the premises or what interest it has in those premises. If the club does not own the premises then the name and address of the individual or organisation to whom rent is paid needs to be included in the application.

The application also needs to give details of, or incorporate an appendix giving details of, the following items:

(a) Details of any other property which may be used by the club and has not already been included in the details given above, giving the same details as already required.

(b) Particulars of any liability of the club in respect of both principal and interest on monies borrowed by the club or, alternatively, charged on property held by or in trust for the club. These details should include the name and address of the person to whom payment is made.

(c) Particulars of any liability of the club or, alternatively, of any of the trustees of the club and, where any person has given any guarantee or provided any security, details of the guarantee or security, including the name and address of the person giving or providing it.

(d) Where the application is for renewal, then details of any changes since the last application need only be recorded. Where there are no such liabilities, then the application shall say so. (In terms of the Licensing Act, when it talks about liability, it actually includes any future or contingent liability, therefore, any guarantees would be included.)

(e) Where the club occupies leasehold premises and neither the club nor the trustees pay any rent on this but it is paid by a third party, then details of the person making the payment should be included.

(f) The application must give details of any premises not already incorporated in the application which have, within the preceding year, been occupied and regularly used for the purposes of the club. Details of these premises should include the interest held by or in trust for the club in those premises and, if it holds no such interest, then the name and address of any person to whom payment was made for rent under any lease or otherwise for the use of the premises. Again, if there were no such premises then this should be stated in the application.

The application, when submitted, should be signed by the chairman or secretary of the club.

This application is made by lodging it, along with any additional copies required, with the Clerk to the Justices. The Clerk to the Justices will require additional copies to send to any chief officer of police concerned and to the clerk of any local authority concerned.

When an application has been made for a licence, an objection can be lodged in respect of either the issue or the renewal of a registration by the chief officer of the police, the local authority or any person affected by reason of his occupation of or interest in other premises. There are a number of different grounds on which such an objection can be made:

(a) the application does not contain all the information required by the Act;

(b) the premises are not suitable and convenient for the type of club;

(c) the club does not satisfy the conditions set out above;

(d) the club is conducted in a disorderly manner or for an unlawful purpose or the rules of the club are habitually disregarded in respect of the admission of persons to membership or to the privileges of membership or in any other material respect; or

(e) the club premises are habitually used for an unlawful purpose or for indecent displays or as a resort of criminals or prostitutes or that in any such premises there is frequent drunkenness or there have, within the preceding 12 months, been illegal sales of intoxicating liquor to persons not qualified to be supplied with intoxicating liquor (e.g., minors or non-members) and that they are habitually admitted to the premises for the purpose of obtaining it.

Care must therefore be taken to ensure that clubs and associations do comply with the requirements of their rules with regard to members and the selling of alcohol to members of the public.

If the court is satisfied that the grounds for objection are reasonable they may refuse the application. However, before refusing an application or renewing a registration certificate for a shorter time than has been requested, the court will give the club an opportunity to be heard. If no objection is received and the application is in order, then the licence will usually be issued.

Within the provisions of the Licensing Act the fire authorities, environmental health and the police all have the right to inspect the premises on application for a licence and on renewal of the registration certificate. All three offices will usually exercise this right, particularly on initial application. In addition, on first application for a licence an officer of the local authority may visit the premises.

Where any alteration is made to the rules of a club registered in respect of any premises the secretary of the club must give written notice of the alteration to the chief officer of police and the clerk of the local authorities.

The Licensing Act also contains provisions relating to opening hours and applications for extensions which must be adhered to.

4.2.2 Suspension of licence

Section 47 of the Licensing Act 1964 deals with the power of the licensing authority to order disqualification of premises. Effectively, if the magistrates' court cancels or refuses to renew the registration certificate for a particular club premises due to one of the following conditions:

(a) the club does not satisfy the registration conditions set out in **4.2.1** above; or
(b) the club is conducted in a disorderly manner or for an unlawful purpose or the rules are habitually disregarded in respect of the

admission of a person to membership or the privilege of membership, i.e., non-members may be served alcohol; or
(c) the premises are habitually used for unlawful purposes;

then the court may also order that the premises cannot be occupied and used for the purposes of any registered club. The period of restriction shall not exceed one year unless the premises have previously been the subject of an order under s47.

4.2.3 Register of clubs

The Clerk to the Justices needs to keep a register of clubs holding registration certificates for premises in the area. This register contains details of the premises that are registered and the hours fixed by the rules (where appropriate). The register shall be open at all reasonable times for inspection on payment of a fee by any person.

Written notice of any change in the particulars of the club which are required to be contained in the register and which must be signed by either the chairman or the secretary, needs to be sent to the Clerk of the Justices.

4.3 The Gaming Act 1968

4.3.1 Bingo

The Gaming Act 1968 allows clubs which satisfy certain conditions not to register in order to undertake gaming activities such as bingo.

In order to qualify for this exemption the following conditions have to be met:

(a) only one payment can be made for a player in respect of all games played on any one day. A limit is set for this payment which currently stands at £3;
(b) there is a limit to the total value of prizes and awards that can be distributed in respect of the games. The current limit is £300;
(c) if any expenses are charged then these must not be excessive, i.e., they must be a reasonable reflection of the cost of the facilities provided for the purpose of the games.

In addition, once prizes have been distributed, any balance remaining must be paid into the club funds and utilised for the purposes of the club. The above exemption is under Part IV of the Act.

There is another exemption from registering under this Act available which exists provided the following conditions are met:

(a) all money paid by way of stakes must be repaid to the participants as winnings;
(b) any charge made for a right to take part in the game must not exceed 50 pence on any one day. This amount may be increased from time to time.

The above exemption is available via Part II of the Act.

The former classification is gaming entertainment and the latter is classified as a gaming activity. There is nothing to preclude a club from carrying out a gaming entertainment and a gaming activity on the same day.

If bingo is played on the club premises then members are able to play along with associates and guests, provided such people have been admitted in accordance with the rules of the club. Therefore, any person wishing to play would either have to be a member or an associate or be introduced by a member to the premises.

4.3.2 Fruit machines

The Gaming Act 1968 also governs the use of fruit machines on the premises. The provisions are contained in Part III of the Act. In order to have fruit machines on the premises, an application for registration should be made to the Clerk to the Justices. A copy of the application must be sent to the local police who are the only people who have the right to object to a licence being issued. The magistrates have the discretion to grant the application without any hearing.

The club would have to pay a fee for the registration of the licence in addition to the annual licence fee. Their registration will initially be for a period of five years and it is then renewed in five-yearly intervals. There are certain other conditions in the Act which may be relevant. Section 31(3) of the Gaming Act 1968 places a restriction on the amounts that can be paid for a game. This can be increased from time to time by the Secretary of State.

The provisions contained in section 28 of the Act prevent a club from entering into a profit-sharing agreement in respect of gaming machine income. The amount paid for the machine cannot depend upon the extent to which, or the manner in which, it is used. It is, however, perfectly acceptable for a club to purchase or enter into straightforward rental agreements for these machines.

Section 31(4) states that any prize received must be by way of coin or coins delivered by the machine.

Section 31(7) states that there shall be displayed on any machine on the premises the following details:

(a) a statement specifying the value of the maximum prize which can be won by playing a game once on a machine;
(b) if there are any special circumstances in which that prize cannot be won a statement of those circumstances; and
(c) a statement of a percentage which will be the percentage or minimum percentage of the takings of the machine which it is designed to pay out.

Although the usual number of machines on a premises will be two, which is the maximum usually allowed, s32 of the Gaming Act 1968 does give the licensing authority power to authorise more than two machines on application. If no such application is made then once the club is registered it has the right to have two machines available for gaming. It may have more than two machines on the premises but only two of them can be in use at any one time.

Section 36 of the Act contains provisions relating to the removal of money from machines. It actually stipulates that this must be done by an officer or member of the club.

Theoretically, anyone who is lawfully on the premises is able to play the machines even though that person may be under the age of 18. However, it is a serious offence for the machines to be in operation when members of the public are on the premises.

An annual fee is payable for the machine licence to Customs & Excise. The licence must be displayed on the premises, usually by the side of the machines.

4.4 The Lotteries and Amusements Act 1976

A club can exempt itself from the provisions of the Lotteries and Amusements Act 1976, as updated by the National Lottery, etc. Act 1993, by undertaking a private lottery (s4). A club would qualify under s4 of the Act as holding a 'private' lottery on the basis that the sale of tickets or chances by the promoters is confined to members of the club and is promoted by those same members. The amendment to the Lotteries and Amusements Act 1976 made by the National Lottery, etc. Act 1993 requires a society to have authorisation in writing from its governing body to promote a private lottery. In practice, this authorisation can be by the committee, but it must be in writing. These lotteries will not be unlawful but certain conditions have to be observed in connection with its promotion and conduct which are laid out in s4(3) Lotteries and Amusements Act 1976.

Those provisions are as follows:

(a) the whole proceeds, after deducting any expenses incurred for printing and stationery, should be devoted to the provision of prizes and purchases of tickets or chances, or, in the case of a lottery promoted for the members of the society, should be devoted to:
  (i) the provision of prizes; or
  (ii) purposes which are purposes of the society; or
  (iii) a combination of the two;
(b) there shall not be exhibited or distributed any written notice or advertisement of the lottery other than:
  (i) a notice of it exhibited on the premises of the society for whose members it is promoted or, as the case may be, on the premises on which the persons for whom it is promoted work or reside; and
  (ii) such announcement or advertisement of it as is contained in the tickets, if any;
(c) the price of any ticket or chance shall be the same, and the price of any ticket shall be stated on the tickets;
(d) every ticket shall bear upon its face the name and address of each of the promoters and a statement of the persons to whom the sale of tickets or chances by the promoters is restricted, and a statement that no prize won in the lottery shall be paid or delivered by the promoters to any person other than the person to whom the winning ticket or chance was sold by them, and no prize shall be paid or delivered except in accordance with that statement;
(e) no ticket or chance shall be issued or allotted by the promoters except by way of sale and upon receipt of its full price and no money or valuables received by a promoter shall in any circumstances be returned; and
(f) no tickets in the lottery shall be sent through the post.

If any of the above conditions are not met then each of the promoters of the lottery, and where the person by whom the condition is broken is not one of the promoters that person also, is guilty of an offence.

4.5 Other relevant regulations

4.5.1 Performing Rights Society

Any club which wishes to use copyright music in public must first get the permission of each copyright owner. This is a requirement of the Copyright, Designs and Patents Act 1988. The Performing Rights Society (PRS) is a society of composers and publishers of music. Because it has arrangements with similar societies throughout the world it can license virtually the whole worldwide repertoire of copyright music.

Whether the performance of music is live or through the use of a record player, tape player, CD player, jukebox, radio, video, television sets or even karaoke, a PRS licence will be necessary.

If a licence is not obtained then the PRS have the right to obtain permission from the court to forbid any musical performances and to award damages against the club.

It is important to know that although a television licence gives you the right to receive programmes it does not authorise the holder of the licence to use copyright music on television for public performances. In addition, any local authority entertainment licence does not cover performance of copyright music. For this reason virtually every club will need to have a licence with the PRS.

4.5.2 Phonographic Performance

Phonographic Performance Ltd (PPL) for all intents and purposes is very similar to the PRS, however, the PRS deals with composers' and music publishers' rights, whereas PPL is a non-profit-making company established by the recording industry to administer public performances and broadcasting rights centrally. Its members assign their rights to the PPL so that, on their behalf, it licenses all the UK. All of the PPL income from licences goes back to its members and to performers and artists.

An annual licence should be obtained from PPL (as well as the PRS) in order to have any music played on the premises. The exemptions from obtaining a PPL licence are very limited but in certain instances a charity may not need a licence. This is not likely to cover any music played on the premises by clubs. Similar to the situation with the Performing Rights Society, failure to obtain a licence could result in the PPL obtaining an injunction against the club, stopping it from playing any music and then obtaining legal costs and damages.

Chapter 5 – Accounts and accounting records

As most clubs and associations are predominantly cash businesses, there is a need for setting up and maintaining good records along with adequate controls. As set out in **2.17** and **3.2**, both the Friendly and Industrial and Provident Societies Act 1968 and the Friendly Societies Act 1974 require clubs and associations to maintain adequate records. It is essential that systems are set up to enable the club to demonstrate that their records present a true and fair view of transactions entered into by the club.

5.1 Maintenance of books and records

Most clubs and associations will maintain manual records. The following is guidance on the recording of income and expenditure and controls that should be put into place to ensure that an auditor can satisfy himself that it is a full and accurate record of the transactions entered into by the club or association.

5.2 Bar income

Till rolls should be maintained for inspection. A record should be maintained detailing the till readings taken (which can be checked back to the till rolls), the actual cash in the till, any cash expenditure (but see **5.10**), the net amount available for banking and an explanation of any variances between the till reading and the actual cash.

Controls should be encouraged to ensure that the 'Z' reading is taken at least weekly by the treasurer, secretary or a member of the committee. In addition, the key should be maintained in a secure place, so that 'Z' readings cannot be taken at other than the designated times.

5.3 Fruit machines

A record should be maintained detailing, where appropriate, the machine reading, the cash taken out of the machine, explanations of any variances, the amounts of any top-ups, the signature of the person emptying the machine and if possible, the signature of one or two members of the committee or other club members who have witnessed this. The Gaming Act 1968 actually requires the machine to be emptied by an officer or member of the club (see **4.3.2**). If possible, one or more of the persons witnessing the emptying of the machine should differ from week to week.

This book should also contain a column for recording details which could explain reasons for any fluctuations in income, for example, where there have been more than the usual number of jackpot payouts in the week or a machine has broken down.

The club will need to consider whether it wishes to buy or rent the fruit machines. Although it may not enter a profit-sharing relationship for fruit machines, it may still prefer to rent as the machines can then be changed more regularly, optimising the level of income.

5.4 Tote, raffles and bingo

The club should be maintaining a record of the income received from each of these ventures, along with the income that has been paid out. There should be a record of the number of tickets which can be reconciled back to the actual ticket issues.

There should also be a record of the prize money so that it is possible to demonstrate that the relevant laws have been adhered to (see **4.3** and **4.4**).

5.5 Door income

The doorman should give out a ticket to all guests. Ticket sales can be reconciled to the income recorded. There is also a requirement for all guests to sign a visitors' book and the income should be agreed to this.

Control over entrance to the club is essential to enable the club not only to demonstrate that all income has been recorded, but also to ensure that only people who are entitled to have entered the club and purchased alcohol. Failure to do this can cause problems, both in terms of demonstrating mutuality and also with the licensing authorities (see **4.2**).

5.6 Subscription income

The club will maintain a register of members which should record the category of membership along with the income receivable. This can then be reconciled to the actual income reported in the cash book.

5.7 Other sources of income

A club may have a number of other 'relatively immaterial' sources of income, such as receipts from telephone, cigarette machine, juke box, etc. These machines should be emptied on a regular basis and the income recorded in a book. All the income could be recorded in the same book, but it should be done as individual items, and not all grouped together. The same controls need to be put in place as for the emptying of the fruit machine.

For some of these sources of income some clubs will have an agreement with a supplier that rather than purchasing the machine, they 'rent' the machine. The way these agreements tend to work is that someone from the company will come into the club on a regular basis (usually weekly) and empty the machine. The company will then pay the club usually half of the income in the form of site rental and retain the rest itself. With these agreements generally, the company will pay over half of the net receipt and will account to Customs & Excise for the VAT on the full amount retrieved from the machine. Therefore, from the club's point of view, it must ensure that this is *not* included in vatable income or VAT will have been paid twice. It should be noted that this type of agreement cannot be entered into for fruit machines (see **4.3.2**).

Where this system is in operation, the club should ensure that someone is present when the machine is emptied.

There are pros and cons of both forms of receipt of machine income. There is less risk attached to renting, but the club may make more money out of purchasing its own machines.

5.8 Cash book

It is usually appropriate to keep an analysed cash book reflecting the different types of income, making sure that those that are either zero rated or exempt from VAT are separately identified to facilitate easy preparation of VAT returns.

In addition, in order to enable a club to demonstrate that it is complying with the rules for mutuality, if it receives any income from non-members this should be recorded separately. There are an increasing number of clubs which are renting out rooms for functions and conferences. Where this is to people who are not members of the club and, more importantly, when people who are not members are able to buy alcohol, the profits made are subject to corporation tax. Where there are functions at which alcohol is sold, then not only should the income be separately identifiable, but also the expenditure.

The expenditure side should be analysed between bar purchases, wages and other significant categories of expenditure. Where an analysed cash book is maintained, a column can be given over to each of the expense headings used in the financial statements.

5.9 Goods received

The steward will be required to keep a record of deliveries received. This will be used by the stocktaker when preparing his report (as will the record of bar takings detailed in **5.2**). It should contain details of the precise quantities of orders received on the date from a particular supplier. There should also be evidence to show that invoices received have been checked to the goods received book, to ensure that charges have not been made for items that were not received.

5.10 Petty cash

Clubs should be encouraged to bank all income gross, in fact, generally their rules will stipulate that they must bank gross. Therefore, where there are significant levels of cash payments, for example where wages are paid in cash, they should be encouraged to maintain an imprest petty cash system.

It should be impressed upon the secretary, treasurer and the committee that from a control point of view it is preferable to pay as much as possible by cheque rather than cash. Having identified those areas where cash has to be paid, the club should endeavour to calculate the level of cash that is likely to be needed to be held to meet those expenses. On the basis that they will need to bank at least once a week (more frequently if at all possible), then someone (usually the treasurer) is going to be making a regular visit to the bank and therefore the level of petty cash held does not need to be too high.

A petty cash book should be maintained analysing the expenditure and recording the receipt of any income. This should be balanced every time more income is issued.

5.11 Wages

Full wages records need to be maintained. Details of what has to be maintained for each type of employee can be found in Chapter **10**, but in summary, a P11 or equivalent should be maintained for each member of staff paid above the tax and/or National Insurance level during the course of the year. For any other staff where they are paid below this level, for example, perhaps the cleaning staff, details of their names and addresses and the amounts paid should be maintained. The club also needs to ensure that it retains a signed P46 form wherever required. It is absolutely essential that this is done, as the penalties for failing to apply the PAYE procedures properly are fairly onerous, and this is a common problem area within many clubs.

5.12 Fixed asset register

The club is likely to have material fixed assets, even considered apart from any property. As these are likely to be material, in order to comply with the requirements of the Friendly and Industrial and Provident Societies Act 1968 and the Friendly Societies Act 1974, a fixed asset register should be maintained. In reality, these details are frequently maintained by the auditor or accountant. Where maintained by the club, such a register should include details for each category of asset of the cost, estimated residual value, depreciation and net book value of each asset. Obviously, the depreciation and net book value would need to be updated each year.

5.13 Cash flow management

As clubs tend to be working in a relatively low margin area (they are mutual trading organisations and therefore are not trading to make substantial profits), it is important that they maintain adequate control over income and expenditure to ensure that they do not become loss-making. Generally speaking, fairly good accounting records will be maintained, and therefore it should be relatively easy for them to project forward and know what their expenditure is likely to be. They will have a level of fixed costs related to the premises and the steward, and they must make sure that the margins charged are sufficient to cover these costs and contribute to the variable costs. A careful watch needs to be maintained, to ensure that bar prices are put up as soon as the breweries increase their prices and that the gross profit percentage required by the club to maintain a profit is maintained. Where they have regular stocktakes, this will be easy to gauge.

Generally, the accounts will have sub-categories looking at the different sources of income and trying to identify the precise expenditure attached to these. These should be reviewed and monitored very carefully, to ensure that any loss-making area is reviewed and if necessary, ceased.

The finance committee of the club would be responsible for setting budgets and reviewing the club's performance against them. This may even be one of their specific duties in the rules. If the committee is not currently doing this, it may require input from the accountant to help set up some standard forms by which it can review the performance of the club.

5.14 Sources of finance

When a club wishes to raise money, for example, to refurbish its premises, the most common sources of finance will be the bank or a brewery. As most clubs are major consumers of beer and alcohol, breweries are generally very keen to lend money on favourable terms, even more so since the restrictions have been introduced on the number of tied houses a brewery can have. These loans are a way to increase the level of sales with the club without it being classified as a tied house. There are two main types of brewery loan, repayment loans and barrelage loans, and these are considered below.

5.14.1 Repayment loans

Breweries may offer straightforward repayment loans at favourable rates of interest. These will normally be drawn up in such a way that the rate of interest will rise if the club does not purchase a certain amount of products, usually beer, from the brewery. It is essential that the terms are checked in detail, because quite often the level of 'barrelage' that the club will need to purchase from the brewery will be in excess of what it currently buys. Where the club is using other suppliers, this may be acceptable because, potentially, it can change supplier for some of its beer. However, if the requirement is that it increases its level of beer sales, it needs to ensure that it has budgeted properly, and that it is happy that this is sustainable. In most cases, if the barrelage (a barrel is 36 gallons) is not actually achieved, the penalties can be fairly punitive and the club may find itself having an expensive loan.

In addition, if the club thinks that it can increase sales of one brewery's beers simply by purchasing less of another, while still giving members free choice, it needs to consider whether this is going to be achievable. If the members prefer the beer of one brewer, they will not necessarily transfer over to another just to benefit the club. The committee may then need to make the decision to withdraw the beer of the favoured brewer to force the issue, which could be an unpopular move. The other way of achieving preference for their favoured brewer would be to reduce the prices, but this could have a detrimental effect on margins.

5.14.2 Barrelage loans

Barrelage loans or advance discount loans are set up in such a way that the club does not have to make any formal repayments. Effectively, the loan is written off on the basis of the purchases made by the club during the course of the year. It is, therefore, a discount. However, as with a repayment loan, the club will have to achieve certain targets in order to be able to reap the benefits. The chances are that the agreement will be such that, should they not achieve the barrelage targets, they will have to make some form of repayment, sometimes at fairly onerous interest rates.

It is also worth looking up the price the club will have to pay for the brewery's beer. There is no such thing as something for nothing, and there have been instances, particularly when interest rates are low, when the club might have been better to have raised finance from elsewhere, such as the bank, and negotiated with the brewers to achieve better discounts. On the basis that the breweries are trying to gain influence with this type of organisation, if the club is not tied to them in some way, through a loan or a barrelage loan, then there is the possibility it can get some very good deals, just so that the brewery can encourage the club to sell its beer.

5.14.3 Bank loans

The other major source of finance for a club would be bank loans. These can be achieved on normal commercial terms from any of the major banks. In order to obtain such a loan, the club would need to put forward a formal business plan showing all areas of income and expenditure. This would be unlike dealing with the breweries where they are much more interested in the level of beer sales. The bank would only lend to the operation if they thought it was commercially viable.

5.15 Format and content of accounts

As already explained in **2.18** and **3.3**, there are no detailed requirements for the format of club accounts in either the Friendly and Industrial and Provident Societies Act 1968 or the Friendly Societies Act 1974. However, the Registrar of Friendly Societies issues guidance on what type of information he considers should be included in the accounts of the club or association. In addition, there is an overriding consideration that any accounts produced must show a true and fair view. This in itself would necessitate compliance with all major Statements of Standard Accounting Practice (SSAPs) and Financial Reporting Standards (FRSs).

A pro-forma set of accounts together with an accounts disclosure checklist are shown in Appendices 1 and 2. However, the following notes provide background information on some considerations that should be made.

5.16 General accounting requirements

The accountant should follow the profit and loss account and balance sheet formats as prescribed by the Registrar of Friendly Societies, as well as giving the details required for the notes to the accounts. However, items which are considered immaterial need not be shown separately.

The prescribed format is very similar to that required for companies registered under the Companies Act 1985.

It is acceptable to provide the members with more information than is prescribed by the guidance notes, but not less.

The principles set out in Statements of Standard Accounting Practice and Financial Reporting Standards are considered in the guidance notes issued by the Registry of Friendly Societies generally to be relevant to clubs. However, the guidance notes also state that the exemptions conferred by FRS 2 *Accounting for Subsidiary Undertakings* cannot override the provisions in the Acts.

Some of the provisions of the SSAPs and FRSs would not be relevant to many clubs, but many of them are and are frequently not applied.

The following SSAPs and FRSs are most likely to be relevant to clubs.

5.16.1 SSAP 2 *Disclosure of Accounting Policies*

This will be relevant to all clubs and full disclosure should be made of the accounting policies applied. Consideration should also be given to the fundamental accounting concepts when drawing up the accounts.

5.16.2 SSAP 4 *The Accounting Treatment of Government Grants*

This will apply to any club receiving a grant or equivalent from an outside agency. This SSAP is important to remember where a club has received a barrelage loan from a brewer. Where a loan has been received for the purposes of, for example, refurbishment, it is fairly common for the cost of the refurbishment not to be incorporated in the financial statements. This would not adhere to the principles of SSAP 4. Where this happens the full amount should be capitalised and treated in the same way as a grant. The amount involved would probably be written off on the basis of so much per barrel of beer purchased, and the relevant amount of income could be taken to the profit and loss account each year.

5.16.3 SSAP 5 *Accounting for VAT*

This will be applicable and, irrespective of the adequacy of the accounting records, the accounts should be prepared net.

5.16.4 SSAP 9 *Stocks and Long Term Contracts*

The provisions of this SSAP should be adhered to when dealing with the valuation and disclosure of stocks in the accounts.

5.16.5 SSAP 12 *Accounting for Depreciation*

The cost or valuation of all fixed assets should be depreciated to the residual value over the useful economic lives.

When recording cost, it should be recorded gross. No deduction should be made for any grants or other incentive received.

5.16.6 SSAP 17 *Accounting for Post Balance Sheet Events*

Any adjusting post balance sheet events should be adjusted in the accounts. Non-adjusting, material post balance sheet events should be disclosed.

5.16.7 SSAP 18 *Accounting for Contingencies*

Any contingent liabilities identified should be disclosed.

5.16.8 SSAP 21 *Accounting for Leases and Hire Purchase Contracts*

The standard accounting treatment should be applied for any hire purchase or finance lease contract.

5.16.9 SSAP 24 *Accounting for Pension Costs*

Where the club is involved in a pension scheme, this SSAP should be adhered to.

5.16.10 FRS 1 *Cash Flow Statements*

Any club or association which, if registered under the Companies Act, would be entitled to file small company abbreviated accounts can take advantage of the exemption available from producing a cash flow statement. Any club or association which has turnover, etc. above the small company limits would have to produce a cash flow statement.

5.16.11 FRS 3 *Reporting Financial Performance*

All the provisions of this FRS will be appropriate to clubs and associations. Therefore, as a minimum there should be a statement regarding the recognised gains and losses at the bottom of the profit and loss account along with the statement on continuing activities, and a reconciliation of members' funds in the balance sheet notes. A more detailed account of recognised gains and losses would be required in such instances where there had been a revaluation of property or a prior year adjustment, for example.

5.16.12 FRS 4 *Capital Instruments*

This FRS is unlikely to have a bearing on most sets of financial statements for clubs and associations. However, the 'credit' side of the balance sheet should be classified as 'members' funds'. In addition to the above, any long-term loans should be disclosed analysing the maturity of the debt between amounts falling due:

(a) in one year or less, or on demand;
(b) between one and two years;
(c) between two and five years;
(d) in five years or more.

5.16.13 FRS 8 *Related Party Transactions*

The provision of this FRS may be relevant to certain types of clubs and associations, for example, farmers' co-operatives, where there may be a number of related organisations.

5.17 Balance sheet disclosure

In addition to complying with the relevant SSAPs and FRSs the guidance notes issued by the Registrar of Friendly Societies require the following disclosures to be made:

(a) The method of arriving at the value of fixed assets, i.e., cost or cost and valuation.
(b) A split of the tangible fixed assets between land and buildings, distinguishing between freeholds, long leaseholds and short leaseholds (short leaseholds being defined as those with less than 50 years

to run); plant and machinery; motor vehicles; fixtures and fittings; payments on account and assets in the course of construction.

(c) For each class of tangible asset the details of cost, depreciation, additions, disposals, revaluations and transfers in the year should be shown.

(d) Where there are assets that have been revalued, then the comparable amounts should be disclosed at historic cost. In addition, details of any transfers to or from any revaluation reserve must be disclosed.

(e) There should be a breakdown of investments between listed and unlisted investments.

(f) For listed investments the aggregate market value of those investments should be disclosed.

(g) For unlisted investments there should be disclosure to show how much consists of investments in other Industrial and Provident Societies or Friendly Societies and the names and amounts invested in subsidiaries, where relevant.

(h) Stocks should be broken down between refreshments, other bar stocks and other stocks.

(i) Separate disclosure is needed in respect of creditors (for amounts falling due within one year) of the amount due for mortgages, bank overdrafts and other creditors and accruals. The same disclosure should be made for amounts falling due after more than one year.

(j) For each item included under creditors and loans, there is a requirement to show the aggregate amount of secured liabilities giving an indication of the security given.

(k) Any provisions for liabilities and charges should be split between pensions and similar obligation, taxation including deferred taxation, and other provisions.

(l) Where there are land and buildings or any other fixed asset which has been revalued, the amount of any surplus arising from the revaluation should be disclosed separately under the heading 'revaluation reserve'.

(m) For transfers between reserves, the following disclosure is required:
   (i) the amounts of reserves or provisions as at the date of the beginning of the financial year and as at the balance sheet date respectively;
   (ii) any amounts transferred to or from reserves or provisions during that year; and
   (iii) the source and application respectively, of any amounts transferred.

(n) Where there are capital commitments then the aggregate amount or estimated amount of contracts for capital expenditure not provided for and the aggregate amount or estimated amount of capital expenditure authorised by the committee of management but not contracted for should be disclosed.

(o) Where the club or association has contingent liabilities not provided for, disclosure should be made of:
  (i) the amount of the liability;
  (ii) the legal nature of the liability;
  (iii) whether any valuable security has been provided by the club
  in connection with that liability and if so, what?

5.18 Disclosure relating to the income and expenditure account

The following additional disclosures are required for income and expenditure items:

(a) Disclosure should be made of the method by which turnover stated
is arrived at.
(b) The amounts of remuneration (including fees and expenses) paid to
members of the committee of management must be disclosed.
Expenses may include free drinks, etc.
(c) The amount of staff (including officers') salaries and wages.
(d) The amount of auditors' remuneration.
(e) The amount of depreciation.
(f) The amount of interest payable and similar charges, showing
separately how much consists of:
  (i) interest on bank loans, overdrafts, mortgages and other loans
  wholly repayable within five years;
  (ii) interest on each class of members' loans and deposits;
  (iii) interest on other loans and mortgages.
(g) The basis on which the charge for corporation tax and income tax
is computed.
(h) In relation to extraordinary items, whether extraordinary income
or charges, the net of these two items and the tax on the net
amount should be shown separately. It should, however, be noted
that under FRS 3 it is unlikely that there would be any extraordinary items.

Chapter 6 – Carrying out the audit

The audit of any club and association should be approached in the same way as any other statutory audit of a cash business. It has many similarities and also several peculiarities but, in the main, if approached logically, it should be relatively straightforward. It should be noted that this chapter and the following chapters are aimed towards dealing with clubs and associations.

Included in this chapter is a section on things to look out for during the course of the audit, along with a suggested approach for each of the main audit sections. Specific audit programmes for stock, statutory records and income can be found in Appendix 4, and there are also several forms to aid the planning and completion of the audit.

6.1 Planning

As with every other audit, planning is the key to carrying out an efficient and effective audit, as well as being a direct requirement of the auditing standards.

There are several stages to the planning, and these are detailed below.

6.2 Letter of engagement

Before commencing the audit the letter of engagement should be reviewed to ensure that it is appropriate and up-to-date. An example of a specifically tailored letter can be found in Appendix 3.

It is important to ensure that all aspects of the work undertaken for the client are covered. The new client checklist in Appendix 4 covers appropriate areas to ensure that all relevant issues are covered in the letter of engagement.

Another point to consider here is that if the firm wishes to undertake any corporate finance work for a club or association registered as an Industrial and Provident or Friendly Society or even for an unregistered society then the firm would need to have at least a category B registration.

6.3 Permanent file

A copy of the rules should be maintained on the permanent file and these should be reviewed to ensure that there is nothing within them that will have a bearing on the audit. Most clubs and associations will have a standard set of rules which could occasionally result in audit complications. For example, most standard rules will preclude a body corporate from acting as auditor. Although this is no longer precluded by the Friendly and Industrial and Provident Societies Act 1968 or the Friendly Societies Act 1974, the rules would take precedence. If the audit practice is incorporated, in order to continue as auditors the rules would need to be changed.

The permanent file should contain a record of the systems, including a record of all the different forms of income received by the club and the means of recording this. The systems notes should reflect the flow of documents through the system stating how a sale is first recorded and a liability first recognised. A thorough appreciation of the club or association's system is essential if the auditor is to gain adequate assurance on completeness of income and completeness of creditors.

There should be a register of significant laws and regulations (see Chapters **2–4**); this should include details of any laws and regulations that can have an impact on the business of the club or association and/or on the audit. The details contained in Chapters **2–4** are the most common laws and regulations that will be encountered by the auditor of a club or association, but it is not necessarily a fully comprehensive list. The audit staff must have a basic understanding of the requirements of such things as the Licensing Act, as failure to comply with these requirements could easily result in a substantial liability and/or the cessation of business.

A pro-forma permanent audit file index for clubs and associations has been included in Appendix 4. In addition to the items outlined above, the following information should be contained on this file:

(a) Some background information on the client – this can be recorded on the background information sheet contained in Appendix 4.
(b) Details of bankers and professional advisers, giving details of bank accounts and building society accounts held by the club or association, along with details of any other professional advisers that they might use such as stockvaluers, solicitors, etc.
(c) Some general background notes on the client's business should be placed on the file. This can be a history of the club, along with the types of activities it enters into, for example, whether the club runs bingo sessions, has separate senior citizens' divisions, etc. You would also place in this section details of any affiliated body such as the

Working Men's Club and Institute Union Limited or the Royal British Legion. In the latter case, you would need to obtain details of the reporting requirements to this body along with any specific rules which will apply.

(d) For any new client entering the practice, a new client acceptance form should be completed. A pro-forma can be found in Appendix 4. Not only does this provide you with a checklist to ensure that you have obtained all the information necessary from the client, but it also contains relevant information with regard to such things as money laundering.

(e) Details of the membership and trustees of the club should be held on the file.

(f) Details of any brewery loans or other loans should also be maintained on the file. It is important that these are considered and that a full appreciation of any potential contingent liability is recorded.

(g) The accounts disclosure checklists should also be maintained on this file.

The permanent file should be reviewed on an annual basis to ensure that the details held therein are up-to-date. It is important that it is considered as a working document that helps staff to gain an appreciation of the client they are dealing with. Many clubs are very similar but most of them have their own little peculiarities and these can be highlighted on the permanent file to ensure that best service is given. It is a requirement of the standards that a knowledge is gained of the client before an audit is commenced and this can be recorded via the permanent file.

6.4 Professional independence questionnaire

The first step in the audit is to ensure that the independence of the partner has been maintained. The main areas of risk regarding independence for clubs would relate to the family or other personal relationships, i.e., in certain circumstances the partner may be involved as a member of the club. There is a potential risk relating to provision of other services. It is quite common for the management committees in these operations to rely fairly heavily on the auditor for help and support, so the auditor needs to be careful that he does not become too involved in the management of the club, effectively becoming a 'shadow officer'.

In addition, it must be remembered that the firm is precluded from acting where an employee of the practice is an officer or servant of the society. Therefore, this issue should be considered before the audit commences. A tailored professional independence questionnaire has been incorporated in Appendix 4 for use on clubs and associations, covering the issue of employees acting as either officers or servants of the society. It is also suggested that the practice should circularise details of any clubs and associations they act for to all relevant staff, advising them to declare whether they undertake any paid or unpaid work for these societies. In addition, the firm may wish to put something in its terms and conditions of employment precluding staff from working for any of these bodies. Although this provision in the Acts may seem to be excessive, there is, apparently, at the moment no intention to bring the Acts in line, in this respect, with the Companies Act. It should also be noted that the Acts refer to any employees of the practice, therefore, all staff including administrative staff will need to confirm that they do not act as an officer or a servant for any of the clubs or associations which are clients of the practice.

6.5 Preliminary analytical review

A preliminary analytical review should be undertaken either from a review of the figures or discussions with the officers. The results of this review should be considered when planning the rest of the audit. Further details of the types of procedures that can be applied can be found in Chapter **7**, Analytical Review.

6.6 General risk assessment

The assessment of risk is obviously determined by the exact nature of the client and, therefore, it is difficult to indicate what it is likely to be. However, as there is an external interest in the accounts and it is primarily a cash business, then one would expect to see justification where it is treated as anything other than a medium or high risk audit.

Special consideration needs to be given to the likelihood of there being an error in the accounts as a result of fraud or error, which will include a review of the systems the client has in place to minimise the risk. As the clubs and associations being considered within this publication are primarily cash businesses, the risk of fraud is high unless there are exceptional controls in place. Guidance on the types of accounting systems the auditor should be encouraging the club or association to maintain can be found in Chapter **5**.

Although the general risk assessment will be undertaken at the beginning of the job, it is important that it is reconsidered at every stage of the audit. If anything arises during the course of the audit that would result in the firm reassessing its view, then this should be taken into consideration. If a revision of the risk is necessary, then the auditor needs to consider whether sufficient work has been done on areas that have already been completed, prior to the revision being made.

6.7 Materiality

The auditing standards require materiality to be determined for all clients. Calculations should be made using whatever standard system is applied by the practice. For most clubs and associations a turnover-based parameter for the calculation of materiality will be more appropriate than a gross assets base, although obviously for a housing association, for example, which is outside the scope of this publication, the gross assets parameter may be more appropriate. The materiality should be set on draft figures (or best estimate figures) at the beginning of the job and should be reassessed throughout the audit.

When the audit is completed a final assessment of materiality should be made and where the materiality set at the final stage differs significantly from that used during the course of the audit, the auditor should consider whether sufficient work has been undertaken to enable him to form an opinion on the accounts.

6.8 Systems overview

As well as the record of accounting systems maintained in the permanent file, some sort of overview needs to be placed on the current audit file, as this helps to concentrate the minds of the people undertaking the planning. In addition, the form should contain a conclusion regarding the adequacy of the accounting records and whether the auditor is likely to be able to rely on the figures produced from those records.

A standard form that can be used for undertaking this process can be found in Appendix 4.

6.9 Specific risk assessment

Each of the audit sections needs to be considered so that the appropriate approach can be made to the audit.

Each of the main sections has been listed below giving some guidance on the major risks and the approach that should be taken.

6.9.1 Intangible assets

It is unlikely that the club or association will have material intangible assets. If they have then the nature of these assets should be considered and, where appropriate, a standard audit programme should be used.

If the amounts involved are immaterial, then the auditor should ascertain the nature of the intangible asset, the basis of capitalisation and the basis and period of amortisation. Each of these should be considered to ensure that the asset can properly be capitalised, meets any audit standard requirements and is being amortised over a reasonable period.

6.9.2 Tangible fixed assets

Tangible assets are likely to be a medium risk in the audit of a club or association. The risk will result from the possibility of there being items scrapped in the period or obsolete items on the fixed asset register. In most cases, the use of a standard audit programme will be appropriate as the club is likely to have material fixed assets. It is particularly important that existence tests are carried out, checking items from the fixed asset register to ensure that they exist, which will minimise the risk of there being a material misstatement in the financial statements due to assets that are no longer owned or used by the club being recorded in the books.

In addition, if the club itself does not maintain a fixed asset register and/ or one is not maintained by the practice, then the club's ability to demonstrate compliance with the requirements to maintain proper books and records should be considered.

The auditor also needs to ensure that the following aspects are adequately dealt with:

(a) The fixed asset register and analysed cash book should be reviewed for any large and unusual items in respect of fixed assets and additions and disposals. Any such items identified should be researched and their treatment verified. Given that one of the major risks is that assets may be scrapped or fall permanently into disuse rather than being resold, it is also important to consider, where additions have been made to items such as tills, what happened to the old ones.

(b) The ownership of any freehold property should be determined and any security ascertained. Where the club or association has, for example, a brewery loan this may be charged on the property.

(c) A sample of fixed asset additions should be vouched to the supporting documentation. Obviously, where an accounts preparation assignment is undertaken, this work may have been covered by the work done in preparing the accounts.

(d) Any disposals should be vouched to supporting documentation. In addition, the secretary and committee should be asked to confirm that no assets were scrapped during the year or have fallen permanently into disuse, or they should provide the auditor with details of these. The auditor may also wish to enquire specifically on the disposal of assets which may have been scrapped when new assets were purchased during the year.

(e) Where grants have been received in respect of fixed assets, the auditor needs to ensure that these have been correctly accounted for. This also includes the receipt of brewery money for refurbishment. It is not unusual for breweries to pay for the refurbishment of premises and to treat this like a barrelage loan (see **5.14.2**). It is important that where this has occurred, the full value of the refurbishment is incorporated in the books of the club and written off over its useful life. The 'loan' from the brewery can then be released to the profit and loss account over the same period or, alternatively, if it is a pure barrelage loan (see **5.14.2**), it can be written off in accordance with the agreement and the statement received from the brewer on an annual basis.

(f) The rates of depreciation should be considered to ensure that they are in accordance with the accounting policies, have been applied correctly and are reasonable. Where there are freehold premises that have not been depreciated then the file should contain adequate consideration as to whether this treatment is reasonable.

6.9.3 Other investments

These, where they exist, are likely to be a low specific risk. A standard audit programme should only be adopted where these are material. It is important to ensure that sufficient information is obtained to facilitate adequate disclosure in the financial statements.

Where material investments do exist, then the following detailed audit procedures should be applied:

(a) A review should be undertaken for large and unusual items. Where these exist, details should be ascertained and investments verified.

(b) Share certificates should be reviewed or, if these are not available and perhaps in the case of building society share accounts or investments in other Industrial and Provident or Friendly Societies, third party verification should be obtained, where appropriate.

(c) All additions should be vouched to supporting documentation.

(d) Where there are material investments which are not convertible to cash, then the valuation of these investments needs to be considered.

(e) Any income received should be vouched to available evidence.

(f) The rules should be reviewed to ensure that investments are only made in those bodies authorised by the rules.

6.9.4 Stock and work in progress

This area is likely to be low risk and the club or association is only likely to have stock and not work in progress. In most cases the stock will be valued by a professional valuer and so a standard programme will not be appropriate. Appendix 4 contains a tailored programme which can be adopted where a professional valuer has undertaken a stocktake. It is important to remember that although some reliance can be placed on the professional valuer, the auditor must ensure that the company used is competent and independent from the club. In addition, the make-up of the figures must also be checked. It is not sufficient merely to accept the figure without being satisfied that it is actually reasonable.

Where a professional valuation has been undertaken and these are done at regular intervals during the year, the information obtained from the stock reports can actually provide some audit comfort in other areas as well. Once the auditor is satisfied as to the completeness and accuracy of the information in the reports then a reconciliation of the recorded bar income to that obtained from the stock report would provide some comfort to the completeness of income. In addition, a reconciliation of bar purchases to the stock reports can give comfort on the accuracy of the cost of sales figure.

The following audit procedures should be applied:

(a) The stock reports for the year should be analysed and reviewed for any large or unusual items. Any such items identified, along with all adjustments, should be investigated and care should be taken to ensure that they are treated correctly. For example, the turnover should be grossed up for free drinks for staff and committee members and, these figures should then be shown as an expense item in the accounts.

(b) The auditor should ascertain details of deliveries around the year end and ensure that these have been incorporated in the correct report, i.e., that the correct cut-off has been applied.

(c) The reasonableness of any allowances given by the stocktaker on the report should be considered. For example, is the allowance given for wastage (ullage) reasonable and in line with the auditor's expectations? There have been instances where these types of allowances have been attacked by Customs & Excise when they have been excessive.

(d) The reasons for any material deficits and surpluses should be investigated with the club. Sometimes these will occur due to cut-off errors, but if they are happening on a regular basis the auditor needs to consider whether this is a warning that some problem exists in the accounting procedures or if it is merely an indication that the stocktaker is not doing a very good job.

(e) Tests should be undertaken on the pricing to ensure that the stock-taker has valued the stock correctly and, when computing the sales, has applied the correct selling price. These tests can be applied throughout the year as it provides more comfort when seeking to undertake an overall reconciliation of sales and cost of sales to reports.

(f) A sample of the brewer's delivery notes, invoices and statements should be scrutinised to see whether any free goods have been received by the club which have not been entered in the reports by the stocktaker. This could be a possible explanation where the club is recording regular surpluses. If the club is regularly receiving free beer which is not being recorded by the stocktaker, and it is not recording regular surpluses, then the auditor needs to consider whether and where this income is being recorded.

(g) If the stocktake is carried out on a date other than the year-end date, then a reconciliation of the figure to the year end should be undertaken. Adjustments should be made for any deliveries received during the period and the cost of any sales made. The sales adjustment should be the actual net sales discounted for the average gross profit during the period.

Where stock has not been taken by a professional valuer, or where the audit of a farmers' co-operative, for example, is being undertaken, a standard programme should be used, provided stock is material.

6.9.5 Debtors and prepayments

This area is likely to be low risk. It is unlikely that most clubs and associations, as they are predominately cash businesses, will have material trade debtors. Where an accounts preparation assignment is undertaken, the prepayments would have been prepared by the practice. It is unlikely to be necessary to use a full audit programme on this section and it will usually be sufficient to carry out an analytical review on the prepayments. The auditor should take steps to satisfy himself that all material prepayments have been recognised. Any other material debtors should be vouched to supporting documentation.

6.9.6 Bank and cash

This area can be high risk due to the large cash balances often maintained by clubs and associations. It will be appropriate to use some form of standard audit programme. It is also appropriate to ensure that a cash-count is undertaken. If the auditor does not attend the premises at the year end this can be done during the course of the audit and the balance reconciled back to the year-end cash. It is important to check that any outstanding lodgements at the period end have cleared promptly in the new year. Adequate consideration should be given to the possibility of some sort of teeming and lading fraud. This fraud is particularly prevalent in this type of business.

If possible, it may be appropriate to undertake a cash-count at a stage where one is not expected.

A cash certificate should be obtained from the client for the cash held at the year end and any floats maintained in the bar, the fruit machines and any other machine in the club. Bank and building society certificates should be obtained for all accounts held. The auditor should review to ensure that all accounts are actually held in the club's name and not on behalf of the club by members of the committee. If the latter is the case, then he needs to ensure that there is adequate protection to prevent the individuals involved from absconding with any cash. There may be a bond held, and the club will usually have fidelity insurance. In addition, where accounts or in some cases investments are held in the name of individual members of the committee, any books and certificates should be maintained in a secure place on the club's premises, not by the individual concerned. Therefore, as part of the routine audit procedures the auditor should ask to see such documents.

The size of any cash balances maintained by the club or association should be considered. The holding of excessive volumes of cash may well be the result of some sort of fraud being undertaken. In addition, it is not best practice and frequently clubs can find themselves being underinsured should there be a burglary. The auditor should consider these aspects and make sure that any comment is recorded in writing to the club.

6.9.7 Creditors and accruals

This area is likely to be low risk. However, as the club or association is likely to have material creditors it will usually be appropriate to use a standard audit programme.

Brewery creditors should be vouched to supplier statements and the clubs should be reminded to retain these at the year end. It is quite often useful to send out a pre-year-end letter reminding clubs that these should be retained.

Care should be taken to ensure that all brewery creditors have been fully recorded, as it is fairly common for extended credit periods to be given by breweries to encourage clubs to buy more alcohol approaching the festive season. These purchases will not always be recorded on statements until early in the new year. This aspect can be covered by the testing undertaken on the goods received book and delivery notes.

Analytical review should be undertaken on the accruals, as well as the expenditure side of the profit and loss account to ensure that no material accruals have been missed.

6.9.8 Taxation

This area is likely to be low risk, so it is unlikely that a full audit programme will be required. In most cases the auditor will only need to calculate the liability on non-exempt income, i.e., interest, rent, etc. However, during the course of the audit consideration needs to be made as to whether substantial income is being received from non-members which could result in the club becoming liable to corporation tax.

The auditor should also consider whether the rules over admitting non-members, etc. are being followed.

Apparently, the Inland Revenue are looking very closely at the whole issue of mutuality for this type of organisation and there have been a number of examples of situations where income has been assessed for corporation tax when it has been received from non-members. The club's rules are likely to be very specific in terms of their treatment of visitors, to the extent that they will stipulate that non-members are unable to purchase drink and the auditor needs to ensure that this rule is followed. If the club has decided that the cost of maintaining someone on the door exceeds the income received from affiliates and visitors then the auditor needs to satisfy himself that the club has adequate controls in place to ensure that no non-members are served at the bar, as the cost of losing its mutual trading status would be much more significant than the cost of paying someone to 'man' the door. It may be that the club is happy that the steward has a knowledge of all members and will ask to see the appropriate membership or affiliate card of anyone he does not recognise. If this is the case the auditor needs to consider whether he is satisfied that this is an adequate control and this consideration should be recorded on the file. The auditor should remember that the serving of alcohol to people who are not entitled to purchase alcohol on the premises could not only cause problems from a tax point of view but also could cause difficulties with the licensing authorities.

6.9.9 Capital and reserves

This is likely to be a low risk area. A standard audit programme will not be appropriate as the statutory requirements for clubs and associations are different from those of a limited company. A tailored programme can be found in Appendix 4.

The specific areas that need to be addressed within this section are:

(a) The reserve accounts should be scheduled and any movements vouched and reconciled. A number of clubs and associations are likely to have reserve funds over and above the profit and loss account and their treatment needs to be considered and agreed.

(b) Minutes of meetings of the full committee and the finance committee should be reviewed and any items relevant to the audit extracted and cross-referenced to any other relevant section in the file.

(c) Where the auditor is dealing with an Industrial and Provident Society then a reconciliation of members should be undertaken, cross-referenced to the accounts subscription income and the members' register. It is important to ensure that the shares of any member who has left have been properly cancelled where the rules state that they are not repayable to a member on leaving the club.

6.9.10 Long-term loans

These are likely to be a low risk area and in most cases a standard audit programme should be applied, if relevant. Where the club has significant loans outstanding to breweries, direct confirmation of the balances should be sought. These loans could be in the form of repayment loans or advanced discounts (barrelage loans) (see **5.14.1** and **5.14.2**).

Where barrelage loans have been obtained then it is important that any discount is adequately disclosed. Any write-off of the loan in the form of discount allowed should be set off against cost of sales and not shown as income in the profit and loss account. Not incorporating it in the cost of sales calculation can distort the gross profit percentage.

The loan agreements should also be reviewed to see what the conditions are. Where the club has entered into a barrelage loan or, alternatively, a preferential interest rate loan, then the chances are that the preferential rates received will be tied in some way to the amount of business undertaken with the particular brewery. Very often the agreements have fairly punitive clauses in place where the purchase targets are not achieved. The auditor needs to be aware of these and to review the transactions with the breweries to determine whether any additional charge needs to be made in the accounts and/or any contingent liabilities should be recognised in the notes to the accounts. As a bare minimum the possibility that the club or association may need to make an additional payment will usually need to be disclosed.

6.9.11 Provisions and contingencies

This will normally be a low risk area. In most cases the use of the standard audit programme will be appropriate.

In addition to considering whether there is adequate disclosure of any potential liability resulting from the existence of a brewery loan or any grant received, the auditor needs to consider whether the failure to comply with the requirements of any relevant laws and regulations (as detailed in Chapters **2–4**) could result in any liability or cause any going concern problems.

When considering going concern the auditor needs to examine whether the committee has looked at the club or association's ability to continue trading into the future. This should be done by review of budgets where these exist, and/or discussion with the relevant members of the committee. Where a period of less than 12 months has been considered by the committee then this should be disclosed in the audit report.

The auditor also needs to consider in this section whether the club or association has adequate insurance cover. In particular, the issues of whether it has adequate cover for the cash usually held on the premises and whether there is adequate fidelity insurance in respect of cash held by the steward and other officers of the club or association should be considered. Where no fidelity insurance is maintained and this is a requirement of the rules, this fact should be brought to the attention of the committee.

6.9.12 Profit and loss – income

This area is a high risk area. The risk is that as it is a cash business, income will not be fully recorded. A tailored programme to help audit this area has been included in Appendix 4. It is important that full consideration is made of each material type of income and whether the auditor can satisfy himself that the amounts recorded are a fair reflection of the income received. The first stage in the audit process is to ascertain all the different types of income received and the methods of recording. The auditor then needs to consider whether this method is likely to give adequate comfort on completeness of income if it has been applied properly. If that is the case then the auditor should test to ensure that the system has been upheld for each material category of income.

Where the auditor does not feel that the system is adequate or the results are unsatisfactory then consideration should be given to the effect that this will have on the audit report. Any shortfall must be reported to the committee and instruction given to improve their system to rectify this. There have been instances where the Registrar of Friendly Societies has returned accounts to a club where there is an audit qualification on the grounds that inadequate books and records had been maintained stipulating that this is a breach of the requirements of the Act.

Therefore, the auditor must ensure that the club or association is aware of the possible repercussions where it has not maintained an adequate record of income. Details of the type of records a club may maintain can be found in Chapter **5**.

6.9.13 Profit and loss – expenses

This is likely to be a low risk area and in most cases a standard audit programme should be used.

Where the accountant undertakes accounts preparation, it may well be that the work undertaken during the course of the accounts preparation in conjunction with detailed analytical review on the movements on the profit and loss account will be sufficient to give him audit comfort. However, where this is not the case then the auditor must ensure that the following items are covered:

(a) A sample of expense items from the nominal ledger, if available, or from the final point of entry if not, should be selected and vouched through to supporting documentation. The auditor may wish to extend this test to consider paid cheques. This test is particularly important in this type of organisation as there is an external interest in the accounts.
(b) A sample of cash purchases needs to be selected and vouched through to any supporting documentation.

The auditor may wish to look at expense items separate from the cost of sales, as the sample size selected for cost of sales can be reduced significantly provided that a reconciliation from the cost of sales in the accounts to the stock reports has been successful.

6.9.14 Profit and loss – wages

This is another high risk area; the risk being that there will be casual labour employed without the proper P46 procedures, etc. being applied. These procedures should be checked and any appropriate checklists completed. A report should be made to the committee of management if the relevant procedures are not being followed. The procedures for casual labour have been recorded in Chapter **10**.

Where the wages have been computed by the client themselves, a sample of payments made should be calculated to ensure that they have been calculated correctly. Particular emphasis should be placed on making sure that the correct National Insurance tables have been applied and that the correct PAYE tables have been used where there has been a change in rate. During any visit to the premises, the auditor may wish to see if there are any members of staff present on the premises who have not been recorded in the wages book.

In addition, the cash book should be scrutinised to identify any items of expenditure which should be classified as wages but are being analysed elsewhere. It is fairly common for wages being paid to the cleaner to be incorporated in a cleaning charge. Where this is the case, then the auditor needs to ensure that an adequate record is maintained.

6.9.15 Post balance sheet events

This area is also likely to be low risk, and in most cases a standard audit programme will be appropriate. On a rare occasion where there is a significant delay between the completion of the field work and the approval of the accounts and signing-off of the audit report, a further review should be undertaken.

The auditor should review the bank statements and cash book in the new period, discuss the issue with the secretary and members of the committee and, where appropriate, put a suitably worded paragraph into the letter of representation for signature by the committee.

6.9.16 VAT

This area is likely to be low risk and in most cases it will be appropriate to use a standard audit programme, along with any supporting checklists.

However, it is also important to ensure that the staff working on the job are aware of the VAT treatment of specific forms of income received by the club. This can be included in the records maintained on the permanent audit file.

6.10 Review/finalisation

6.10.1 Checklists

Standard checklists should be used at the end of each job to ensure that all relevant areas have been dealt with. These will include checklists to ensure that all the auditing standards have been complied with. A critical review of accounts questionnaire has been included in Appendix 4 to help demonstrate compliance with the relevant auditing standards.

6.10.2 Letter of representation

The points for a letter of representation that have arisen during the course of the audit should be collated. This should be drafted and then discussed with the secretary and, potentially, the committee before it is signed. A pro-forma letter of representation has been included in Appendix 5.

6.10.3 Analytical review

An overall analytical review needs to be carried out at the end of the job in addition to any analytical review that has been undertaken during the course of the audit. The accounts should be looked at in total to see whether the results obtained make sense in view of the audit evidence obtained and the auditor's knowledge of the client. In the profit and loss account section, the auditor should have considered the relationship between the different types of income, for example, it is quite usual for there to be a correlation between the fruit machine income and bar sales. However, as an overview, it is still appropriate to complete some form of final analytical review. The ratios that are likely to be meaningful in this type of business are the gross profit percentage, stock turnover and liquidity. An analytical form has been included in Appendix 6, and more detailed guidance on the application of analytical review can be found in Chapter **7**.

6.10.4 Audit highlights

The member of staff working on the job should be encouraged to complete some sort of audit highlights report. This should go through the salient points of the audit, explaining what problems have been encountered, how these have been dealt with and what the overall results and conclusions are on each of the main audit sections. The report should contain an assessment of the impact of any unadjusted errors which have been identified and recorded on the file. The report should then carry on to form an overall conclusion on the job. This conclusion needs to consider the type of audit report that should be given to the client, i.e., whether it should be 'clean' or 'qualified'. A specimen form of justification of audit report has been incorporated in Appendix 4 for use in drawing this final conclusion. Where it is considered that an audit qualification is necessary, this should be designed and discussed in full with the committee. An example of the officers' responsibility statement and an unqualified audit report is contained in the model accounts in Appendix 1. The following two example audit reports can be used in the most common cases of qualification, either on the basis of incomplete accounting information or concern over the ability of the club or association to carry on as a going concern.

6.10.5 Specimen audit report with an inherent uncertainty relating to going concern

REPORT OF THE AUDITORS TO THE MEMBERS OF ....

We have audited the financial statements on pages . . . to . . . which have been prepared under the historical cost convention (as modified by the revaluation of certain fixed assets) and the accounting policies set out on pages . . . and . . . .

Respective responsibilities of officers (committee of management) and auditors
As described on page . . . the society's officers (committee of manage-ment) are responsible for the preparation of financial statements. It is our responsibility to form an independent opinion, based on our audit, on those accounts and to report our opinion to you.

Basis of opinion
We conducted our audit in accordance with the auditing standards issued by the Auditing Practices Board. An audit includes examination, on a test basis, of evidence relevant to the amounts and disclosures in the accounts. It also includes an assessment of the significant estimates and judgements made by the officers in the preparation of the accounts, and of whether the accounting policies are appropriate to the society's circumstances, consistently applied and adequately disclosed.

We planned and performed our audit so as to obtain all the information and explanations which we considered necessary in order to provide us with sufficient evidence to give reasonable assurance that the accounts are free from material misstatement, whether caused by fraud or other irregularity or error. In forming our opinion, we also evaluated the overall adequacy of the presentation of information in the accounts.

Fundamental uncertainty

In forming our unqualified opinion, we consider that we should draw your attention to the following matter referred to in Note . . . .

† The society meets its day-to-day working capital requirements through an overdraft facility which, in common with all such facilities, is repayable on demand. The society is currently trading within its agreed overdraft facility which is due for review in . . . .

On the basis of our discussions with the society's officers (committee of management) and other information of which we became aware during our audit, we consider that it is appropriate for the society's officers (committee of management) to prepare accounts on a going concern basis.

Opinion

In our opinion the accounts give a true and fair view of the state of affairs of the society as at . . . and of the profit for the year then ended and have been properly prepared in accordance with the Industrial and Provident Societies Act 1965 and the Friendly and Industrial and Provident Societies Act 1968/the Friendly Societies Act 1974*.

† *This would need to be adapted for the specific needs of the client. Another example can be found in example 11 to the standard.*

* *delete as appropriate*

Registered Auditors   Address
Date

6.10.6 Specimen qualified audit report resulting from limitation in scope – cash sales

REPORT OF THE AUDITORS TO THE MEMBERS OF . . . . . .

We have audited the financial statements on pages . . . to . . . which have been prepared under the historical cost convention (as modified by the revaluation of certain fixed assets) and the accounting policies set out on pages . . . and . . . .

Respective responsibilities of officers (committee of management) and auditors

As described on page . . . the society's officers (committee of management) are responsible for the preparation of financial statements. It is our responsibility to form an independent opinion, based on our audit, on those accounts and to report our opinion to you.

Basis of opinion

We conducted our audit in accordance with the auditing standards issued by the Auditing Practices Board. An audit includes examination, on a test basis, of evidence relevant to the amounts and disclosures in the accounts. It also includes an assessment of the significant estimates and judgements made by the officers in the preparation of the accounts, and of whether the accounting policies are appropriate to the society's circumstances, consistently applied and adequately disclosed.

We planned and performed our audit so as to obtain all the information and explanations which we considered necessary in order to provide us with sufficient evidence to give reasonable assurance that the accounts are free from material misstatement, whether caused by fraud or other irregularity or error. However, the evidence available to us was limited because £. . . of the society's recorded turnover comprises cash sales, over which there was no system of control on which we could rely for the purpose of our audit. There were no other satisfactory audit procedures that we could adopt to confirm that cash sales were properly recorded.

In forming our opinion, we also evaluated the overall adequacy of the presentation of information in the accounts.

Qualified opinion arising from limitation in audit scope

Except for any adjustments that might have been found to be necessary had we been able to obtain sufficient evidence concerning cash sales, in our opinion, the financial statements give a true and fair view of the state of the society's affairs as at . . . and of its profit for the year then ended and have been properly prepared in accordance with the Industrial and Provident Societies Act 1965 and the Friendly and Industrial and Provident Societies Act 1968/the Friendly Societies Act 1974*.

In respect alone of the limitation on our work relating to cash sales:

- we have not obtained all the information and explanations that we considered necessary for the purpose of our audit; and
- we were unable to determine whether proper accounting records had been maintained.

* *delete as appropriate*

Registered Auditors   Address
Date

6.10.7 Review

When carrying out the review the auditor needs to ensure that the main risk areas identified at the planning stage have been adequately dealt with and will not themselves result in a qualification being necessary.

Any points arising during the audit which need to be brought to the attention of the committee of management should be included in a letter of comment which may need to be discussed in detail with the committee before it is sent.

Where necessary, disclosure checklists should be completed to ensure that the accounts contain all necessary disclosures. A specimen accounts disclosure checklist can be found in Appendix 2.

The audit principal needs to ensure that there is adequate evidence of his involvement in the job and that he is happy that the audit report can be signed and all relevant standards have been complied with. A partner completion form, which helps to provide some of this evidence, has been incorporated in Appendix 4 for use by the partner at the end of the job, before the audit report is signed.

Chapter 7 – Analytical review

7.1 Introduction

Analytical review is being recognised more and more as a powerful audit tool. The principles of analytical review do not solely relate to audit assignments. Certain of the procedures considered can equally be applied for clubs and associations which can now submit an independent accountant's report. Analytical review has to be used on audit assignments at the planning and the review stage. However, this chapter also looks at how analytical review techniques can be used to cut down on other substantive audit work and how analytical review can give the auditor/accountant an improved probability of picking up errors during his work.

The most logical place to look for a definition of analytical review is in the new auditing standards. Below the auditing standard, SAS 410 *Analytical Procedures* (in other words, analytical review) is considered. Within this standard, 'analytical procedures' (analytical review) is defined as 'the analysis of relationships:

(a)   between items of financial data, or between items of financial and non-financial data, deriving from the same period; or
(b)   between comparable financial information deriving from different periods or different entities,

to identify consistencies and predicted patterns of significant fluctuations and unexpected relationships, and the results of investigations thereof'.

Perhaps it can be put in a simpler way by saying that analytical review is all about analysing information, investigating the results and drawing reasonable conclusions thereon.

All three of these ingredients are critical for good analytical review. Information must be analysed, investigated and then concluded on.

The other salient point to note at this stage is that the definition talks about comparing not only items of financial data but items of financial and non-financial data. Normally, the key item of non-financial data will

104

be the accountant's own knowledge of the client and, importantly, the client's business.

7.2 SAS 410 *Analytical Procedures*

Before moving on to look at how the auditor/accountant can practically use analytical review it is worth recapping on the SAS to set out the ground rules and guidance which should be followed.

The first standard within the SAS simply says that 'auditors should apply analytical procedures at the planning and overall review stages of the audit' (SAS 410.1).

The guidance notes then go on to detail the situations where analytical procedures can be used. The guidance states that they are 'designed primarily to assist in planning the audit and as part of the evaluation of the financial statements'. The evaluation of the financial statements should happen at the end of the audit. This latter requirement really was contained within the old auditor's operational standard. However, the requirement to use analytical procedures in the planning of the audit is being prescribed for the first time although this has always been best practice for most audits. This aspect will be considered in more detail later on.

The standard also states that analytical procedures can be used to obtain audit evidence on certain material financial statement assertions. In other words, analytical review can be used as a substantive test to gain audit evidence. Again this will be examined in more detail later on.

There are then some notes on the nature of analytical procedures. Firstly, the auditor/accountant is told that analytical procedures include the consideration of comparisons of an entity's financial information with the following examples:

- comparable information from prior periods;
- anticipated results of the entity from budgets or forecasts;
- predictive estimates prepared by the auditors;
- similar industry information.

The guidance notes then go on to say that analytical procedures 'also include consideration of relationships:

- between elements of financial information that are expected to conform to a predicted pattern based on the entity's experience such as the relationship of gross profit to sales;

105

- between financial information and relevant non-financial information, such as the relationship of payroll costs to number of employees'.

Really, these notes just formalise on paper what most people have been doing on analytical review in the past. The SAS continues to say that 'the auditors' choice of procedures, methods and level of application is a matter of professional judgment'. This is the case as long as the auditor does clearly evidence analytical review at the planning and review stage of the audit.

7.3 Analytical review at the planning stage – procedures where you are given draft accounts

A situation where a client produces its own accounts is, in theory, the easiest situation for adopting analytical procedures at the planning stage. Clearly, this particular part of the standard can be adopted as long as the client does produce the accounts for audit. This would also include situations where the club or association presents the auditor/accountant with a reasonably accurate trial balance. This may not happen very frequently but will occasionally occur where a professional stocktaker is employed and they run a book-keeping agency.

The types of procedures that one would typically adopt when conducting analytical procedures at the planning stage will primarily be the completion of the analytical review form which can be found in Appendix 4.

The main purpose behind conducting analytical procedures at the planning stage is to identify the figures and ratios which have changed significantly since the last accounting period. This should also of course include situations where the auditor/accountant would have expected certain figures and ratios to have changed, but they have not.

A simple example would be a club which you know has opened a second bar during the year, but there has no been corresponding increase in the stock figure.

The auditor/accountant would then potentially assess these areas as being medium or high risk for audit purposes or, at the very least, ensure that such areas are given priority when conducting the audit field work.

It is worth pointing out at this stage that conduct of the preliminary analytical review does not constitute extensive analytical review procedures and, therefore, sample sizes on substantive tests cannot be reduced.

106

Also, just as the auditor/accountant would discuss the results of the final analytical review with the client, it is important to discuss the results of the planning analytical review with the client and obtain any explanations for significant changes which were unexpected. The auditor/accountant would then substantiate these as part of his audit work.

The results obtained and explanations given should then be borne in mind when assessing risk.

An additional point to make, is that when assessing general risk the auditor should evidence his consideration as to whether or not the client would be able to continue as a going concern for the foreseeable future. Clearly, if any management accounts presented to the auditor by the client indicated a decline in the financial health of the club or association, then this particular area would need to be highlighted as being a potential risk. The auditor/accountant would then have to devote more time to the consideration of the applicability of the going concern basis.

7.4 Budgets

The auditor/accountant can use procedures similar to those described above when comparing any management accounts or trial balance produced by the club or association to budgets, rather than previous years' accounts.

The budgets do not necessarily have to have been set by the club or association. Any form of financial forecasting can be used. The most common example of this would be any cash flow and profit forecast produced by the auditor/accountant on behalf of the club or association. This work has become more common for clubs and associations due to financial pressures.

If the accounts that are available at the planning stage show significant departures from the forecasted financial statements then this could potentially lead to those areas being identified as having a medium or high risk of being materially misstated.

Therefore, any significant departures from budgets or forecasts in the figures or the ratios calculated from any draft accounts presented to the auditor/accountant must be looked into with explanations sought. The auditor/accountant must remember to substantiate any explanations as part of the audit procedures.

7.5 Analytical review at the planning stage – procedures where there are no draft accounts

As long as draft accounts are available at the planning stage, conducting analytical procedures at the planning stage really only involves the application of common sense.

The guidance notes to SAS 410 say that 'for those entities with less formal means of controlling and monitoring performance, it may be possible to extract relevant financial information from the accounting system (perhaps when preparing the draft financial statements), VAT returns and bank statements. Discussions with management, focused on identifying significant changes in the business since the prior financial period, may also be useful'.

What the standard suggests that the auditor/accountant should do in this particular scenario is to look at whatever records the client has in order to assess if there are any particular changes indicated by the books and records that the club or association actually keep.

For example, if it can be seen from looking at the bank statements that the club or association appears to be trading at a level at or around its overdraft limit, then this could indicate a potential going concern problem that should be addressed.

Although many clubs and associations may not be able to produce full financial accounts for audit, they may well prepare certain schedules for the auditor/accountant to prepare the accounts from. A potential example of this would be a daily takings book. The auditor/accountant could then assess whether or not the daily takings book indicated sales on a seasonal basis consistent with expectations and previous years.

At this stage the club or association may also have available the stock-taker's report for the auditor/accountant to examine. This would contain basic bar sales information. From these reports the auditor/accountant may be able to calculate certain ratios such as gross profit percentage and spillage allowances (ullage).

If it is not possible for the auditor/accountant to complete full analytical review at the beginning of the job, then the auditor/accountant should be looking to calculate and complete the analytical review form outlined in Appendix 4 as and when the relevant information becomes available during the accounts preparation work. If the figures and ratios vary significantly from previous periods and this cannot be adequately explained, then potentially the risk assessments relating to that particular area need to be reconsidered and possibly amended.

The other form that the analytical review at the planning stage may take is a discussion with the club or association to see how it feels it has performed over the last accounting period. If the auditor/accountant talks to the right person within the club or association, the auditor/accountant will usually find that he will have a reasonable idea as to how the club or association has fared in the last 12 months.

When conducting this discussion the auditor/accountant needs to ensure that as much information as possible is collected in respect of significant changes to the club or association. This is so that the auditor/accountant can obtain from the management committee the changes to the figures that they would expect to see in this year's accounts. This is probably best evidenced as narrative notes on the auditor/accountant's discussions with the club or association as to what its expectations are and what the accounts will show for the accounting period in question.

This actually achieves two things – not only does it help the efficiency and effectiveness of the audit but it will also help client relations if the auditor/accountant shows willingness to discuss the results with the club or association before the work commences. The best time for this to be done is somewhere around the year end so that the accounting year is fresh in the mind of the club's management.

7.6 Risk assessments

As stated above, once the planning analytical review has been carried out, the auditor/accountant must carefully consider any unexplained figures or ratios in the accounts which vary from what the auditor/accountant and the club or association would expect.

For example, there may not be an adequate explanation why the stock turnover ratio has worsened from last year. This, combined with a steady gross profit percentage, when the club or association had told the auditor/accountant that it had decreased its selling prices in order to increase volume of sales, could lead the auditor/accountant to the conclusion that stock could, potentially, be overstated. The auditor/accountant would then either assess or re-assess the risk assessment on stock as possibly being medium or high. At the very least, the auditor/accountant would want to ensure that the audit objective of overstatement of stock was fully satisfied.

The same principle applies when the auditor/accountant has no accounts to look at. The club or association's expectations must be examined and risk assessments drawn thereon.

7.7 Analytical review at the completion stage

This is the basic critical review of the accounts and should always take place at the end of the audit. SAS 410 expects that analytical procedures will play a part in completing the audit. SAS 410.3 says that 'when completing the audit, auditors should apply analytical procedures in forming an overall conclusion as to whether the financial statements as a whole are consistent with their knowledge of the entity's business'.

Linking this in with the audit documentation contained within Appendix 4, this would involve completing the critical review of the accounts questionnaire and the main analytical review form.

The critical review of the accounts, however, does not end with the simple completion of the forms and the calculation of the various ratios. It is imperative that any unexpected variations and, indeed, any unexpected consistencies, are properly followed up, explained and substantiated. The conclusion that the auditor/accountant should be trying to arrive at in the critical review of the accounts, is that the accounts 'make sense'. It is, therefore, important that the auditor/accountant does explain any variations.

With certain societies, it will not really help the critical review of the accounts to complete the analytical review form outlined in Appendix 4. This is because the ratios that are calculated when completing the form do not really mean anything to that particular type of society. In these situations, it is up to the auditor/accountant to develop his own indicators and ratios that should be calculated and critically examined every year.

The guidance notes within this part of the SAS state that the conclusion that the auditor/accountant arrives at, i.e., that the accounts make sense, is intended to corroborate the other conclusions that the auditor/ accountant has arrived at during the audit.

It is also stressed that this closing analytical review may identify areas requiring further procedures.

From experience on cold file reviews, practices do not have any difficulties in calculating ratios, but interpreting the results and properly following up unexpected fluctuations is not well done in many cases.

It must be remembered, however, that the calculation of, and follow-up on, these basic ratios does not constitute extensive analytical review. The auditor/accountant needs further analytical review evidence to cut down on sample sizes.

7.8 Significant fluctuations

The next part of the SAS that needs to be considered is the section on fluctuations, or what procedures are needed when the accounts do not appear to make sense. The SAS tells us that:

'when significant fluctuations or unexpected relationships are identified that are inconsistent with other relevant information or that deviate from predicted patterns, auditors should investigate and obtain adequate explanations and appropriate corroborative evidence.' (SAS 410.4)

This means that where the auditor/accountant does have any unexpected results that are thrown up by the analytical review, these must be fully investigated. Proper explanations for the deviations should be obtained and the auditor/accountant should also consider obtaining other audit evidence to back up the explanations that have been received.

The guidance notes in this particular section of the SAS state that the follow-up of changes on an analytical review usually begin with enquiring of the management why these changes have occurred. This must then be 'followed by corroboration of management's responses'.

This corroboration can be done by comparing the explanation to the auditor/accountant's knowledge of the club or association and with 'other evidence obtained during the course of the audit'. However, if the deviations relate to analytical procedures that the auditor/accountant has carried out as substantive tests on particular sections of the audit, the auditor may need to undertake additional detailed testing to confirm the explanations received.

Finally, if the society is unable to prove an explanation as to why certain changes have occurred, then the auditor needs to conduct audit procedures to obtain an explanation for the changes.

The importance of obtaining explanations for any unexpected results and also the need to substantiate any explanations that are given to the auditor cannot be over-emphasised. It is also, of course, imperative that adequate notes are made of these steps on the audit file.

It is also worth remembering that sometimes the auditor/accountant may expect significant deviations from previous years' figures, due to a change in the club or association's circumstances. It is important that the auditor/accountant also properly follows up situations where there are expected fluctuations but they do not appear to be occurring.

7.9 Analytical review substantive procedures

7.9.1 When should it be used?

The simple answer to this question is as often as possible. However, there is no actual standard contained within the section of SAS 410 on using analytical procedures as a substantive test during the audit fieldwork. The auditor should really carry out extensive analytical review procedures wherever this will be considered necessary or effective. Carrying out extensive analytical review procedures can lead to excellent audit assurance from certain areas and, if successful, should reduce the extent of the transaction/balance testing.

This section only contains guidance on when analytical review can be used to obtain some of the audit evidence within particular audit sections. The section starts by stating that it is up to the auditor's own judgement as to whether or not use is made of analytical procedures during the detailed substantive testing.

The only guidance given is that the auditors should assess the expected 'effectiveness and efficiency of the available procedures in reducing detection risk for specific financial statement assertions'. Therefore, at the planning stage the auditor needs to make an assessment as to whether or not analytical review is going to be used as a substantive test on particular audit sections.

The auditor will usually be aware of the sort of information that is available from the client on which the auditor can base any analytical review on individual sections. It is also acceptable to use financial information that is prepared by the club or association when using analytical procedures as a substantive test. However, if the auditor is going to do this, then it is clear that the auditor needs to document to his satisfaction that 'such data is properly prepared'.

It therefore follows that extensive analytical review can be utilised as a substantive audit tool even when it is used on accounting information drawn up by the auditor.

Extensive analytical review procedures can also provide alternative audit procedures enabling appropriate reliable audit evidence to be derived from a combination of transaction testing and analytical review, from which, for example, it can be concluded that all sales have been properly recorded in the accounting records.

7.9.2 How it should be used

The types of analytical procedure that are being considered here are detailed examination of particular sections of the audit through analytical review in order to cut down the amount of other substantive work that needs to be undertaken.

A typical examination would be a thorough review of the third party stock reports on a club. The auditor would be able to reconcile the information from the reports to sales and cost of sales. This can then be used to cut down the amount of audit work the auditor would perform on detailed bar income and costs of sales testing.

The notes on the SAS then state that when intending to use analytical review as a substantive procedure on individual audit sections, the auditor needs to consider a number of factors. They are given as follows:

- 'the plausibility and predictability of the relationships identified for comparison and evaluation' (in other words, is there a close relationship between two sets of figures that you were looking at);
- 'the objectives of the analytical procedures and the extent to which their results are reliable;
- the degree to which information can be disaggregated' (basically the more broken down figures can be, the more reliable they are. If a club or association has a number of product lines then the auditor should look at the gross profit of each line rather than any change in the gross profit as a whole);
- 'the availability of information, both financial . . . and non-financial;
- the relevance of the information available, for example whether budgets are established as results to be expected rather than as goals to be achieved' (if it is the latter then perhaps the information available is not so relevant);
- 'the comparability of the information available; and
- the knowledge gained during previous audits.'

Basically the factors that are outlined in the SAS are really just matters of common sense that need to be borne in mind when using analytical review as part of the substantive procedures.

7.9.3 Guidelines and ground rules

The SAS also comments that the analytical procedures could be relied upon more when the information used comes from sources 'independent of, rather than internal to, the entity'. If it is produced internally within the entity, then reliability is enhanced when the information comes from a source independent of the accounting system. Reliability is also enhanced if 'there are adequate controls over its preparation' by the accounting system within the entity.

If the auditors do not feel that they can wholly rely on the information to be used during the analytical review procedures, then they may need to obtain other evidence to check on the reliability of this information. The necessity of this will depend on the results of the other substantive procedures within that particular section and the importance of the results of the analytical procedures within that particular audit section.

There is then some guidance on the extent of reliance that the auditor should place on the results of analytical procedures when used as substantive tests. The factors that should be considered when looking at the extent of reliance will include:

(a) 'The number of other audit procedures directed towards the same financial statement assertions.' (The particular example given in the SAS is where analytical review is carried out on the detailed aged debtors listing but after date cash testing is also carried out.)
(b) 'The accuracy with which the expected results of analytical procedures can be predicted.' (The example given here is that the relationship of gross profit to sales is easier to predict than comparing advertising to sales.)
(c) 'The frequency on which a relationship is observed.' (The more frequently the relationship is looked at the better the evidence.)

There is one final note on this particular section of the standard which says that if the auditor is going to rely on the results of analytical review then the auditor needs to specifically state and consider at the planning stage whether or not analytical review will pick up a material misstatement in the particular area where it is being used as a substantive procedure.

If there are differences between the auditor's expectation of what figures should show and what the figures actually show, then the auditor should perform further analysis and, more usually, enquire from the client if there are any explanations for the differences. Such explanations tend to relate to unusual transactions or accounting or business changes.

It is not just a question, however, of obtaining explanations for these differences. The explanations must be substantiated. Usually, explanations can be substantiated in one of two ways. The auditor would either use his understanding of the business (including knowledge gained when performing audit work both in the present and in the past) and/or, potentially, some checking of other evidence supporting any explanations given.

The key point to remember when conducting detailed analytical review procedures as part of the substantive testing is to ensure that the amounts tested, the results (including any explanations and corroborative evidence for any unexplained fluctuations) and a proper conclusion on the analytical review are all properly documented.

7.9.4 Sampling

As far as most sampling systems are concerned, using extensive analytical review can enable the auditor to cut sample sizes by varying amounts. It is important, though, to bear in mind that only certain analytical procedures could be considered to be 'extensive'.

For example, calculating an overall gross profit percentage would not constitute extensive analytical review and, therefore, merely calculating this figure and obtaining explanations for a significant change would not enable the auditor to cut down on sample sizes.

The remainder of the chapter contains the main examples of extensive analytical review procedures which can be used to reduce the extent of substantive testing and perhaps, depending on the size of the amounts involved, eliminate the need for detailed substantive testing altogether.

Care must be taken in the analysis of the results of extensive analytical review procedures. It would be wrong to assume that extensive analytical review procedures result in automatic reduction in the extensive detailed testing. Only if the results of the procedures are satisfactory can the extent of substantive testing be reduced.

If, as may often be the case, extensive analytical review indicates unexpected variations which cannot be explained, this would require investigation of the variations and the directing of audit attention accordingly. In such circumstances it might be inappropriate to reduce the level of substantive testing.

As has been said above, using extensive analytical review could lead the auditor to be able to eliminate detailed substantive testing altogether on certain sections of the audit. There are a number of scenarios where detailed analytical review on certain areas could, if successful, lead to there not being a requirement to conduct detailed account balance testing. The exact application of this principle is very much up to individual firms and can be flexed on individual audits.

Generally speaking, there are potentially three different scenarios whereby detailed testing could be replaced by analytical review. The first case involves small amounts.

For example, if stock is around the materiality level that is set at the planning stage then extensive analytical review could be wholly relied upon to assess whether or not stock is fairly stated. The types of analytical review procedures that could be used are described below but generally the auditor would perhaps look at changes in value on individual stock lines or stock types. This particular principle could be extended to amounts of, say, two to three times materiality.

The particular principle itself could be extended further if the auditor would restrict the detailed substantive testing to items above the tolerable error level and other key items. In this scenario, extensive analytical review and detailed testing restricted to items above tolerable error and other key items could lead to there not being a requirement to audit a random sample of the remaining balances.

Another reason for eliminating detailed testing by using detailed analytical review procedures would potentially be due to the level of accounts preparation work undertaken. A good example of this would be expenses and wages testing on the profit and loss account. One could say that due to the level of checking that was carried out at the accounts preparation stage, a certain amount of comfort can be drawn. Therefore, the auditor only needs to evidence his comparison of this year's expenses to previous years' expenses (and possibly budgets) as additional audit evidence.

The ground rules for the use of analytical review have now been set. There follows a look at the types of extensive analytical review procedures that can be used to make auditing clubs and associations more efficient, effective and importantly, interesting.

7.10 Use of analytical review on the balance sheet audit – fixed assets

Fixed assets is actually quite a difficult area to apply extensive analytical review procedures on. However, below are listed a number of procedures which can be used to give additional audit comfort as to whether or not fixed assets are fairly stated.

7.10.1 Additions

The auditor can compare the level of additions to fixed assets during the year to, potentially, many other pieces of information. It should be borne in mind, though, that on an accounts preparation audit this may not necessarily be that useful as the auditor may well have vouched the vast majority of additions to invoices as part of the accounts preparation work.

What is certainly a very weak correlation is to compare this year's level of fixed asset additions to previous years. Inherently, this figure is subject to significant variations.

However, societies will usually have to have authorisation for additions. Some may even have budgeted levels of capital expenditure, to which the fixed asset additions figure for the accounting year can be compared. It is also likely in such scenarios that the club or association would document any departure from capital expenditure budgets and, therefore, this can be used to corroborate any explanations for differences given to the auditor by the committee.

The auditor may also be on the look-out for expected increases in capital expenditure. A typical example of this would be the opening of a second bar. Obviously, when such expansion occurs it would be usual for a certain level of additions to fixed assets to be made. The auditor's understanding of the club's business should lead the auditor to be able to estimate roughly the level of fixed assets that would be required in the second bar. The question that the auditor would then have to answer is whether or not the level of fixed asset additions shown in the accounts is reasonable.

Depending on the replacement policy of the society, the auditor may also be able to deduce that if certain assets are disposed of, then additions should be made to replace them. Finally, there will be a correlation between the level of capital expenditure and the repair policy of the club or association. If the club or association decides to repair more of the fixed assets rather than replace them, the auditor may well expect to see a downturn in the level of capital expenditure.

7.10.2 Disposals

Disposals of fixed assets will be, by their very nature, one of the more erratic figures in the accounts.

However, the auditor may be able to compare disposals with other information. If a club or association has a formal or informal replacement policy then the level of disposals in a year may be compared to this. Also, for the reasons described above, the auditor may be able to tie in disposals to particular additions.

7.10.3 Fixed asset utilisation

There is a standard ratio of fixed assets utilisation that can be calculated. This is actual sales: fixed assets, however for clubs and associations this ratio would not be particularly useful as the level of fixed assets, aside from the building, can be difficult to predict. Therefore, comparing this ratio to other clubs and associations may not be that useful an exercise.

7.10.4 Depreciation

There is not much that the auditor can do with depreciation from an analytical review point of view. The auditor can assess the reasonableness of depreciation charges on categories of fixed assets when compared to the accounting policy notes and previous experience of that club or association. In addition, there is also the fact that depreciation would usually be calculated as part of the accountancy work.

The auditor can potentially look at depreciation as a percentage of gross cost of the fixed assets (Depreciation/Gross Cost $\times$ 100 per cent). This can then be analysed through fixed asset categories.

Potential explanations for changes in this percentage from year to year, other than errors in calculation, could possibly include the age of the assets, the different depreciation methods used, the level of fully depreciated assets included in the figures and any change in the depreciation rates used.

Obviously, if any of these factors are relevant then the explanations can easily be corroborated. This would just be done by reference to the auditor's knowledge of the club or association.

Another ratio which can be used to assess the reasonableness of the depreciation charge and also the reasonableness of any additions/disposals, would be to compare fixed assets at net book value to fixed assets at original cost, as a ratio (Fixed Asset at NBV: cost). This effectively gives the unexpired life of the fixed assets. Again, this can be split into different fixed asset categories. Potential explanations for any changes to this ratio would include a change in the repair and maintenance policy of the society, a change in the depreciation rates and/or methods used on depreciation, or expansion/downsizing of the club or association. Again, any of these explanations could easily be corroborated with reference to the auditor's knowledge of the club or association.

7.11 Use of analytical review on the balance sheet audit – stocks

7.11.1 Stock turn ratio

This is the most basic of the analytical review ratios that can be interpreted with stock. The auditor should always calculate it as part of the final review of the accounts. However, with the onset of SAS 410 it would be more usual to calculate the stock turn ratio (if the figures are available) at the planning stage. Certainly, the ratio should be examined as soon as practically possible.

The ratio may be expressed in two ways. Firstly cost of sales over stock. This measures the amount of time during the year that stock flows through the club or association. The second ratio is stock over cost of sales multiplied by 365 – this gives the average number of days taken for the stock to flow through the club or association. The quicker the stock turns over, the better for most organisations..

Generally speaking, a worsening stock turnover ratio indicates that stock could be overstated. There may be a number of legitimate reasons for this that would be provided to the auditor by the club or association. It is important for the auditor then to corroborate them. Generally speaking, there may be a change in the stock-holding policy. This could be for reasons such as potential future expansion, bulk-buying to take advantage of discounts and seasonal factors (especially if the club or association has changed year ends).

An improving stock turn ratio could also indicate a potential problem with the stock figure in the accounts. In this case, though, the auditor would be looking for a potential understatement. One reason for an improvement could be a concerted effort by the club or association to reduce stock levels to keep down financing costs.

7.11.2 Analysis

On a society stock section, the main form of analytical review as a substantive procedure to cut down on the sample size on the stock testing is to look at significant changes in values on the various types of stock commonly held at the bar. The auditor needs to ensure that he has gained from the client reasons for the changes and he also needs to corroborate the explanations given.

Generally speaking, the auditor will be able to trace this on a monthly or quarterly basis from the stocktaking reports. If applicable, the auditor also needs to follow up on any changes of the level of stock-holdings that he would have expected to see following his discussions with the club or association at the planning stage.

7.11.3 Provisions

Analytical review is also useful in determining the reasonableness of stock provisions. If there have been increases in the level of stock held without an adequate explanation and there has been a worsening of the stock turn ratios, then, potentially, this could lead one to the conclusion that the level of stock provision needs to be increased. However, with most clubs and associations the issue of stock provision is one that requires some addressing, although it does not usually lead to a problem.

7.12 Use of analytical review on the balance sheet audit – debtors

7.12.1 Prepayments

On the basis that the bulk of most clubs' and associations' debtors will be prepayments, an auditor can usually justify that it is sufficient to conduct analytical review on the prepayments via a reasonableness check. The logic behind this is that most of the work would have been done whilst preparing the accounts, and in any case the amounts involved with prepayments may not even approach the materiality figure. Therefore, a comparison of prepayments to the previous accounting period would usually be sufficient.

7.13 Use of analytical review on the balance sheet audit – creditors

7.13.1 Creditors' settlement

The main figure that is usually calculated as part of the general analytical review which has to be done is the creditors' settlement days' ratio:

$$\frac{\text{trade creditors}}{\text{cost of sales}} \times 365$$

This gives the average number of days the society takes to pay its creditors. However, adjustments do have to be made for VAT, as trade creditors includes VAT, whilst cost of sales does not.

Changes in this particular ratio are not straightforward to interpret. Indeed, in many ways because of this it is not that useful a ratio. It is important, though, that this particular ratio is discussed with the club or association if significant changes are noted. If a reduction in the creditors' days figure is detected then this could indicate a potential understatement of creditors. A significant increase in the figure could indicate potential solvency problems as creditors are not being paid as they fall due.

Perhaps the auditor needs to discuss the creditors' settlement ratio with the club or association, taking particular note of the sort of settlement days ratio they would expect the club or association to have.

If the creditors' days ratio has decreased as outlined above then another procedure could potentially be used to assess whether or not the creditors' cut-off has been correctly observed.

One of the reasons for potential understatement of creditors is that some purchases may not be recognised until the following accounting period. In this case, what you may be able to do is to look at the post-year-end creditor listing (if it is kept by the society) and compare the figures there to the year-end figures that you are working with. A significant increase in trade creditors after the year end could indicate a potential cut-off problem.

7.13.2 Purchase ledger analysis

The main analytical procedure that can be used to cut down on the sample sizes with trade creditors testing is to compare individual creditor balances to previous accounting periods. Any significant changes would be explained by the club or association and potentially then be chosen for the detailed substantive testing.

Computerised purchase ledgers will have a facility for reviewing purchasing activity with particular suppliers. Obviously, this can also be referred to when comparing individual creditor balances on a year-on-year basis.

The auditor should also look for the situation whereby the level of purchasing activity has increased significantly but there has not been a corresponding increase in the level of the amounts owed to the creditor. Indeed, this is the type of creditor on which the auditor should be looking to conduct detailed testing.

7.13.3 Accruals

Turning to accruals, obviously in most cases these figures are produced by the auditor/accountant as part of the accounts preparation work. However, the figure also needs to be audited.

It may well be that the audit has already been conducted on accruals by accounts preparation. This is the case if the auditor has looked into payments and invoices after the year end to identify the accruals. However, it would also be a useful process to compare the accruals that have been identified and calculated to what the auditor would expect to see in the accounts and also the accruals that the club or association has provided for in previous years.

7.14 Use of analytical review on the profit and loss account audit – sales

7.14.1 Bar takings

Obviously, the auditor would usually examine the gross profit percentage on bar takings. However, merely examining the gross profit percentage on an overall basis and comparing it to previous periods of the same club would not necessarily lead the auditor to cut down on sample sizes on transaction testing. If the auditor had a number of clubs or associations as clients, then obviously the auditor could compare the gross profit percentage enjoyed by one to the others. This is actually fairly strong analytical review evidence.

However, if the auditor uses the stocktaker's report to maximum effect then a good deal of comfort can be drawn from a number of analytical review procedures. The auditor can put together schedules on monthly or quarterly stock deficits or surpluses and also, potentially, monthly or quarterly gross profit percentages.

The auditor can also assess the percentage of each type of bar sale made compared to previous periods. This may help the auditor to highlight where particular problems seem to be occurring.

This could pick up something as potentially simple as someone creaming off profit on their own bottle of spirits rather than the club's.

It may also be useful to examine the daily or weekly takings records to assess whether or not they seem to be reasonable given the society's trading patterns. Are the peaks and troughs of the business where the auditor would expect them to be given previous years' figures and his knowledge of the client?

7.14.2 Other income

Given the usual relative immateriality of the other income, then extensive analytical review evidence can be drawn by comparing the contributions made by other forms of income as a percentage of gross profit. The auditor can then compare this to previous accounting periods and, potentially, other clubs.

However, it should be remembered that any variations do need to be investigated, explained and corroborated before the extensive analytical review can be relied upon.

7.15 Use of analytical review on the profit and loss account audit – expenses

7.15.1 Overhead comparison

One form of analytical review that is probably conducted on every audit is comparing the detailed breakdown of overheads to the comparable figures for previous years. This is probably not just done on all audit clients but for all jobs. It is important that it is evidenced on the file if this work is undertaken.

It can be argued that auditors can rely solely on the analytical review of expenses for audit purposes in a situation where they have prepared the accounts. A certain amount of vouching will have been carried out during the accounts preparation and, therefore, there is no need for detailed expenditure testing to be carried out.

7.15.2 Wages and salaries

With normal, run-of-the-mill audits it is possible to conduct analytical review on the wages charge in the profit and loss account. This will potentially be done by putting together an expected wages charge for the year from last year's figure, any change in the number of employees and any change in the rates of pay. This would then be compared to the actual figure with any differences being followed up.

However, with a club this particular form of analytical review could be more difficult. Tracing changes in the number of employees during the year would actually be very difficult. However, unless the level of trading by the club or association has increased significantly, then the number of employees should have actually stayed the same (or very similar) from one year to the next. Therefore, potentially the auditor could conduct an analytical review on the wages charge by taking last year's wages charge and multiplying it by any increase in the rates of pay. This would then be compared to the actual figure with any differences being followed up. For example, a potential reason for any increase would be an increased level of trade by the club.

What the auditor would probably do in addition to this is to take the level of wages and salaries as a percentage of the bar takings. This should be a relatively consistent ratio which, if consistent and comparable to other clubs and societies could be relied on to say that wages appear to be fairly stated.

Chapter 8 – Independent accountant's reports

8.1 Introduction

For periods of accounts commencing after 1 September 1996 the Deregulation (Industrial and Provident Societies) Order 1996 will come into
force. This contains several deregulation measures one of which is the
introduction of higher levels of audit exemption for Industrial and
Provident and Friendly Societies. Full details of the provisions can be
found in **2.25** and **3.17** of this publication.

As with limited company exemptions there are two levels of audit
exemption, i.e., total exemption and then a halfway house where an
independent accountant's report is required.

The aim of this chapter is to supply guidance on the procedures that
need to be undertaken to ensure that exemption is only being taken
where appropriate and also on the work procedures that should be
undertaken during the course of an independent accountant's report
assignment.

8.2 Preliminary procedures

The practice should identify those clubs and associations that it deals
with that should be entitled to the exemption. These will be the ones
that satisfy the financial criteria (as set out in **2.25** and **3.17**) i.e., have
turnovers of between £90,000 and £350,000 and gross assets of less
than £1,400,000 and do not fall into one of the categories where
exemption is not available. Having identified these clients, the accountant should be approaching these clubs and associations to ascertain
whether they are intending to take advantage of the exemption. If the
answer is yes then there are a number of practical issues that need to
be dealt with.

8.2.1 Audit exemption

Firstly, the legislation stipulates that the members should vote on the
society's right to opt out of an audit. Should either 10 per cent of the
membership who are entitled to vote or 20 per cent of the persons

present at the meeting decide that an audit should be undertaken then one must be carried out. Therefore, a meeting should be held of the members to vote on whether they want to take advantage of the exemption. This vote should be undertaken on an annual basis at the annual general meeting.

As the provisions come into force for accounting periods commencing on or after 1 September 1996, the first accounts it will apply to are for year ends after 31 August 1997. In addition, the qualification will be based on the figures for the previous year end. Therefore, when completing the audit for year ends after 31 August 1996, the auditor will know whether the club will qualify. If they do, then a motion should be laid before the annual general meeting at which the accounts are approved.

If the club actually wants to take advantage of the audit exemption, on the basis that it feels it will save the club money, then for most working men's clubs the idea will have to be 'sold' to the members. It needs to be made clear to the members that there is nothing underhand in the plan to take advantage of the exemption. It also needs to be made clear to them what assurance the independent accountant's examination will give. They may feel that as it is still being undertaken by a qualified accountant, more reliance can be placed upon it than the auditor would like. As the auditor and independent accountant have the right to receive notice and to attend all general meetings of a club or association they may feel it is worth attending such a meeting so that they can be happy that there is no misunderstanding. It may be for some clubs and associations that a halfway house is agreed where the audit exemption is taken advantage of but the terms of engagement of the independent accountant are such that a limited amount of work on the income side of the profit and loss account including tests on the adequacy of the committee controls would be undertaken.

8.2.2 Rule changes

Secondly, the rules of a club or association are the equivalent of the Memorandum and Articles of Association of a limited company. Where standard rules have been adopted these will invariably contain rules relating to the appointment of auditors and also a rule (as required by the Act) requiring the club or association to display a copy of the last balance sheet together with the report of the auditor in a conspicuous place at the registered office. The latter rule along with the rule relating to the appointment of auditors would cause problems for clubs wishing to take advantage of the audit exemption. Therefore, if they wish to take advantage of the exemption, the procedure for rule change would have to be followed.

The practical way of doing this will be to instigate the rule change at the same general meeting where the resolution for taking advantage of the exemption is tabled. The procedure for amending the rules will be laid down in the rules of the society. It is important to note that this change could result in a reasonable amount of cost to the society. In order to change the rules, the details of the proposed change would need to be posted with notice of the meeting to which the amendments will be submitted. In addition, at least two-thirds of the members present and voting at the meeting must agree to the change. From a practical point of view this will not be a problem, as, if the members agree to abolish the audit, there will be the necessary majority needed to change the rules.

For societies that are registered with an organisation such as the Royal British Legion they may have to obtain prior endorsement from its Council in order to make a change. In addition, no change is valid until it has been registered with the Registrar of Friendly Societies. This registration will incur cost for the society. The Registrar of Friendly Societies, on enquiry, has said he has no plans at the moment to waive any fee for registering a rule change to enable clubs to take advantage of the audit exemption. In addition to the registration fee, new copies of the rules will need to be printed and distributed to members, or at least an addendum will need to be distributed. Although a small charge (a maximum of 10 pence) can be made for this it is unlikely to meet the printing costs.

If the rules are going to be changed then it may well be appropriate to use this occasion to review them to remove any other 'anomalies'. For example, it is likely that the rules of a number of clubs and associations will still contain a provision stating that any auditor of the society cannot be a body corporate. This is no longer a provision in the Friendly and Industrial and Provident Societies Act 1968 or the Friendly Societies Act 1974 and therefore could be removed from the rules.

Where the club or association has adopted rules originally drafted by one of the promoting bodies, it is probably appropriate to go back to those bodies for proposed wording rather than drafting the rules itself. It is also appropriate as the registration of a format of rules which has already been agreed by the Registrar of Friendly Societies will be easier and cheaper.

Having established that the society has the right to opt out of audit, then an amended letter of engagement should be issued to the society. Pro-forma letters for Industrial and Provident and Friendly Societies have been reproduced in Appendix 3. These letters are designed to supplement the full letter of engagement that should already be in place with the club. This letter should be discussed with the committee, and it should be reinforced with them that it is their responsibility to ensure that the accountant is informed should they become ineligible to take advantage of the exemptions. It is also important that the committee and the members are aware of the practice's responsibilities as reporting accountants so that their expectations of the comfort they can obtain from the report are not unrealistic.

8.3 Work procedures for an independent accountant's report assignment

The ultimate objective of such an assignment is to produce a report on the accounts which considers the following:

(a) whether the accounts and balance sheets are in agreement with the books and records maintained by the society;

(b) that on the basis of the information contained in the books and records the revenue account or accounts and balance sheet comply with the requirements of the Act; and

(c) whether in the accountant's opinion the financial criteria for the exercise of the power have been met (as explained at **2.25** and **3.17**, this is a more onerous requirement than for companies registered under the Companies Act 1985, and it will require additional procedures to be applied where societies are approaching the exemption limits).

When undertaking the assignment the Statement of Standards for Reporting Accountants should be followed. The work should be properly planned, controlled and recorded. The following is a breakdown of the procedures that should be applied by the reporting accountant.

8.4 Planning

8.4.1 Independence

In order to undertake an independent examination, the person carrying out the examination must be independent. Therefore, the same independence criteria as applied to the audit should be considered before commencing. The independence form reproduced in Appendix 4 should be utilised.

8.4.2 Qualification

Having established independence the accountant needs to consider whether a club or association is actually eligible to take advantage of the exemption. He needs to satisfy himself on a number of issues:

(a) that the club or association will meet the financial criteria, i.e., that its turnover did not exceed £350,000 and its gross assets £1.4 million in the preceding year. In reality, this procedure will have been done at the end of the previous year's assignment;

(b) that the members have agreed to the club or association taking advantage of the exemption. If the accountant did not attend the meeting held then a copy of the minutes and passed resolutions should be obtained;

(c) that its rules have, where necessary, been appropriately amended and such amendments have been filed with the Registrar of Friendly Societies, and an acknowledgement of the change has been received;

(d) that they are not ineligible by virtue of having been or being:
   (i) for Industrial and Provident Societies:
   - a credit union;
   - a housing association;
   - a member of a group;
   - an organisation preparing accounts under the Insurance Accountants Directive (Miscellaneous Insurance Undertakings) Regulations 1993 (A); or
   - an organisation which holds or has at any time since the end of the preceding year of account, held a deposit within the meaning of the Banking Act 1987 (B), other than the deposit and withdrawable share capital;
   (ii) for Friendly Societies, a society which holds, or has, at any time since the end of the preceding year of accounts, held, a deposit within the meaning of the Banking Act 1987.

The independent accountant should consider completing an assessment form assessing the risk of the club or association failing to meet the requirements for audit exemption on the grounds of any of the above. This form should have a 'catch-all' question at the end asking whether there are any other special factors which could result in a club or association requiring an audit. This could, for example, be required by a brewery where a loan exists or by the bank if there is a loan or if the club has a large overdraft on its current account. The club may need to enquire of such bodies whether an audit will be required. When deregulation for companies first came in, many breweries were stipulating that they required an audit where loans existed.

Where the accountant has identified a particular area of risk he should carry out procedures to satisfy himself that the club or association is still entitled to take advantage of the exemption. Generally speaking, this will be done through discussion with the officers of the club or association and although the issues will all be included in the letter of engagement it may be appropriate to send out a letter prior to the year end asking the officers to confirm that they are still entitled to take advantage of the exemption. This letter should cover all of the issues outlined above. In addition, if the club or association is approaching the exemption levels it may be appropriate to point out to them the consequences of them not having an audit one year and then requiring one in the next. This may not be as significant as it would be for a limited company because even if they fail to have an audit, it is likely that most clubs or associations will still have professional stock valuations undertaken to help control bar income and stock. This would mean that it could be possible to carry out procedures in subsequent years that would give sufficient comfort to ensure that an audit qualification would not be necessary. In addition, as the qualification for exemption is on the preceding year's figures, where an accountant is aware that the club will not be able to qualify in the subsequent year due to the level of turnover and/or gross assets in the current year, then he should consider approaching the club to suggest that an audit could be undertaken on the current year's accounts to avoid any future problems.

8.4.3 Terms of engagement

The engagement letter should be reviewed to ensure that it is up-to-date and valid.

It is important to review the letter of engagement in detail to ensure that the responsibilities of the independent accountant and the management committee are clear.

8.4.4 Permanent file

The permanent file and any correspondence should be reviewed to familiarise the accountant with any information surrounding the client that may be of interest.

8.5 Work programme

A work programme would need to be designed and agreed.

No audit procedures needs to be undertaken, but the work programme needs to be sufficient to satisfy the accountant that the club or association is entitled to take advantage of the exemptions concerned and that the accounts as prepared are in agreement with the accounting records.

The same procedures as adopted for any limited company client can be applied. However, in certain circumstances the members of the club may wish the accountant to undertake limited audit type procedures to provide assurances on, for example, completeness of income. This is something that should be determined through discussion with the committee and included, where appropriate, in the letter of engagement.

Where the accountant is preparing the accounts from the cash book, there will be no necessity for him to check entries back to invoices, etc., however, at the end of the job the accountant will need to look at the accounts and consider whether the amounts appear reasonable in view of his knowledge of the client. Details of analytical review procedures which can be applied can be found in Chapter **7**.

The accountant may wish to have a work programme on the file detailing the accounting procedures that need to be undertaken. The emphasis will be slightly different depending upon whether a full accounts preparation job or a pure independent examination is being undertaken.

8.5.1 Accounts preparation assignment

For an accounts preparation assignment the programme should include consideration of the following issues.

For the balance sheet areas:

(a) agreeing the opening balances to the previous year's financial statements;
(b) preparing a lead schedule which is cross-referenced to the financial statements;
(c) preparing, where appropriate, a list of balances which agree to a control account;
(d) reviewing invoices, credit notes, despatch notes, stock records, etc. to ensure that all items have been properly incorporated in the control account;
(e) determining the level of any provisions;
(f) preparing lists of prepayments and accruals from invoices;
(g) obtaining the stock certificates;
(h) preparing a summary of movements on fixed assets and investment accounts;

(i)   scheduling any items that need to be included in a letter of representation;

(j)   recording any items which may need to be included in the independent accountant's report on a points for partner schedule;

(k)   considering the impact of any unadjusted errors recorded on the society's ability to take advantage of the exemptions in the next period and considering what impact, if any, this would have on the accountant's report;

(l)   concluding on the section on whether:

      (i)   for the area in question the amounts disclosed in the accounts are in agreement with the accounting records; and

      (ii)   all the necessary information has been collected for the preparation of the statutory financial statements.

For the profit and loss account:

(a)   agreeing opening balances to the previous year's financial statement;

(b)   preparing a lead schedule which is cross-referenced to the financial statements;

(c)   preparing a schedule of income received from all sources;

(d)   preparing a note considering, where the company is approaching the turnover threshold, whether there is a risk of unrecorded sales and whether any income not included in turnover is correctly classified;

(e)   preparing a schedule of expenditure from the invoices or other record;

(f)   preparing a summary of wages and salaries;

(g)   scheduling any items that need to be specifically mentioned in the letter of representation;

(h)   recording any items which may require an explanatory paragraph in the independent accountant's report on a points for partner schedule;

(i)   considering the impact of any unadjusted errors recorded on the society's ability to take advantage of the exemptions in the next period and considering what impact, if any, this would have on the accountant's report;

(j)   concluding whether the profit and loss account is in agreement with the accounting records and whether all the necessary information has been collected for the preparation of the statutory financial statements.

Obviously, this work programme may need to be amended if the club wishes the accountant to undertake more detailed work on, for example, completeness of income. In addition, it is important not to lose sight of the practice's role as professional adviser to the organisation and even though detailed tests may not be undertaken on wages, for example, it is still important that the committee is made aware of any breaches of regulations which could prove punitive to them in future.

8.5.2 Pure examination

Where a pure examination assignment is being undertaken the accountant can place a great deal of reliance upon the records prepared by the club or association. The work programme should include the following procedures.

For balance sheet areas:

(a) lead schedules should be drawn up or obtained and cross-referenced to the final accounts;
(b) the opening balances should be agreed to the previous year's financial statements;
(c) all items in the accounts should be agreed to the final trial balance and the nominal ledger accounts;
(d) a sample of items should be traced from the nominal ledger accounts to the underlying accounting records (such as the cash book);
(e) any items that need to be specifically mentioned in the letter of representation should be scheduled;
(f) the impact of any unadjusted errors recorded on the society's ability to take advantage of the exemptions in the next period should be considered and this should result in a conclusion considering what impact, if any, this would have on the accountant's report;
(g) any items which may require an explanatory paragraph in the report should be recorded on a points for partner schedule;
(h) the member of staff should conclude on whether the balance sheet items disclosed in the accounts are in agreement with the accounting records and whether their disclosures are in accordance with the requirements of the relevant Act.

For profit and loss account areas:

(a) a lead schedule should be obtained and cross-referenced to the final accounts;
(b) the statutory profit and loss account should be agreed to the final trial balance in the nominal ledger accounts;
(c) a sample of items should be traced from the nominal ledger accounts to the underlying accounting records;
(d) any items that should be included in the letter of representation should be scheduled;

(e) the impact of any unadjusted errors recorded on the society's ability to take advantage of the exemptions in the next period should be considered and this should result in a conclusion considering what impact, if any, this would have on the accountant's report;

(f) any items requiring mention in an explanatory paragraph in the independent accountant's report should be recorded on a points for partner schedule;

(g) the member of staff should conclude on whether the profit and loss account is in agreement with the accounting records and whether the disclosures are consistent with the requirements of the relevant Act.

8.5.3 Additional procedures where the society is approaching the limits

As the independent accountant is required to form an opinion on whether the society has met the financial criteria for the exercise of the power to opt out of audit, i.e., in the preceding year, then where the society is approaching either the turnover or the gross assets limits, the accountant should undertake a limited amount of audit-type procedures to enable him to establish that the exemption can be taken.

For the income side, a review of the procedures for recording income along with analytical review and some limited testing of individual figures should suffice.

In respect of gross assets, the accountant should also carry out analytical review along with a limited amount of cut-off testing to establish that there are not sufficient errors to move them above the exemption limit. He should also review accounting policies to ensure that these have not been changed to suppress either the turnover or gross asset amount.

8.6 Completion

When the field work has been completed, an analytical review should be undertaken to satisfy the accountant that the figures appear reasonable. The partner needs to consider any points raised by the staff working on the assignment which could result in an explanatory paragraph having to be put in the report. He also needs to evidence their consideration of the total unadjusted errors.

As well as ensuring that the file is fully cross-referenced to the accounts, the reviewer should consider whether all the adjustments, etc. have been put through and whether a letter of representation has been drafted which contains confirmation of all representations on which the accountant wishes to rely. This letter should be discussed in detail with the committee to reinforce its responsibilities – this is particularly important as they are not required to sign a statement on the balance sheet.

The file also needs to contain an overall conclusion on the following:

(a) whether the accounts are in agreement with the accounting records;
(b) whether the accounts have been drawn up and are consistent with the requirements of the relevant Act;
(c) whether the client is eligible for exemption from an audit;
(d) where there are any items that require an explanatory paragraph that these have been dealt with properly.

8.7 Reports

The report should be drawn up in line with the accounting standard and some examples have been included below.

8.7.1 Unqualified report

Under s9A of the Friendly and Industrial and Provident Societies Act 1968 or s39A of the Friendly Societies Act 1974 (whichever is appropriate), an unqualified independent accountant's report should be used where no qualification issues have been encountered and no issues requiring an explanatory paragraph have arisen.

Accountant's report to the members on the unaudited accounts of XYZ Social Club Limited

We report on the accounts for the year ended .... set out on pages ... to ....

Respective responsibilities of officers and reporting accountant
The society's officers are responsible for the preparation of the accounts, and they consider that the society is exempt from an audit. It is our responsibility to carry out procedures designed to enable us to report our opinion.

Basis of opinion
Our work was conducted in accordance with the Statement of Standards for Reporting Accountants, and so our procedures consisted of comparing the accounts with the accounting records kept by the society, and making such limited enquiries of the officers of the society as we considered necessary for the purposes of this report. These procedures provide the only assurance expressed in our opinion.

Opinion

In our opinion:

(a) the accounts are in agreement with the accounting records kept by the society under s1 of the Friendly and Industrial and Provident Societies Act 1968/s29 of the Friendly Societies Act 1974*;

(b) having regard only to, and on the basis of, the information contained in those accounting records, the accounts have been drawn up in a manner consistent with the accounting requirements of the Act; and

(c) the society satisfied the conditions for exemption from an audit of the accounts for the year specified in s4A(1) Friendly and Industrial and Provident Societies Act 1968/s32A(1) Friendly Societies Act 1974* and did not, at any time within that year, fall within any of the categories of societies not entitled to the exemption specified in s4A(3) Friendly and Industrial and Provident Societies Act 1968/s32A(3) Friendly Societies Act 1974*.

Name   Address

Reporting Accountants and Chartered Accountants

Date

delete as appropriate

8.7.2 Qualification on the grounds of limitation in scope

Under s9A of the Friendly and Industrial and Provident Societies Act 1968 or s39A of the Friendly Societies Act 1974 (whichever is appropriate) an independent accountant's report with a qualification on the grounds of limitation in scope should be used where something has occurred during the course of the assignment about which the reporting accountant is uncertain.

Accountant's report to the members on the unaudited accounts of XYZ Social Club Limited

We report on the accounts for the year ended .... set out on pages ... to ... .

Respective responsibilities of officers and reporting accountants

The society's officers are responsible for the preparation of the accounts, and they consider that the society is exempt from an audit. It is our responsibility to carry out procedures designed to enable us to report our opinion.

Basis of opinion

Our work was conducted in accordance with the Statement of Standards for Reporting Accountants, and so our procedures consisted of comparing the accounts with the accounting records kept by the society, and making such limited enquiries of the officers of the society as we considered necessary for the purposes of this report. These procedures provide the only assurance expressed in our opinion.

Owing to flood damage, certain accounting records relating to sales for the first month of the year have been destroyed, and so we have been unable to compare the sales shown in the accounts with those accounting records.

Opinion

In our opinion:

(a)   except for the uncertainty relating to sales, which arises from the limitation of the scope of our work described above, the accounts are in agreement with the accounting records kept by the society under s1 of the Friendly and Industrial and Provident Societies Act 1968/s29 of the Friendly Societies Act 1974*;

(b)   having regard only to, and on the basis of, the information contained in those accounting records, the accounts have been drawn up in a manner consistent with the accounting requirements of the Act; and

(c)   the society satisfied the conditions for exemption from an audit of the accounts for the year specified in s4A(1) Friendly and Industrial and Provident Societies Act 1968/s32A(1) Friendly Societies Act 1974* and did not, at any time within that year, fall within any of the categories of societies not entitled to the exemption specified in s4A(3) Friendly and Industrial and Provident Societies Act 1968/s32A(3) Friendly Societies Act 1974*.

Name   Address

Reporting Accountants and Chartered Accountants

Date

delete, as appropriate

8.7.3 Unqualified report with explanatory paragraph

Under s9A of the Friendly and Industrial and Provident Societies Act 1968/s39A of the Friendly Societies Act 1974 (as appropriate), an unqualified independent accountant's report with explanatory paragraph should be used where something has occurred during the course of the assignment which the accountant feels should be brought to the attention of the society's members.

Accountant's report to the members on the unaudited accounts of XYZ Social Club Limited

We report on the accounts for the year ended .... set out on pages ... to ... .

Respective responsibilities of officers and reporting accountant

The society's officers are responsible for the preparation of the accounts, and they consider that the society is exempt from an audit. It is our responsibility to carry out procedures designed to enable us to report our opinion.

Basis of opinion

Our work was conducted in accordance with the Statement of Standards for Reporting Accountants, and so our procedures consisted of comparing the accounts with the accounting records kept by the society, and making such limited enquiries of the officers of the society as we considered necessary for the purposes of this report. These procedures provide the only assurance expressed in our opinion.

SSAP 21

In carrying out our examination, it has come to our attention that the society has entered into hire purchase contracts for the purchase of new equipment costing £15,200 which have not been capitalised. This is in conflict with generally accepted accounting principles and the society's previous accounting policy. Our opinion is not qualified in this respect.

Opinion

In our opinion:

(a) the accounts are in agreement with the accounting records kept by the society under s1 of the Friendly and Industrial and Provident Societies Act 1968/s29 of the Friendly Societies Act 1974*;

(b) having regard only to, and on the basis of, the information contained in those accounting records, the accounts have been drawn up in a manner consistent with the accounting requirements of the Act; and

(c) the society satisfied the conditions for exemption from an audit of the accounts for the year specified in s4A(1) Friendly and Industrial and Provident Societies Act 1968/s32A(1) Friendly Societies Act 1974* and did not, at any time within that year, fall within any of the categories of societies not entitled to the exemption specified in s4A(3) Friendly and Industrial and Provident Societies Act 1968/ s32A(3) Friendly Societies Act 1974*.

Name   Address

Reporting Accountants and Chartered Accountants

Date

* *delete as appropriate*

Chapter 9 – Audit exemption

9.1 Introduction

For periods of account commencing on or after 1 September 1996 the Deregulation (Industrial and Provident Societies) Order 1996 will come into force. This Order, as described in **2.25**, **3.17** and Chapter **8** brings in two levels of audit exemption. Details of the procedures to be applied for societies with turnovers exceeding £90,000 but less than £350,000 who meet the other criteria have been laid out in Chapter **8**. Societies which satisfy all of the other criteria and whose turnovers are below £90,000 will be able to take advantage of full audit exemption. There is no requirement for them to have either an audit or an independent examination of their accounts.

When such an assignment is being undertaken the following procedures should be applied.

9.2 Preliminary procedures

The society will have to go through the procedure of voting on whether the members wish to take advantage of the exemption or not and will also, if necessary, have to change the rules of the society to enable them to take advantage of the exemption. The procedures for doing this have been laid out in **8.2**.

9.3 Planning

At the start of the job a risk assessment should be completed to assess the ability of the society to take advantage of the exemption. The following items should be considered:

(a) whether the society's turnover was under £90,000 in the preceding year;
(b) whether the gross assets of the society were less than £1.4 million in the preceding year.

Where the answer to either of the above two questions is no then the society would be unable to take advantage of total exemption.

In addition to the financial criteria, the following issues need to be considered:

(a) whether the society is at risk of losing the exemption by entering into one of the business categories where exemption is not available;
(b) whether there are any other factors which could result in the society requiring an audit (such as the presence of brewery loans).

The answers to the above questions can be ascertained through the accountant's knowledge of the client and discussion with the members of the committee. In certain circumstances the accountant may wish to send a letter to the committee asking them to confirm that there are no reasons why they would be unable to take advantage of the exemptions.

The accountant may well have attended the initial meeting voting on whether the exemption should be taken but in subsequent years if he does not attend such a meeting then he should have a record of the minutes of the meeting on file so there is no confusion.

9.4 Work programme

Having satisfied himself that the society is eligible for the exemption the accountant can plan the work. There is no equivalent independence requirement for this type of assignment.

No specific work programme is actually necessary. This assignment should be treated in the same way as any other accounts preparation assignment undertaken by the practice. Work programmes will have been designed for independent accountant's report assignments and where accounting work is undertaken the accountant may wish to use these programmes to record evidence of the work being done, but this is not strictly necessary. However, as with any client, the accountant should prepare the accounts with due skill and attention and ensure that any problems or potential problems are brought to the attention of the committee of management.

If the society is approaching the turnover or gross asset parameter in the current year, the accountant may need to carry out limited audit-type procedures similar to those laid out in **8.5.3** to satisfy himself that the society will be entitled to total exemption from audit the following year.

9.5 Completion

At the end of the assignment an analytical review should be undertaken to ensure that the figures in the accounts makes sense in view of the accountant's knowledge of the client. In addition, the accountant should ensure:

(a)   that there is an up-to-date letter of engagement;
(b)   that the file has been cross-referenced and agreed to the accounts;
(c)   that any problems or queries have been properly cleared and dealt with adequately;
(d)   that a satisfactory VAT turnover reconciliation has been completed, where necessary; and
(e)   that a letter of representation has been drafted and sent to the client.

It is important on this type of assignment that a letter of representation is obtained as this helps to clarify for the officers of the society their responsibilities for the financial statements. A pro-forma letter has been included in Appendix 5.

Having reviewed the file the partner responsible for the assignment needs to conclude on the following issues:

(a)   whether any matters have come to light which cause a concern about the financial statements;
(b)   whether any matters have come to light which give rise to concern about the entitlement of the society to the exemption from audit in the current or subsequent year;
(c)   whether the accountant's report drafted is appropriate and may be signed.

9.6 Accountant's report

The accountant's report used on this type of assignment should be in accordance with the requirements of Audit 1/95 Reports on Accounts Compiled (prepared by accountants). An example report has been incorporated below.

Accountant's report on the unaudited accounts of XYZ Social Club Limited

To the officers of XYZ Limited

You are responsible for the preparation of the accounts for the year ended ...., set out on pages ... to ..., and you consider that the society is exempt from an audit under s4A of the Friendly and Industrial Provident Societies Act 1968/s39A of the Friendly Societies Act 1974*. In accordance with your instructions, we have compiled these

unaudited accounts in order to assist you to fulfil your statutory responsibilities, from the accounting records and information and explanations
supplied to us.

Name   Address

Chartered accountants

Date

* delete as appropriate

Chapter 10 – Pay as you earn

10.1 Introduction

Pay as you earn (PAYE) is the system by which income tax and Class 1 National Insurance is deducted at source from employees' earnings that are assessable under Schedule E. PAYE must be operated in respect of all employees of UK employers unless they are classified as self-employed. Most clubs and associations using staff would not be able to classify individuals as self-employed.

The definition of earnings is very broad and for Schedule E purposes, emoluments 'shall include all salaries, fees, wages, perquisites and profits whatsoever' (s131 ICTA 1988). PAYE must be operated in respect of all cash payments to an employee, including round sum allowances. Where there is bona fide business use in respect of these allowances, a claim can be made by the employee to the Inland Revenue in order to obtain repayment of income tax suffered on these payments to the extent of the business use. This will be discussed later on in this chapter. It is also necessary for the employer to identify any non-cash considerations given to employees, which are deemed benefits in kind due to their employment, and any expenses reimbursed. These items are recorded using forms P11D and P9D, which are supplementary to the operation of PAYE. The completion of P11Ds and P9Ds by clubs and associations will be considered later in this chapter.

Payments due to the Collector of Taxes in respect of income tax and National Insurance are usually payable within 14 days of the end of the tax month (5th of the month). However, where an employer uses calendar months, the tax is payable by the 19th day of the following month. If an employer's total deductions for staff, under the PAYE system, are below £600 per month, the employer can account for PAYE on a quarterly basis. In the case of small clubs and associations, where there are few staff, this can save time on the administration of PAYE.

10.2 Scope of PAYE

For income tax purposes the scope of PAYE is large, but for National Insurance it is narrower. It is often difficult to ascertain whether there is a charge to National Insurance and this area requires careful consideration. The income usually assessable to PAYE includes the following:

- payments such as salaries, wages, fees, overtime, bonuses, commissions, pensions, honoraria, perks, etc.;
- payments in cash, such as Christmas bonuses;
- statutory sick pay;
- statutory maternity pay;
- round sum allowances;
- payments for time spent travelling;
- cash payments for meals;
- pay in respect of periods of sickness;
- contribution towards or payment of telephone bills.

An area of specific interest to clubs and associations is the payment of honoraria. As indicated above it is taxable and when the club or association has a PAYE scheme, tax should be deducted from the honoraria. The individual in receipt of the honorarium can make a claim under s198 ICTA 1988 and reclaim the tax for an amount equal to his justifiable business expenses. It should be noted that travel costs from home to place of employment are regarded as not being business expenses.

In small clubs and associations that do not have PAYE schemes, it is unlikely in practice that the Inland Revenue will seek to assess small amounts of honoraria. Typically, secretaries and treasurers might receive honoraria, but could possibly justify an amount for expenses of at least the sum concerned. In the circumstances, it will be seen that it would be futile for the Inland Revenue to assess the honoraria only for claims to be made under s198 which would negate the tax charged.

10.3 Employed or self-employed

It is a very difficult area to decide whether someone is employed or self-employed. As employers are aware, employing staff involves a great deal of administration as well as the need to pay employer's National Insurance, so they would often prefer to take on people on a self-employed basis. The Inspector of Taxes will look at the underlying position rather than any agreement or otherwise between the employer and employee. There are many legal precedents that have created the guidelines for assessing a person in this respect. These guidelines suggest that someone who is self-employed will tend to:

(a) decide how to undertake the job and be responsible for timing;
(b) come and go freely;

(c)   work for more than one company;

(d)   raise an invoice for work undertaken;

(e)   be 'set up' with a tax office/VAT office (if applicable);

(f)   have variable income month by month;

(g)   not be part of a business structure, i.e., they will not usually report to anyone or be reported to by employees;

(h)   own their own equipment and tools.

On consideration, it should be clear that most people working for a club or association would not be able to satisfy these criteria. In particular, they would not be using their own equipment to work behind a bar, nor would they be able to come and go as they pleased.

If someone is treated as self-employed but in reality should be taxed under the PAYE system, the employer will be responsible for any PAYE which should have been collected and also may incur penalties and interest.

The rules regarding classification of employment and self-employment differ for the Inland Revenue and the Department of Social Security, so that it is possible for a person to be self-employed for tax purposes and employed for payment of National Insurance!

10.4 Benefits in kind and return of expense payments

Certain cash equivalents of any benefit in kind and expenses reimbursed must be declared on forms P11D or P9D, depending on the category into which the individual falls. A form P11D is required for any director, or an employee who earns at least £8,500 per annum. This rate is calculated after including any potential taxable benefits in kind, therefore it is unusual for any person who receives benefits or expenses payments to be below this rate. If, however, a person does fall below this rate then they are only taxable on certain benefits on form P9D which are discussed later. The definition of director also includes a member of the committee which manages a club or association and any member of a body whose affairs are managed by its members. However, there are various exclusions from the special rules that bring directors within the category for which form P11D is required. Broadly, the effect is that the following are not included within the exclusions:

(a)   full-time working directors of any concern;

(b)   members of committees of unincorporated bodies or non-profit-making concerns;

(c)   directors of charities;

146

provided that the individuals concerned do not receive remuneration at the rate of £8,500 or more in a year and they do not have a 'material interest' in the concern that employs them. (A material interest is defined as one where the individual, together with his associates and relatives, controls more than 5 per cent of the concern.)

10.5 Valuation of benefits for inclusion in form P11D

The general rule for valuing benefits is the cost to the employer, however there are special cases which have their own particular rules and will be discussed shortly. The cost to the employer has now been ruled to represent the marginal cost to the employer since the case of *Pepper* v *Hart*. The following categories represent the main forms of benefits but are by no means an exhaustive list. It is advisable to approach potential benefits as likely to be taxable and then confirm their treatment or exclusion.

10.5.1 Living accommodation

Generally, where an employee is provided with living accommodation a taxable benefit arises. However, in the case of clubs and associations that require a steward to reside on the premises, it is likely to be arguable that a tax charge does not arise. In order to come within the exemption the accommodation must either have been provided;

(a) for the proper performance of the employee's duties; or
(b) for the better performance of his duties and be the type of employment for which it is customary for accommodation to be provided.

It could be justifiable in many clubs and associations that the provision of the steward's accommodation falls within the defined limits.

If the above exemption does not apply, and the employer incurs the cost of normal living expenses, i.e., heating, lighting, cleaning and repairs, a benefit of the full cost will arise to the employee. However, where the exemption does apply, the benefit for living expenses will not exceed 10 per cent of the employee's emoluments.

10.5.2 Cars

The provision of a car for private purposes creates a taxable benefit on the employee or 'director' for its period of availability. This charge is calculated at 35 per cent of the car's original list price and is reduced by a mileage allowance and age allowance. If the business miles are 2,500 or more but under 18,000, the initial charge is reduced by one-third. If the business mileage is 18,000 miles and over, the initial charge is reduced by two-thirds. If the car is four or more years old at the end of the tax year, the charge after deducting the mileage allowance is reduced by a further third.

If the employee makes a capital contribution to the cost of the car, the list price is reduced up to a maximum of £5,000.

If the employer also provides fuel for private motoring, a fixed rate scale charge is applied, unless the employee reimburses the cost of the entire private element.

10.5.3 Private use of a business asset

Where an employee uses an asset, a charge is created based on 20 per cent of the asset's market value at the time that it was made available to the employee, for the length of its use. This rule does not apply to cars and vans.

10.5.4 Mobile/car telephones

If a mobile telephone is made available to an employee and it is used for private purposes which are not paid for, a standard scale charge of £200 is created.

10.6 Benefits to be included in form P9D

If an employee's income, expenses and benefits fall beneath the £8,500 level then certain benefits are taxable, irrespective of the remuneration that the employee receives. They are taxable at the cash equivalent value, i.e., the amount for which they could be sold on the open market.

These benefits are as follows:

- provision of living accommodation;
- personal expenses met by the employer;
- vouchers;
- anything convertible into money.

Therefore, with respect to clubs and associations, the main benefit will be the provision of free drinks to employees and officers. In addition, the provision of live-in accommodation for the steward should be declared on the P11D or the P9D, whichever is appropriate. If an employee receives a subsidised or free meal, this is not taxable as long as all the employees are able to receive this.

10.7 Expenses

Where an employer reimburses business expenses, these must be shown on the P11D, but not the P9D if they related purely to business. A P11D employee can then submit a claim under s198 ICTA 1988 to state that these business expenses were incurred wholly, exclusively and necessarily in the performance of his duties of employment. An employer can apply to the Inspector for dispensations covering certain expenses, for example lunch allowances, which alleviates some of the end of year form-filling that is required by employers operating PAYE. At present, there is no requirement for an employer to provide an employee with details of the entries in form P11D. However, when self-assessment comes for the tax year 1996/97, employers will be required to provide such information to employees.

10.8 Dispensations

If the Inspector is certain that there are no profit elements within the rates of expenses, a dispensation should be granted. Expenses, for which dispensations have been granted, do not have to be included in the P11D and the employee will not need to make a s198 claim. It must be remembered, however, that these dispensations are reviewed regularly and always need to be agreed by the Inspector if the rate is changed. Mileage allowances have a separate regime known as the fixed profit car scheme.

10.9 Fixed profit car scheme

The Revenue have set rates at which an employer can pay mileage rates to its employees. These rates are deemed not to include any profit element. From 1996/97 an employee can make a claim for losses if their employer pays them at a rate which is lower. Any employer/firm needs to inform the Revenue of its rates and have them agreed before it can operate this scheme.

10.10 Benefits and National Insurance

The rules in relation to which benefits create an NI liability are complex. Generally, if the benefit relates to the settling of the employee's liability, both employee's and employer's NI is due. Whereas only employer's NI is payable on cars provided for employees and taxed as a benefit.

10.11 Casual labour

One area which often gives rise to problems for clubs and associations is the amount of casual labour that they employ. Generally, PAYE should be operated for any employee unless they will be working for less than a week and are unlikely to work for the club at any other point within that tax year.

If the employee will be working for more than a week, but does not have a P45, he must complete a form P46. If the employment is not his main job, he must be included on a P11 deductions sheet and taxed at basic rate. If it is his first job, he needs to be included on a P11 and taxed using the cumulative emergency code (376L for 1996/97). If it is his only job, he must be included on the P11 and taxed on a week 1/month 1 basis using the emergency code.

If the employee earns below the tax threshold, the employer keeps the P46, but still fills in a P11 for the employee. If, however, the employee earns below the National Insurance threshold, the employer need only make a note of the pay and the employee's name and address.

If the employee will be working for one week or less, a P46 is not needed and the following applies:

(a) if the employee has other employment, a P11 is prepared and tax is deducted at basic rate;

(b) if it is not known whether it is the employee's only job, a P11 is prepared and tax is calculated using the emergency code on the week 1/month 1 basis;

(c) if the employee's pay is below the tax threshold, a P11 is prepared but if the pay is below the NI threshold, a P11 is not required and the employer only needs to make a note of the pay, employee's name and address.

The concern here for the employer, is the risk that if the PAYE regulations are not properly adhered to, when the Inland Revenue carry out an audit, it is usually the employer who suffers. Where, for example, P46 procedures were not followed correctly, e.g., a casual employee did not bring the leaver form P45 from the previous employer and did not sign form P46, the new employer is liable for the tax and NI if it is not correctly deducted from the employee's earnings. In such circumstances, the result is that the employer not only has to pay the employee's tax and NI, but is also charged interest and penalties (see **10.12**).

10.12 Penalties

Any monthly payments of PAYE attract interest charges if not paid within 14 days of the end of the tax month (19 days for calendar month payments). If the end of tax year returns are not submitted by 19 May following the tax year, penalties arise.

Indeed, where the PAYE system is not operated correctly and accurately, there is a danger that a visit will be made by the PAYE auditors, and depending upon what they find, further interest and penalties could be charged.

In respect of P11Ds and P9Ds, which are due for submission by 6 June following the tax year, if these are late, a penalty of £300 is incurred, rising by £60 for each additional day that they are late. An error or omission on a form P11D can incur a hefty penalty of up to £3,000. The Revenue might not distinguish between errors due to mistakes and fraud. It is therefore imperative that P11Ds are filled in correctly and submitted on time.

Chapter 11 – Direct taxation

11.1 Introduction

A club or society can either be constituted as an incorporated body or as an unincorporated association. In either event it is liable to corporation tax on certain of its income and capital gains. In particular, it is liable for corporation tax on interest received and profits made from trading with non-members.

The term 'unincorporated association' is not defined in the Income and Corporation Taxes Act 1988 or elsewhere in tax statute. In the case of *Conservative and Unionist Central Office* v *Burrell (Inspector of Taxes)* [1982] STC 317, at page 318 it was held that 'an unincorporated association . . . was an organisation which had rules that identified in whom the control of it and its funds rested and in which two or more persons were bound together for one or more common purposes (not being business purposes) by mutual undertakings, each having mutual duties and obligations'. It can be seen that many small members' clubs fall within this definition.

11.2 Mutual trading

One of the fundamental concepts of direct taxation is that it is not possible to make a profit out of oneself. Although this general rule was contradicted by the case of *Sharkey* v *Wernher* 36 TC 275 it is still of fundamental importance to the direct taxation of clubs and societies. The concept of 'mutual trading' is an extension of the principle that one cannot make a taxable profit out of oneself to the group situation where a group of members cannot be taxed on any profits they make from trading with themselves. As an example, if a social club operates a members' bar, and that bar runs at a profit, no corporation tax is payable on that profit as it is derived from 'mutual trading'. However, where a members' club makes available its facilities to non-members and makes a surplus from these activities they are clearly not derived from 'mutual trading' and hence such profits are subject to corporation tax. For example, if a members' social club rents out a function room and provides catering for, say, a wedding reception, strictly some proportion of overall catering profits should be subject to corporation tax. Hence, where supplies to non-members are profitable, and more

152

than insubstantial, these should be declared to the Inland Revenue as subject to corporation tax as trading profits.

11.3 Interest received

The main area where coporation tax is actually paid by clubs and associations is on investment income, and in particular, on interest received.

11.4 Returns

It is clear that incorporated clubs and associations come within the corporation tax 'Pay and File' system. Hence, corporation tax needs to be paid on investment income and profits from trading with non-members within nine months of the end of each accounting period and the form CT200 submitted within 12 months of the end of 12-month accounting periods. However, the Pay and File regime applies equally to unincorporated associations and therefore small unincorporated members' clubs are potentially liable to substantial penalties for failure to comply with the many onerous obligations placed on them.

Under s11(5) of the Taxes Management Act 1970, an unincorporated association which makes up a set of accounts for a period longer than 18 months is required to file its Pay and File return within 30 months from the date of commencement of the period for which the accounts are made up. For example, if a members' club was formed on 1 November 1993 and prepared its first set of accounts for a period of 29 months to 31 March 1996 it would be required to complete its first Pay and File return covering the year ended 31 October 1994 by 30 April 1996.

Chapter 12 – Indirect taxation

12.1 Introduction

On the whole, indirect taxation causes substantially more difficulties for clubs and associations than direct taxation. This is because the UK VAT legislation makes no allowance for the concept of mutual trading. Therefore, supplies by a members' club to its members can be subject to VAT even if any profits generated are not subject to corporation tax. This is provided for in s94(2)(a) VATA 1994 which specifically includes in the definition of 'business' the provision by a club, association or organisation (for a subscription or other consideration) of the facilities or advantages available to its members. However, it was held in the case of *Notts Fire Service Messing Club* v *Commissioners* [1977] VATTR1 that to come within this legislation a club needed to have a certain minimum level of formalities such as a constitution, rules, management committee or officers. In practice, most unincorporated associations with turnover in excess of the VAT registration threshold are likely to be considered to be sufficiently organised to fall within the above legislation, even in the absence of a written constitution.

12.2 Practical difficulties

The commercial operation of essentially cash businesses such as bars and catering operations frequently give rise to disputes with HM Customs & Excise regarding the completeness of recorded income. This problem is often exacerbated for clubs and associations due to the use of members as unpaid bar staff and semi-honorary positions such as club treasurer. There are numerous examples of VAT tribunal cases where members' clubs have been found liable to substantial arrears of VAT based on 'business economics' models of projected taxable turnover compared with recorded turnover. Where the systems for control over stock and cash are inadequate it can prove extremely difficult to demonstrate that any assessment is not made to the required standard of the officer's 'best judgement'. If it can be demonstrated that apparent underdeclarations arise from theft of stock this should not give rise to an additional output VAT liability. Conversely, theft of cash after the making of taxable supplies is no defence against an assessment for underpaid output tax because the supplies in question would actually have taken place.

154

A good example of a club's successful argument against such an assessment can be found in the case of *Gloucester Old Boys' Rugby Football Social Club* Tribunal Ref. 437. The Tribunal concluded that although the club was run inefficiently, VAT was not a tax on inefficiency and that the club should not be regarded in the same way as a licensee of licensed premises. In addition, it found that 'free' drinks to members who volunteered to serve as bar staff were not subject to VAT. However, recently Tribunals have been rather less sympathetic of the special difficulties faced by clubs and a more typical case would be that of the *Merton Rugby Football Club* Tribunal Ref. 5880.

It should also be noted that another substantial source of income of many clubs is susceptible to VAT assessment, being takings from gaming machines. It is essential that clubs establish and maintain adequate systems for demonstrating completeness of takings records from such machines. In the case of *Moorthorpe Empire Working Mens Club* Tribunal Ref. 1127, an assessment representing underdeclared gaming machine takings of £24,405 was upheld by the VAT Tribunal as representing the Commissioners' best judgement.

12.3 Subscriptions

Prior to 1 January 1990 the vast majority of subscription income received by clubs would be considered to be wholly standard-rated. However, since that date many subscriptions to non-profit-making sports clubs have become exempt due to the implementation in the UK of Article 13A1(m) of the EC Sixth Directive. This provides for a compulsory exemption with direct effect in Member States. The consequences of this change of VAT status are considered at **12.4** below.

As a general rule, joining fees are treated as having the same VAT liability as the subsequent subscriptions.

Where a subscription provides a club member with an entitlement to receive a regular book or magazine which is VAT zero-rated then it would generally be appropriate to apportion the subscription between the standard-rated benefits of membership and the zero-rated publications. Generally this apportionment should be based on market value and should be agreed with Customs & Excise. Legal authority for this approach can be found in the case of the *Automobile Association* [1974] STC 192.

12.4 Exemption for certain sporting and physical education services

On 1 April 1994 Customs & Excise issued VAT Notice 701/45/94. This notice acknowledged VAT exemptions available to non-profit-making sports clubs to cover supplies such as subscriptions to members' golf clubs and charges for various sporting facilities. As a result of this exemption and the availability of backdating to 1 January 1990 many members' sports clubs received substantial VAT refunds and interest supplements. Subsequent case law has indicated that members do not have an individual entitlement to a share of their club's VAT refund unless the majority of members, in accordance with the constitution, decide to make individual repayments.

The main area of contention following the issue of the above notice was the exclusion of boat mooring, berthing and parking charges which Customs & Excise contended were not covered by the exemption even when provided by non-profit-making yacht and sailing clubs. However, as a result of the decision in *Swansea Yacht and Sub Aqua Club* Tribunal Ref. 13938, Customs & Excise have now accepted that the exemption for sporting facilities does extend to all boat and board storage fees charged to members by eligible clubs. Such clubs should review any VAT reclaim applications already made to establish if they are enhanced by this decision.

In addition to members' clubs set up primarily for the purpose of sports it is possible that other members' clubs are eligible for VAT refunds due to this exemption. In particular, social clubs making charges to members for snooker and pool facilities are likely to be eligible for VAT refunds where charges to members have previously been treated as standard-rated. All members' clubs should obtain a copy of the above notice and refer to Annex D which sets out the activities which are considered to be sports for the purposes of the exemption. However, the list currently excludes darts although this may be subject to a legal challenge.

12.5 Exemption for fundraising events

Many clubs and associations hold fundraising events on a regular and recurring basis. Group 12 Schedule 9 VATA 1994 was specifically enacted to provide exemption for certain fundraising events organised for charitable purposes by charities. In addition, the supply of goods and services by a 'qualifying body' in connection with a fundraising event organised exclusively for its own benefit is also covered by the exemption. A non-profit-making club or association could qualify for this exemption if it is established for the principal purpose of providing facilities for participating in sport or physical education.

Only certain fundraising events are covered by the exemption and these are fetes, balls, bazaars, gala shows, performances and similar events which are separate from and not forming part of any series or regular run of like or similar events. This definition contained in Note 1 of the above Group has caused considerable confusion, particularly as one of the most common forms of fundraising events would be a club's annual dinner. However, Customs & Excise have made it clear that they consider that an annual event such as an annual dinner is not excluded from the exemption.

The Tribunal decision in the case of *Blaydon Rugby Football Club* Tribunal Ref. 13901 has provided clear, if somewhat unhelpful, guidance on the scope of the exemption. In that case the club was assessed for output tax on supplies relating to club events such as stag nights, annual dinners, barbecues and various parties. Customs & Excise argued that the events did not qualify as fundraising events for the purpose of the exemption. The Tribunal did not accept the club's contention that the main purpose of the events were fundraising for the club. It took the view that any fundraising was merely an incidental purpose and hence exemption was not available. On this basis many club social events would fall outside the exemption if they are budgeted to break even, rather than to create surpluses and this would be even clearer where social events were subsidised from general club funds. The Tribunal also considered the Commissioners' alternative argument that the events organised by the club were in fact a series of events as they had the common quality of being social events for the club. It accepted that the exemption had to be construed strictly and therefore to qualify for exemption fundraising events had to be exceptional and not merely events which were routine in the life of the club.

This ruling, if applied strictly by Customs & Excise, could greatly reduce the scope of this otherwise helpful exemption.

The Appellant in the case of *Reading Cricket and Hockey Club* Tribunal Ref. 13656 received a far more favourable hearing from the VAT Tribunal than the above rugby football club. The Reading Cricket and Hockey Club organise a three-day annual real ale and jazz festival. In this case Customs chose not to contend that any fundraising was an incidental purpose and neither did they argue that the annual nature of the festival took the event outside of the exemption as 'part of a series or regular run of like or similar events'. Customs in fact chose to dispute the exemption solely on the grounds that the three consecutive days of the festival themselves represented a series or regular run of like events. The Tribunal found that the festival should be considered properly as a single event and not as a series of three separate performances, which would have been the case if, say, the same theatrical play had been put on for three consecutive nights.

As can be seen from the two above contrasting decisions, this is a particularly difficult area and clubs and associations should seek written rulings from Customs & Excise for all major fundraising and social events.

12.6 Raising of capital funds

Another area of potential dispute with Customs & Excise is where clubs and associations choose to raise capital funds from their members. These funds can be raised in numerous different ways and with resulting different VAT treatments. At the simplest level, if a number of members make voluntary interest-free loans to their clubs or associations any concessional treatment they receive in terms of reduced subscriptions is effectively cancelled out for VAT purposes. For example, if a member's standard-rated subscription is halved because of a voluntary interest-free loan, the interest forgone on that loan is deemed to be a taxable consideration 'topping up' the subscription to the full rate.

The situation is rather more complex where compulsory interest-free loans are involved. The leading case considering this is *Exeter Golf and Country Club Limited* v *Customs & Excise* [1981] STC 211. In that case it was decided that the notional interest the club would have paid to borrow the interest-free loans from a bank represented the VAT-inclusive consideration provided by members. Hence, output VAT was calculated on this basis.

By far the greatest difficulty comes where a club issues shares or debentures to its members. Customs' position is that these are either treated as interest-free loans by members to the club and VAT calculated as above or alternatively as additional one-off subscriptions or levies, and hence taxed in accordance with the taxation of the club's subscription.

12.7 Constitutional arrangements

The internal constitution arrangements of clubs and associations can have a profound effect on the treatment of VAT. By way of example, if a sports club has, say, separate cricket, hockey and tennis sections and each of these sub-sections are financially independent and managed as separate units, with their own properly constituted committees and bank accounts, then potentially these are separate 'taxable persons' for VAT purposes and do not form part of the main sports club registration.

12.8 Input VAT recovery

The implementation of exemptions to cover many of the income sources of non-profit-making clubs can have an adverse impact on input VAT recovery and affected clubs should consider their 'partial exemption' position carefully, particularly when embarking on major capital projects.

12.9 Conclusion

The substantial VAT refunds received by many members' clubs have usefully concentrated members' minds on the importance of VAT in the running of their clubs. They would be well advised to consider VAT compliance and planning as equally important for the future.

Appendix 1 – XYZ Social Club Limited financial statements

XYZ Social Club Limited – club information

Club No:

Chairman:

Vice Chairman:

Secretary:

Treasurer:

Committee:

Registered office:

Auditors:

Bankers:

Solicitors:

Trustees:

XYZ Social Club Limited statement of committee's responsibilities

Law requires the committee to prepare financial statements for each financial year which give a true and fair view of the state of affairs of the club and of the profit or loss of the club for that period. In preparing those financial statements, the committee is required to:

- select suitable accounting policies and then apply them consistently;
- make judgements and estimates that are reasonable and prudent;
- prepare the financial statements on the going concern basis, unless it is inappropriate to presume that the club will continue in business.

The committee is responsible for keeping proper accounting records which disclose with reasonable accuracy at any time the financial position of the club and to enable it to ensure that the financial statements comply with the Industrial and Provident Societies Act 1965 and the Friendly and Industrial and Provident Societies Act 1968/Friendly Societies Act 1974*. They are also responsible for safeguarding the assets of the club and hence for taking reasonable steps for the prevention and detection of fraud and other irregularities.

* delete as appropriate

Auditor's report to the members of XYZ Social Club Limited

We have audited the financial statements on pages 5 to 14 which have been prepared under the historical cost convention (as modified by the revaluation of certain fixed assets) and the accounting policies set out on page 7.

Respective responsibilities of management committee and auditors

As described on page 3 the committee is responsible for the preparation of financial statements. It is our responsibility to form an independent opinion, based on our audit, on those statements and to report our opinion to you.

Basis of opinion

We conducted our audit in accordance with auditing standards issued by the Auditing Practices Board. An audit includes examination, on a test basis, of evidence relevant to the amounts and disclosures in the financial statements. It also includes an assessment of the significant estimates and judgements by the committee in the preparation of the financial statements, and of whether the accounting policies are appropriate to the club's circumstances, consistently applied and adequately disclosed.

We planned and performed our audit so as to obtain all the information and explanations which we considered necessary in order to provide us with sufficient evidence to give reasonable assurance that the financial statements are free from material misstatement, whether caused by fraud, or other irregularity or error. In forming our opinion, we also evaluated the overall adequacy of the presentation of information in the financial statements.

Opinion

In our opinion the financial statements give a true and fair view of the state of the Club's affairs at 31 December 199X and of its profit/loss* for the year/period* then ended and have been properly prepared in accordance with the Industrial and Provident Societies Act 1965 and the Friendly and Provident Societies Act 1968/Friendly Societies Act 1974*.

CHARTERED ACCOUNTANTS
AND REGISTERED AUDITORS

DATE:

* *delete as appropriate*

Profit and loss account for the year ended 31 December 199X

	Note	199X	199W
		£	£
Turnover			
Cost of sales		——	——
Gross profit			
Administrative expenses		——	——
Trading profit/(loss)			
Other operating income	2		
Interest payable and similar charges	3	——	——
Profit/(loss) on ordinary activities before taxation	4		
Tax on profit/(loss) on ordinary activities	5	——	——
Profit/(loss) for the financial year		——	——
Profit/(loss) b/f		——	——
Profit/(loss) c/f		══	══

The notes on pages 7 to 14 form an integral part of these financial statements.

There are no other gains or losses other than those disclosed above for both financial years.

There are no acquisitions and discontinued operations during the current or preceding year.

Balance sheet at 31 December 199X

	Note	199X		199W	
		£	£	£	£
Fixed assets					
Investments	**8**				
Tangible assets	**9**				
Current assets					
Stocks	**10**				
Debtors	**11**				
Cash at bank and in hand		_____		_____	
Creditors: Amounts falling due within one year	**12**	_____		_____	
Net current assets/liabilities		_____		_____	
Total assets less current liabilities					
Creditors: Amounts falling due after more than one year	**13**	_____		_____	
		══════		══════	
Capital and reserves					
Share capital					
Profit and loss account					
Revaluation reserve					
Other reserves		_____		_____	
Members' funds	**17**	══════		══════	

The notes on pages 7 to 14 form an integral part of these financial statements.

The financial statements were approved by the committee on .... (date)

              – CHAIRMAN/COMMITTEE MEMBER

              – SECRETARY

              – COMMITTEE MEMBER

Notes to the accounts for the year ended 31 December 199X

1 Accounting policies

The financial statements have been prepared under the historical cost convention.

Turnover
Turnover represents monies received (excluding value added tax) from bar sales.

Tangible fixed assets and depreciation
Depreciation is provided by the club to write off the cost less the estimated residual value of the tangible fixed assets over their useful economic lives as follows:

Freehold property	Over 50 years
Leasehold property	Over the terms of the lease
Fixtures and fittings	Over 5 years
Plant and machinery	Over 5 years
Motor vehicles	Over 3 years

Stocks
Stocks are valued by a professional valuer at the lower of cost and net realisable value. Cost is computed on an average cost basis.

Taxation
The club is treated for corporation tax purposes as being mutually trading and is not liable to UK corporation tax on its trading profits. The charge for taxation is based on investment income for the year. No provision for deferred taxation is made if there is reasonable evidence that such deferred taxation will not be payable in the foreseeable future.

Finance and operating leases
Assets obtained under hire purchase contracts and leases which result in the transfer to the club of substantially all the risks and rewards of ownership (finance leases) are capitalised as tangible fixed assets at the estimated present value of underlying lease payments and are depreciated in accordance with the above policy. Obligations under such agreements are included in creditors net of finance charges allocated to future periods. The finance element of the rental payments is charged to the profit and loss account over the period of the lease or hire

purchase contract so as to produce a constant rate of charge on the outstanding balance of the net obligation in each period.

Rentals paid under other leases (operating leases) are charged against income on a straight line basis over the lease term.

Pension

The club operates a pension scheme, whereby the club agrees to pay a defined contribution into the pension scheme for eligible employees. The pension charge represents contributions payable by the club for the year. The club's liability is limited to the amount of the contribution.

2 Other operating income

	199X £	199W £
Other sources of income		

3 Interest payable and similar charges

	£	£
On bank loans, overdrafts, mortgages and other loans repayable within five years		
Interest on each class of members' loans and deposits		
On other loans		

4 Profit/(loss) on ordinary activities before taxation

	199X £	199W £
Profit/(loss) on ordinary activities before taxation is stated after charging:		
Amounts written off fixed assets		
Depreciation for year		
Operating lease rentals – fixtures & fittings		
Auditors' remuneration		

5 Taxation

	199X £	199W £
Tax on investment income at X%		
Tax on non-mutual trading at X%	───	───
	═══	═══

6 Staff costs and numbers

	£	£
Staff costs:		
Wages and salaries		
Social Security costs	───	───
	═══	═══
Average number of persons employed:		
Bar staff and cleaner		
Administration	───	───
	═══	═══
Remuneration of committee members	£	£
Emoluments including fees and expenses	───	───
	═══	═══

7 Pension costs

Defined contribution scheme

The club operates a defined contribution scheme. The assets of the scheme are held separately from those of the club in an independently administered fund. The pension cost charge represents contributions payable by the club to the fund and amounted to £X (199W: £X).

Contributions totalling £X (199W: £X) were payable to the fund at 31 December 199X, and are included in creditors.

8 Investments

	199X £	199W £
Listed investments		
Unlisted investments	───	───
	═══	═══

168

The aggregate material value of listed investments is £ _____ for 199X.

The unlisted investments include investments in clubs registered under the Industrial and Provident Societies Act 1965 as follows:

	£
Investment in A	X
Investment in B	X
Investment in C	X

9 Tangible fixed assets

	Long leasehold land and buildings £	Freehold land and buildings £	Fixtures and fittings £	Plant and machinery £	Motor vehicles £	Total £
Cost/valuation						
At 1 January 199X						
Additions						
At 31 December 199X						
Depreciation						
At 1 January 199X						
Charge for the year						
At 31 December 199X						
Net book value						
At 31 December 199X						
At 31 December 199W						

The lease on the property expires in 20XX.

The net book value of assets held under finance leases was £ _____. The depreciation charge for the year was £ _____. (199W: £ _____).

169

10 Stocks

	199X £	199W £
Refreshments and other bar stocks		
Other stocks		

There is no material difference between the replacement cost of stocks and their balance sheet amounts.

11 Debtors: amounts falling due within one year

	£	£
Other debtors		
Prepayments and accrued income		

Prepayments include £X pension contribution prepaid.

12 Creditors: amounts falling due within one year

	£	£
Mortgages		
Bank overdrafts		
Trade creditors		
Other creditors		
Other taxation and Social Security costs		
Accruals and deferred income		
Money received in advance		
Stewards' deposits		

Included in other creditors are amounts owed for finance leases. £ _____ is due within one year.

13 Creditors: amounts falling due after more than one year

	199X £	199W £
Mortgages		
Bank loans and overdrafts		
Other creditors and accruals	════	════
Loan account – ABC Ltd		
Opening balance		
Add: interest paid	───	───
Less: repaid in year	───	───
Closing balance	════	════
The above loan is repayable as follows:		
Within 1–2 years		
Within 3–5 years		
After more than 5 years	───	───
	════	════
Advance discount loan – ABC Ltd		
Loan received	════	════

Included in other loans are amounts owed for finance leases. £X is payable in two to five years' time.

The bank has a charge over the club property in relation to the bank overdraft.

14 Contingent liabilities

There were no contingent liabilities at the balance sheet date.

15 Capital commitments

	£	£
Authorised not contracted for		
Contracted for not provided	───	───
	════	════

Of these commitments £ _____ relates to finance leases and hire purchase contracts.

16 Other financial commitments

Operating lease commitments
The annual commitments under operating leases are analysed according to the period in which the leases expires as follows:

	199X £	199W £
Land and buildings:		
Within one year		
Between two and five years		
Over five years		
	———	———
	═══	═══
Other:		
Within one year		
Between two and five years		
Over five years		
	———	———
	═══	═══

17 Reconciliation of movements in member's funds

	£	£
Member's funds brought forward		
Plus shares issued		
Less shares cancelled/repaid		
Profit/(loss) for the year	———	———
Member's funds carried forward	═══	═══

Detailed trading and profit and loss account for the year ended 31 December 199X

	199X		199W	
	£	£	£	£
Bar sales				
Less: bar purchases	_____		_____	
Gross profit				
Pool table receipts				
Less: expenses	_____		_____	
Gaming machine receipts				
Less: expenses	_____		_____	
Tote/bingo receipts				
Less: prizes and expenses	_____		_____	
Snooker table receipts				
Less: expenses	_____		_____	
Members' subscriptions				
Telephone receipts				
Cigarette machine commission				
Visitor's box receipts				
Juke box/quiz receipts				
Gift	_____		_____	
		_____		_____

Balance carried forward

The following pages do not form part of the audited financial statements.

	199X		199W	
	£	£	£	£
Balance brought forward				

Deduct: expenses

Entertainment account
Staff salaries and wages
Printing, stationery and
   advertising
Telephone charges
Ground rent
Rates and water rates
Insurances
Heating and lighting
Cleaning and laundry
Repairs and renewals
Leasing of equipment
Glasses and bar requisites
Bank charges and interest
TV rental and licence
Draymen's beer
Professional fees
Sundry expenses
Loan interest

Net (loss)/profit before depreciation

Deduct:

Depreciation

Net (loss)/profit to date

Entertainment account for the year ended 31 December 199X

	199X		199W	
	£	£	£	£
Bingo receipts				
Bingo expenses	———		———	
Prize draw and raffle receipts				
Prize draw expenses	———		———	
Racing trip receipts				
Racing trip expenses	———		———	
Concert admission receipts				
Donkey derby receipts – net		———		———
Deduct expenses				
Artists' fees and groups				
Entertainment licence				
Entertainment expenses	———		———	
		———		———
Balance transferred to trading account		══		══

Analysis of repairs and renewals for the year ended 31 December 199X

	£	£
Building repairs/maintenance		
Install kitchen		
Roof repairs		
Install gas supply		
Decorator (office)		
Decorations/repairs (flat)		
Sink fittings and tiles		
Bars for window		
Wallpaper, shelving, paint	_____	
Alarm leasing, maintenance and repairs		
Hand dryer rental and maintenance		
Fire extinguisher and maintenance		
Electrical repairs and maintenance		
Cooler repairs		
Sound equipment		
Plumber and drainage maintenance		
Ball sets, triangle, etc.		
Grass cutting		
Sundry repairs and renewals		_____
		======

Analysis of sundry expenses for the year ended 31 December 199X

	£	£
Club coach expenses		
Less: receipts	——	
Trade refuse		
Accountant's fees		
Stocktaking fees		
VAT return fees		
Rodent control		
Solicitors' fees – re negotiation of loan		
other	——	
Building regulation fees		
Chartered surveyor		
Rule books		
Hospitality		
Committee hospitality		
Restaurant promotion		
Wine promotion		
Sandwiches re funeral		
Others		——

Appendix 2 – Industrial and Provident and Friendly Society checklist

The following checklist should be used when completing a set of accounts for a working men's club. This checklist incorporates the basic standard disclosures only. If any special or unusual transactions occur, reference should be made to the relevant legislation or to alternative checklists. Specifically, the checklists assume that none of the following will apply:

- there are no research and development costs;
- there have been no acquisitions or discontinued activities in the period;
- there are no investment properties;
- there has been no early settlement of debt;
- there have been no reverse premiums;
- there is no deferred tax liability;
- there are no pension commitments or other post-retirement benefits;
- no dividends have been paid by any Industrial and Provident Societies.

This checklist incorporates the disclosures required by the Friendly and Industrial and Provident Societies Act 1968 (F, I & P Act 68), the Friendly Societies Act 1974 (FSA 74), the Registrar's requirements and relevant SSAPs, FRSs and UITFs.

Client:		Prepared by:	Date:	Ref:
Year/period end:	File no.:	Reviewed by:	Date:	

1 Revenue account

1.1 In respect of a club set up under the Friendly Societies Act 1974 and Industrial and Provident Societies Act 1965 every registered society or branch for each year of account shall prepare:

(a) a revenue account which deals with the affairs of the society and branch as a whole for the year; or ⬜

178

(b)   two or more revenue accounts for that year which deal separately with the particular businesses conducted by the society or branch; and ☐

(c)   a revenue account(s) which reflects a true and fair view of the club's activities during the period (s3 F, I & P Act 68; s30 FSA 74). ☐

1.2   Disclose the nature and amount of any adjustment to accumulated depreciation as a result of a change in estimate of an asset's useful economic life (SSAP 12, para 18). ☐

1.3   Disclose the effect, if material, on the depreciation charge of any revaluation in the year (SSAP 12, para 27). ☐

1.4   Where the method of depreciation has been changed, give the effect of and reason for the change, if material (corresponding amounts not required) (SSAP 12, para 26). ☐

1.5   Disclose the aggregate finance charges allocated for the period in respect of finance leases and hire-purchase agreements (SSAP 21, para 53). ☐

1.6   Disclose the total charge relating to operating lease rentals (SSAP 21, para 55). ☐

1.7   Disclose the amount of remuneration (including fees and expenses) paid to members of the committee of management (F, I & P Act 68; FSA 74). ☐

1.8   Disclose the amount of staff (including officers') salaries and wages (F, I & P Act 68; FSA 74). ☐

1.9   Disclose the amount of auditors' remuneration (F, I & P Act 68; FSA 74). ☐

1.10 Disclose the depreciation charge for the period (F, I & P Act 68; FSA 74). ☐

1.11 Disclose the amount of interest payable or similar charges, showing separately how much consists of:

(a) interest on bank loans, overdrafts, mortgages and other loans wholly repayable within five years;

(b) interest on each class of members' loans and deposits;

(c) interest on other loans and mortgages (F, I & P Act 68; FSA 74).

Taxation

1.12 Disclose any special circumstances that affect the overall tax charge or credit for the period, or that may affect those of future periods, and quantify the effects (FRS 3, para 23).

1.13 Disclose the effects of a fundamental change in the basis of taxation separately on the face of the profit and loss account, as part of the tax charge or credit (FRS 3, para 23).

1.14 State any tax attributable to franked investment income (SSAP 8, para 22(a)).

1.15 Disclose the basis on which the charge for corporation tax and income tax is computed (F, I & P Act 68; FSA 74).

FRS 3 primary statements and additional notes

1.16 Present (as a primary statement with the same prominence as the other primary statements) a statement of total recognised gains and losses and its components. If there are no recognised gains or losses other than the profit or loss for the period, include a statement to this effect immediately below the revenue account (FRS 3, paras 27 and 57).

1.17 Include a note of historical cost profits and losses (immediately following the revenue account or the statement of total recognised gains and losses) where the result in the revenue account is materially different from the result on an unmodified historical cost basis, showing:

(a) a reconciliation of the reported pre-tax profit or loss to the equivalent historical cost amount; and ☐

(b) the retained profit for the year on the historical cost basis (FRS 3, para 26). ☐

1.18 Where there are no acquisitions and discontinued operations during the current or preceding year, state this fact immediately below the revenue account (FRS 3, para 14). ☐

1.19 Disclose in relation to extraordinary items, extraordinary income, charges, the net of these two items and the tax on the net amount should be shown separately (F, I & P Act 68; FSA 74). ☐

1.20 When a change in accounting policy is made, disclose an indication of the effect on the current year's results (UITF 14, para 3). ☐

1.21 Where the effect on the current year is either immaterial or similar to the quantified effect on the prior year a simple statement saying this will suffice (UITF 14, para 3). ☐

1.22 Where it is not practicable to give the effect on the current year, that fact, together with the reasons should be stated (UITF 14, para 3). ☐

Prior year adjustments

1.23 State the cumulative effect of the prior year adjustments at the foot of the statement of total recognised gains and losses for the current period (FRS 3, para 29). ☐

1.24 Disclose the effect of prior year adjustments on the results for the preceding year where practical (FRS 3, para 29). ☐

1.25 Disclose the reason for each prior year adjustment (F, I & P Act 68; FSA 74). ☐

2 Balance sheet

General

2.1 The balance sheet should reflect a true and fair view of the club's state of affairs at the end of the financial period (F, I & P Act 68; FSA 74).

2.2 Disclose the date on which the accounts are approved by the committee (SSAP 17, para 26).

2.3 The balance sheet must be signed by the secretary and two committee members on behalf of committee (F, I & P Act 1968; FSA 74).

Investments

2.4 In respect of investments, how much consists of listed investments and unlisted investments (F, I & P Act 68; FSA 74).

2.5 Show the aggregate market value of listed investments (F, I & P Act 68; FSA 74).

Tangible fixed assets

2.6 In respect of tangible fixed assets, how much consists of:

   (a) land and buildings, distinguishing between freeholds, long leaseholds and short leaseholds (short leaseholds are defined as those with less than 50 years to run);

   (b) plant, machinery, motor vehicles, fixtures and fittings;

   (c) payments on account and assets in the course of construction (F, I & P Act 68; FSA 74).

2.7 For each class of tangible fixed assets shown in 2.6 above disclose the gross amounts and accumulated depreciation, including the amount of aggregate additions, disposals, revaluations and transfers in the year (F, I & P Act 68; FSA 74).

2.8 In respect of land and buildings and any other fixed assets which have been revalued, disclose comparable amounts determined according to the historic cost convention or the difference between revaluation and cost ('comparable amounts' covers aggregate cost and aggregate depreciation) (F, I & P Act 68; FSA 74). ☐

2.9 If the society holds assets under finance leases or hire purchase agreements, disclose separately the gross amount of each major class of such asset and the related accumulated depreciation charge. As an alternative, these assets may be combined with owned assets and their net book value and related depreciation charge for the year shown separately (SSAP 21, paras 49 and 50). ☐

2.10 Where the value of an asset is shown in a note because it differs materially from its book amount, the note should also show the tax effects, if any, that would arise if the asset were realised at the balance sheet date at the noted value (SSAP 15, para 42). ☐

2.11 Disclose separately the cost or valuation of any non-depreciable assets (for example land) when combined with a depreciable asset (as in land and buildings) (SSAP 12, para 25). ☐

2.12 Where property assets are valued on a basis which has regard to the trading potential which attaches to the property, the assets concerned should be disclosed separately. The notes to the accounts should make clear that this practice has been followed and that the amount at which the assets concerned are stated does not exceed their open market value (SSAP 22, para 15). ☐

Stocks

2.13 Where different bases have been adopted for different types of stocks, the amount included in the accounts in respect of each type should be stated (SSAP 9, para 14). ☐

2.14 In respect of stocks, show how much consists of:

(a) refreshments and other bar stock; ☐

(b) other stocks. ☐

Such other classifications as may be appropriate to the activities of the club may be substituted for (a) and (b) above (F, I & P Act 68; FSA 74).

Debtors

2.15 Give separate disclosure on the face of the balance sheet of debtors receivable in more than one year where the amount is so material in the context of the total net current assets, that the absence of such disclosure could mislead a reader of the accounts (UITF 4, para 3).

Creditors and provisions

2.16 State the amount of each item included within creditors, an analysis of the maturity of all capital instruments treated as debt, showing amounts falling due:

(i)   in one year or less, or on demand;

(ii)   between one and two years;

(iii) between two and five years; and

(iv)   in five years or more (FRS 4, para 33).

2.17 Disclose separately the amounts owed under finance lease and hire-purchase agreements (SSAP 21, para 51).

2.18 Analyse the obligations under finance lease and hire purchase agreements between amounts payable in the next year, in the second to fifth year inclusive, and the aggregate amounts payable thereafter (SSAP 21, para 52).

2.19 Show separately for creditors due in less than one year and for creditors and loans due in more than one year, how much consists of:

(a)   mortgages;

(b)   bank overdrafts;

(c)   other creditors and accruals (F, I & P Act 68; FSA 74).

2.20 For each item included under creditors and loans, show the aggregate amount of secured liabilities and give an indication of the nature of the security (F, I & P Act 68; FSA 74). ☐

2.21 Disclose separately any provision (F, I & P Act 68; FSA 74). ☐

Share capital and reserves

2.22 Disclose the amount released to general reserves during the year of any revaluation reserve relating to assets which have been sold or, in the case of depreciated assets, that proportion which has been depreciated (F, I & P Act 68; FSA 74). ☐

2.23 Where land and buildings or any other fixed assets of a club have been revalued, the amount of any surplus and deficit arising from the revaluation shall be separately disclosed under the heading revaluation reserve. The treatment for taxation purposes of amounts credited or debited to the revaluation reserve shall be disclosed in a note to the accounts (F, I & P Act 68; FSA 74). ☐

2.24 For each class of provision for liabilities and charges, unless the only movement relates to the transfer out for the purpose for which the provision was established, show:

   (a) the amount at the beginning and end of the year; ☐

   (b) the amount transferred to or from the provision during the year; and ☐

   (c) the source and application of any such movement (F, I & P Act 68; FSA 74). ☐

2.25 For each class of reserves show:

   (a) the amount at the beginning and end of the year; ☐

   (b) the amount transferred to or from the reserve during the year; and ☐

   (c) the source and application of any such movement (F, I & P Act 68; FSA 74). ☐

Other balance sheet disclosures

2.26 For any unprovided contingent liability where it is probable or possible that it may occur, and for any material contingent gain where it is probable that the gain will be realised, disclose:

   (a)   the amount and estimated amount of the liability; ☐

   (b)   the uncertainties that are expected to affect its ultimate outcome; ☐

   (c)   the legal nature of the liability; ☐

   (d)   an explanation of the tax implications, where necessary for the proper understanding of the financial position; ☐

   (e)   whether any valuable security has been provided by the club in connection with that liability and, if so, what (SSAP 18, paras 16, 17, 18 and 20) (F, I & P Act 68; FSA 74). ☐

2.27 Disclose any commitments under finance leases and hire purchase lease agreements in existence at the year end, but whose inception occurs after the year end (SSAP 21, para 54). ☐

2.28 Disclose the amount payable under any commitments under operating leases for the next 12 months, analysed between land and buildings and other operating leases, and splitting each between leases which expire in the next year, in the second to fifth years inclusive, and over five years from the balance sheet date (SSAP 21, para 56). ☐

2.29 Disclose for capital commitments:

   (a)   the aggregate amount or estimated amount of contracts for capital expenditure, so far not provided for; and ☐

   (b)   the aggregate amount or estimated amount of capital expenditure authorised by the committee of management which has not been contracted for (F, I & P Act 68; FSA 74). ☐

2.30 Disclose for any material non-adjusting post balance sheet event, or the reversal of any transactions entered into primarily for window-dressing purposes:

(a) the nature of the event; ☐

(b) an estimate of the financial effect, before taxation, or a statement that it is not practicable to make such an estimate; and ☐

(c) an explanation of the tax implications, where necessary for a proper understanding of the financial position (SSAP 17, para 24 and 25). ☐

2.31 Current assets should be stated at the lower of cost and net realisable value (F, I & P Act 68; FSA 74). ☐

3 Miscellaneous disclosures

3.1 State the accounting policies used for dealing with items which are judged material or critical to the accounts. ☐

The accounting policy note disclosures should include, where applicable:

(a) the method by which turnover stated is arrived at (SSAP 5, para 8); ☐

(b) stocks (SSAP 9, para 32); ☐

(c) operating and finance leases (SSAP 21, para 57); ☐

(d) method of arriving at value of fixed assets, cost or valuation (F, I & P Act 68; FSA 74); ☐

(e) method of accounting for grants and brewery advanced discount loans (SSAP 4, para 28(a)); ☐

(f) for each major class of depreciable asset, disclose the depreciation methods used, and the estimated useful economic life or rate of depreciation (SSAP 12, para 25). ☐

3.2 Where an audit has been undertaken, the accounts need to include a statement of the committee's responsibilities for each financial year to include:

(a) selecting suitable accounting policies and then applying them consistently;

(b) making judgements and estimates that are reasonable and prudent;

(c) preparing financial statements on a going concern
basis, unless it is inappropriate to presume the club
will continue in business;

(d) keeping proper accounting records (F, I & P Act 68;
FSA 74)

(e) safeguarding the assets of the club; and

(f) taking reasonable steps for prevention and detection
of fraud and other irregularities (SAS 600).

FRS 8 *Related party disclosures*

3.3 Disclose material transactions undertaken by the club or
society with a related party, irrespective of whether a
price has been charged.

Disclosures include:

(a) names of transacting related parties and description
of relationship;

(b) description of related party transactions;

(c) amounts involved;

(d) any other elements of transactions necessary for an
understanding of the financial statements;

(e) amounts due to or from related parties at the balance sheet date and provisions for doubtful debts
from such parties at that date; and

(f) amounts written off in the period in respect of debts
due to or from related parties (FRS 8, para 6).

3.4 The transactions with related parties may be disclosed on
an aggregated basis (aggregation of similar transactions

by type of related party) unless disclosure of an individual transaction or connected transactions is necessary for an understanding of the impact of the transactions on the financial statements of the club or society or is required by law (FRS 8, para 7). ☐

Deferred income

3.5 Disclose the effects of grants or brewery advanced discount loans on the results for the period and/or the financial position (SSAP 4, para 28(b)). ☐

3.6 Where the results for the period are affected materially by the receipt of grants or brewery advanced discount loans, disclose the nature of the assistance and, where possible, an estimate of the effect (SSAP 4, para 28(c)). ☐

3.7 Show comparative figures for all the primary statements and notes except where indicated (FRS 3, para 30). ☐

3.8 Show the amount and description of each exceptional item, either individually or as an aggregate of similar items, by way of note or on the face of the profit and loss account if necessary for a true and fair view, together with a statement of the effect of the item (FRS 3, para 19). ☐

3.9 If the financial statements are prepared on the basis of assumptions which differ from any generally accepted fundamental concepts (going concern, accruals, consistency and prudence), or accounting policies are not consistently applied (either within the same accounts or from year to year), then particulars of the departure, the reason for it and the effects must be disclosed (SSAP 2, para 17). ☐

4 Reports

Audit report (SAS 600)

4.1 The audit report should be addressed to the members of the club. ☐

4.2 State that the accounts have been prepared under the historical cost convention, as modified for any revaluations that have occurred. ☐

189

4.3 State where the accounting policies can be found. ☐

4.4 State the responsibilities of the management committee and the respective responsibilities of the auditor. ☐

4.5 Include a basis of opinion paragraph in accordance with SAS 600. ☐

4.6 State in the opinion paragraph whether or not the financial statements give a true and fair view of the club's affairs, and have been prepared in accordance with the Industrial and Provident Societies Act 1965 and the Friendly and Industrial and Provident Societies Act 1968 or the Friendly Societies Act 1974. ☐

4.7 State the pages which have been audited in the audit report. ☐

4.8 The audit report must refer to any significant departure from SSAPs/FRSs:

(a) which is not adequately disclosed in the notes to the accounts; or ☐

(b) with which the auditors do not concur (Foreword to Accounting Standards, para 10(b)). ☐

4.9 Where the detailed statement required under 3.2 above has not been included elsewhere, include these details in the audit report (SAS 600). ☐

4.10 If the auditor is a chartered accountant, state this fact on the audit report. ☐

4.11 Show the date that the audit report was signed on the face of the audit report. ☐

Independent accountant's report

4.12 The independent accountant's report should be addressed to the members of the society. ☐

4.13 The independent accountant's report must state whether, in the opinion of the reporting accountant:

(a) the accounts are in agreement with the books of account kept by the society under s1 of the Friendly and Industrial and Provident Societies Act 1968 or s29 of the Friendly Societies Act 1974; ☐

(b) on the basis of the information contained in those books of account, the accounts have been drawn up in a manner consistent with the requirements of the Industrial and Provident Societies Act 1965 and the Friendly and Industrial and Provident Societies Act 1968 or the Friendly Societies Act 1974 (s9A F, I & P Act 68; s39A FSA 74). ☐

4.14 The report must also state whether the financial criteria for the exercise of the power to opt out of audit were met (s9A F, I & P Act 68; s39A FSA 74). ☐

5 Additional disclosure for Industrial and Provident Societies only

5.1 Give a note reconciling the opening and closing total shareholders' funds (FRS 3, para 28). ☐

5.2 Disclose in respect of unlisted investments how much consists of investments in other Industrial and Provident Societies and show separately the names and amounts invested in subsidiaries (F, I & P Act 68). ☐

Appendix 3 – Letters of engagement

The letter of engagement forms the basis of the contract between the firm and the client. In the event of any dispute or uncertainty this will play a vital part in reaching any agreement. It is essential that the letter is both complete and up to date.

The section relating to investment business treats the client as a corporate finance client. However, it should be noted that in order to undertake any corporate finance work for a registered club or association the firm must be registered under at least category B.

The relevant investment business paragraph should be used depending on the firm's category of authorisation. In addition, when completing letters (a)(i) or (b)(i) for category A firms using paragraph 6.3 or category B firms using paragraph 6.6, where commission is received, the investment business regulations require firms to obtain specific consent for its retention. These paragraphs only give general consent. Therefore, the firm will either need to obtain consent for the retention of each individual receipt, specifying the percentage and amount of commission involved, or, alternatively, it may wish to add a further sentence giving the firm consent to retain commissions up to a certain percentage *and* value without requiring further consent. Any commissions received above these amounts would need to be agreed by the client in writing.

There are six pro-forma letters in this appendix:

(a) For societies registered under the Industrial and Provident Societies Act 1965:
   (i) an audit letter of engagement;
   (ii) a supplementary letter for use where an independent accountant's report assignment is being undertaken; and
   (iii) a supplementary letter for use on a total exemption assignment.
(b) For societies registered under the Friendly Societies Act 1974:
   (i) an audit letter of engagement;
   (ii) a supplementary letter for use where an independent accountant's report assignment is being undertaken; and
   (iii) a supplementary letter for use on a total exemption assignment.

Specimen audit letter of engagement for a society registered under the Industrial and Provident Societies Act 1965

The committee of .... Limited

Dear Sirs,

We are pleased to accept the appointment as auditors of your club/association/society* and are writing to confirm the matters discussed at our meeting (with you/Mr ....*) on ....

We are bound by the ethical guidelines of our professional Institute, and accept instructions to act for you on the basis that we will act in accordance with those ethical guidelines.

1 Audit

1.1 Our function as auditors under the Friendly and Industrial and Provident Societies Act 1968 is to examine and report on the annual accounts of the club/association/society*. The officers are responsible for the preparation of accounts giving a true and fair view, and for the maintenance of proper accounting records and an appropriate system of internal control. You are also responsible for making available to us, as and when required, all the club's/association's/society's* accounting records and all other relevant records and related information, including minutes of all committee and members' meetings.

1.2 Our legal and professional duty is to make a report to the members stating whether in our opinion the accounts of the club/association/society* which we have audited give a true and fair view of the state of the club's/association's/society's* affairs, and of the profit or loss for the year, and whether they comply with the Industrial and Provident Societies Act 1965 and the Friendly and Industrial and Provident Societies Act 1968. In arriving at our opinion we are required by law to consider the following matters, and to report on any matters in respect of which we are not satisfied:

(a) whether proper accounting records have been kept by the club/association/society* and proper returns adequate for our audit have been received from branches not visited by us;

(b)   whether the club's/association's/society's* balance sheet and profit and loss account are in agreement with the accounting records and returns;

(c)   whether we have obtained all the information and explanations which we think necessary for the purpose of our audit.

In addition, we have a professional duty to report if the accounts do not comply in any material respect with Statements of Standard Accounting Practice, or Financial Reporting Standards, unless in our opinion the non-compliance is justified in the circumstances. In determining whether or not the departure is justified we consider:

(a)   whether the departure is required in order for the accounts to give a true and fair view; and

(b)   whether adequate disclosure has been made concerning the departure.

Our professional responsibilities also include:

(a)   including in our report a description of the officers' responsibilities for the accounts where the accounts or accompanying information do not include such description; and

(b)   considering whether other information and documents contained in audited accounts are consistent with those accounts.

1.3   Our auditing procedures will be carried out in accordance with the Statements of Auditing Standards issued by the Auditing Practices Board, and will include such tests of transactions and of the existence, ownership and valuation of assets and liabilities as we consider necessary. We will ascertain the accounting systems in order to assess their adequacy as a basis for the preparation of the accounts. We will need to obtain relevant and reliable evidence sufficient to enable us to draw reasonable conclusions therefrom.

1.4   The nature and extent of our tests will vary according to our assessment of the club's/association's/society's* accounting and internal control systems, and may cover any aspects of the business operations. We shall report to the committee any significant weaknesses in, or observations on, the club's/association's/society's* systems which come to our notice and which we think should be brought to the committee's attention. Any such report may not be provided to third parties without our prior written consent. Such consent would be granted only on the basis that such reports are not prepared with the interests of anyone other than the club/

association/society* in mind and that we accept no duty or responsibility to any other party as concerns the report.

1.5   The responsibility for safeguarding the assets of the club/association/society* and for the prevention and detection of fraud, error and non-compliance with laws or regulations rests with the committee. However, we will plan our audit so that we have a reasonable expectation of detecting material misstatements in the accounts resulting from irregularities, fraud or non-compliance with law or regulations but our examination should not be relied upon to disclose all such material misstatements or frauds, errors or instances of non-compliance as may exist.

1.6   As part of our normal audit procedures, we may request you to provide formal representations concerning certain information and explanations we have received from you during the course of our audit.

1.7   In order to assist us with a review of your accounts, which constitutes part of our audit, we will request sight of any documents or statements which will be issued with the accounts. We are also entitled to attend all general meetings of the club/association/society*, and to receive notice of all such meetings.

1.8   (We appreciate that the present size of your business renders it uneconomic to create a system of internal control based on the segregation of duties for different functions within each area of the business. In the running of the business we understand that, instead, the officers are closely involved with the control of the club's/association's/society's* transactions. In planning and performing our audit work we shall take account of this supervision.)†

1.9   Once we have issued our report we have no further direct responsibility in relation to the accounts for that financial year. However, we expect that you will inform us of any material event occurring between the date of our report and that of the annual general meeting which may affect the accounts.

2 Accounting

2.1   It was agreed that we should carry out the following accounting and other services on your behalf:

(a)   write up the accounting records of the club/association/society*;

    (b)   complete the postings to the nominal ledger; and

    (c)   prepare the accounts for approval by yourselves.

2.2 We understand that you have agreed that your staff will:

    (a)   keep the records of receipts and payments;

    (b)   reconcile the balances monthly with the bank statements;

    (c)   post and balance the purchase and sales ledgers;

    (d)   extract a detailed list of ledger balances; and

    (e)   prepare details of the annual stocktaking, suitably priced and extended in a form which will enable us to verify the prices readily by reference to supplier invoices.

or

provide us with a copy of the valuation produced by your independent stocktakers.

3 Direct taxation

3.1   We have agreed to prepare on your behalf form CT200, your corporation tax return, which is required under the Pay and File legislation. The form CT200, together with our corporation tax computations, will be sent to you for approval and signature before submission to the Inland Revenue.

3.2   We will advise you of the corporation tax payments that are due, and the due date of payment.

3.3   There are strict time limits and penalties relating to the above. In order to avoid these penalties, we will produce statutory accounts within the required period provided that all your records are complete and presented to us within four months of the year end and all subsequent queries are promptly and satisfactorily answered.

3.4   You have asked us to undertake all correspondence with the Inland Revenue on behalf of the club/association/society*. To avoid any problems would you please send to us any forms or correspondence received from the Inland Revenue as soon as you receive them. In particular, would you please ensure that no payments are made to the Inland Revenue without our approval that the demands are correct.

Payroll and year end returns

3.5   You have asked us to maintain your payroll records and to produce your year-end returns. In order to do this we will require from you the following information:

   (a)   Personal details of all employees (i.e., name, NI number, home address, etc.).
   (b)   All P45 forms received by you.
   (c)   If any casual labour is taken on, you are required to operate P46 procedures. The completed P46 form should be passed to us for processing.
   (d)   Notification within two weeks of any employee who is sick for four or more calendar days, including weekends, bank holidays, etc. This will enable us to operate statutory sick pay for you.
   (e)   Notification of any employee who becomes pregnant. This will enable us to operate statutory maternity pay.
   (f)   Details of any money or benefits made available to employees by you or by a third party through you.
   (g)   Hours worked, rates of pay, bonuses, etc.
   (h)   Notification of employees engaged by you or leaving your employment.

   and/or

P11D benefits for officers and higher paid employees

3.6   You have asked us to prepare forms P11D for approval by the officers. To ensure these forms are correctly prepared we will require details of all benefits or perks received by the officers/higher paid employees. (*Note*: A higher paid employee is someone who received (at the current level) £8,500 pa including the taxable value of benefits/perks).

3.7   There are penalties for the late submission of forms P11D. In order to avoid these, you must ensure that we receive complete and accurate details of all benefits and expenses for the tax year (NB, not accounts year) within 14 days of the end of the tax year.

   and

3.8   As detailed above we have agreed to operate your payroll/P11D* system. We can also offer you advice in the following related areas:

   • year-end returns P14/P60 and P35*;
   • casual labour P46*;
   • benefits for employees and officers*.

or

3.9 You have not asked us to become involved in your PAYE system. Should you require it we can offer advice on the operation of all aspects of wages and PAYE.

3.10 We will be pleased to advise on any other taxation matters referred to us.

4 Indirect taxation – value added tax

4.1 You have asked us to undertake the completion of the club's/ association's/society's* VAT returns. You have undertaken that you/your staff will ensure that:

(a) We receive all VAT records within 14 days of the end of the VAT return period. If this deadline cannot be met then we will not be held responsible for any default surcharges arising.

(b) Valid VAT invoices are received for all payments where VAT is being reclaimed.

(c) The VAT rating of supplies is correctly dealt with, i.e., between positive and zero rates, and exempt supplies.

(d) We are notified in writing of any standard-rated own consumption, including free drinks.

(e) Any input VAT on non-business expenditure is clearly marked on supporting invoices.

(f) We are notified each quarter of any payments to or for the benefit of officers or staff for fuel used for private mileage, together with the business mileage for each such person, for each quarter.

(g) All supplies made by the business are shown in the records made available to us.

or

4.2 You/your staff will be responsible for completing and submitting VAT returns. We will not be responsible for checking the VAT treatment of supplies made, i.e., between positive and zero rates, and exempt supplies, unless specifically requested in writing to make a detailed review. We will ensure that the sales figure in your accounts is reconciled to your VAT returns submitted provided you:

(a) let us have copies of all returns submitted; or

(b)   if you do not have access to photocopying facilities, complete our VAT return form which we will let you have on request.

Similarly, we will not specifically check the deductibility of input VAT and the validity of supporting invoices unless specifically requested in writing to carry out a detailed review.

or

4.3   At the time of this letter you are not VAT-registered. We will ensure that you do not register late for VAT provided both:

(a)   you notify us in writing within 14 days of the end of each month of the total value of supplies you have made in that month; and

(b)   you notify us immediately in writing if the value of taxable supplies that you will make in the next 30 days will exceed the annual registration limit then in force.

5 Secretarial

5.1   A club/association/society* is required to file its accounts with the Registrar of Friendly Societies within seven months of the year end. In order to avoid being late, we will produce statutory accounts, suitable for filing, within the required period, provided all your records are complete and presented to us within four months of the year end, and all subsequent queries are promptly and satisfactorily answered.

5.2   We have agreed to:

(a)   submit the accounts to the Registrar of Friendly Societies;

(b)   complete and submit the club's/association's/society's* annual return;

(c)   complete and submit any other forms required by law to be filed with the Registrar of Friendly Societies, provided that you keep us fully informed of any relevant changes or events which are required to be notified to the Registrar of Friendly Societies, within one week of the change or event.

or

5.3   You have agreed to complete all the returns required by law, for example, the annual return. We shall, of course, be pleased to advise you on these and any other secretarial matters if requested.

6 Investment business

For Category A registered firms

6.1 As an incidental part of our services to you, we may advise you on investment matters. We are authorised to carry on investment business by the Institute of Chartered Accountants in England and Wales. As such we are bound by their investment business regulations.

6.2 We may advise you about the availability, attributes and potential suitability of broad types of investments, but not about the attributes or suitability of any particular investment.

6.3 Should you require any specific investment advice, we may introduce you to an independent authorised third party (ATP). We are not authorised to advise or comment on the advice received by you from the independent ATP. You agree that we may receive and retain commission from the ATP and we will notify you of any such commission within 60 days of receipt.

or

For Category B registered firms

6.4 As an incidental part of our services to you, we may advise you on investment matters. In particular, we would be pleased to introduce you to a suitable independent authorised third party (ATP) if you wish. We are authorised to carry on investment business by the Institute of Chartered Accountants in England and Wales. As such we are bound by their investment business regulations.

6.5 We may advise you about the availability, attributes and potential suitability of broad types of investments, but not about the attributes or suitability of any particular investment.

6.6 Should you require us to assist in arranging any of your investment business with the ATP, that ATP will take full responsibility for all aspects of compliance under any regulations required by the Financial Services Act 1986. We will act solely as introducers but we may comment on any advice given by the ATP to you if you so wish. You agree that we may receive and retain commission from the ATP and we will notify you of any such commission within 60 days of receipt.

6.7 Under the Institute's investment business regulations, investment business carried on for a corporate finance client in the course of corporate finance activities is subject to a system of regulation which differs in certain material respects from that for investment business generally, so that if that client agrees to be treated as a corporate finance client he will enjoy the protection afforded to a corporate finance client rather than the protection that may be appropriate for individual investors.

6.8 We are satisfied that we may properly regard you as a corporate finance client. In the course of our corporate finance services to you, we may undertake investment business on your behalf and, further, we consider that such services are likely to be provided to you.

or

For Category C2 registered firms

6.9 As an incidental part of our services to you, we may advise you on investment matters. We are authorised to carry on investment business by the Institute of Chartered Accountants in England and Wales. As such we are bound by their investment business regulations.

6.10 Should you require us to assist in arranging any of your investment business, we will base these arrangements on our knowledge of your financial and non-financial affairs. You must ensure that we are kept fully up to date with any matters which may affect these arrangements.

6.11 Should you require us to conduct specific investment business on your behalf, such as reviewing any investment portfolio or advising on a specific investment, we will send you a separate letter of engagement.

6.12 Under the Institute's investment business regulations, investment business carried on for a corporate finance client in the course of corporate finance activities is subject to a system of regulation which differs in certain material respects from that for investment business generally, so that if that client agrees to be treated as a corporate finance client he will enjoy the protection afforded to a corporate finance client rather than the protection that may be appropriate for individual investors.

6.13 We are satisfied that we may properly regard you as a corporate finance client. In the course of our corporate finance services to you, we may undertake investment business on your behalf and further we consider that such services are likely to be provided to you.

7 Client monies

7.1 We may, from time to time, hold money on your behalf. Such money will be held in trust in a client bank account, which is segregated from the firm's funds. The account will be operated, and all funds dealt with, in accordance with the client money regulations of the Institute of Chartered Accountants in England and Wales.

and

7.2 All client monies will be held in an interest-bearing account. In order to avoid an excessive amount of administration, interest will only be paid to you where the amount earned in any calendar year exceeds £25. Subject to any tax legislation, interest will be paid gross.

or

7.3 If the total sum of money held on your behalf is such that a material amount of interest would arise, or would likely arise, then the money will be placed in an interest-bearing client bank account. All interest earned on such money will be paid to you. Subject to any tax legislation, interest will be paid gross.

8 Other services

8.1 We have agreed to . . .

8.2 However, there are many other areas where we can be of assistance and we shall be pleased to discuss any matters with you. These other services include:

    (a) reports in support of returns or claims, e.g., insurance company certificates, government claims, etc.;

    (b) advice on financial matters;

    (c) management accounting, including such matters as cash flow statements, costing systems, etc. and advice on management;

    (d) advice on the selection and implementation of computer systems;

(e) investigations for special purposes, e.g. examination of specific aspects of your business; and

(f) advice on the selection and recruitment of staff.

8.3 We enclose a copy of our booklet which explains more fully the services that we can provide.

9 Fees

9.1 Our fees, which are based upon the recommendations of the Institute of Chartered Accountants in England and Wales will take account of the degree of skill and responsibility involved and the time necessary to complete the work.

9.2 If it is necessary to carry out work outside the responsibilities outlined in this letter it will involve additional fees. Accordingly we would like to point out that it is in your interest to ensure that your records, etc. are completed to the agreed stage.

9.3 It is our normal practice to request that clients make arrangements to pay a proportion of their fee on a monthly standing order. These standing orders will be applied to fees arising from work agreed in this letter of engagement for the current and ensuing years. Once we have been able to assess the amount of work and time involved we would be grateful if you would agree to pay an amount to us on a regular basis.

9.4 Our terms relating to payment of amounts invoiced [and not covered by standing orders]† are strictly 30 days net. Prompt payment discounts may only be taken if the payment is received by us within 14 days of the date of issue of any invoice. Interest will be charged on all overdue debts at the rate stated on the invoice, which is currently .... % (APR .... %). Settlement of fees by Mastercard and Visa is accepted.

10 Quality control

As part of our ongoing commitment to providing a quality service, our files are periodically subject to an independent quality review. Our reviewers are highly experienced and professional people and, of course, are bound by the same requirements for confidentiality as our partners and staff.

11 Help us to give you the right service

If at any time you would like to discuss with us how our service to you could be improved, or if you are dissatisfied with the service you are receiving, please let us know, by telephoning .... (name).

We undertake to look into any complaint carefully and promptly, and to do all we can to explain the position to you. If we have given you a less than satisfactory service, we undertake to do everything reasonable to put it right. If you are still not satisfied, you may of course take up matters with the Institute.

12 Agreement of terms

Once it has been agreed, this letter will remain effective until it is replaced. We shall be grateful if you could confirm the contents of this letter by signing the enclosed copy and returning it to us immediately.

Yours

I/We* confirm that I/we* have read and understood the contents of this letter and agree that it accurately reflects my/our* fair understanding of the services that I/we* require you to undertake.

Signed on behalf of the committee .... Dated ....

* *delete as appropriate*
† *insert items as appropriate*

204

Specimen supplementary letter for an independent accountant's report assignment for a society registered under the Industrial and Provident Societies Act 1965.

To the officers of ....

Dear ....

We are pleased to accept this appointment as the reporting accountants for your club/association/society*.

The purpose of this letter is to set out the basis on which we are engaged as reporting accountants. This is an additional letter of engagement which is supplemental to the full letter issued to you on .... (date).

1 Accounts examination

Your duties as officers

1.1   As officers of the club/association/society*, you are required to prepare accounts for each financial year which give a true and fair view of the state of affairs of the club/association/society* and of the profit or loss of the club/association/society* for that period. In preparing those accounts, you are required to:

   - select suitable accounting policies and then apply them consistently;
   - make judgements and estimates that are reasonable and prudent; and
   - prepare the accounts on the going concern basis unless it is inappropriate to presume that the club/association/society* will continue in business.

You are responsible for keeping proper accounting records which disclose with reasonable accuracy at any time the financial position of the club/association/society* and to enable them to ensure that the accounts comply with the Friendly and Industrial and Provident Societies Act 1968 (the Act). You are also responsible for safeguarding the assets of the club/association/society* and hence for taking reasonable steps for the prevention and detection of fraud and other irregularities.

1.2 You are also responsible for determining whether, in respect of the year, the club/association/society* meets the conditions for exemption from an audit of the accounts set out in section 4A of the Act, namely:

    (a) a resolution not to have an audit has been passed at a general meeting at which:
        (i) less than 20 per cent of the total votes cast were cast against the resolution; and
        (ii) less than 10 per cent of the members of the society for the time being entitled under the society's rules to vote cast their votes against the resolution;

    (b) notice has not been received from the Registrar of Friendly Societies requiring an audit;

    (c) the society's total turnover in the preceding year is more than £90,000, but not more than £350,000 (£250,000 for charities); and

    (d) the society's balance sheet total (gross assets) for the preceding year is not more than £1.4 million.

1.3 You are also responsible for determining whether, in respect of the year, the exemption is not available for any of the reasons set out in section 4A(3) of the Act, namely that at no time during the year was the club/association/society*:

    (a) a credit union within the meaning of the Credit Unions Act 1979;

    (b) registered in the register of housing associations maintained by the Housing Corporation, Housing for Wales or Scottish Homes;

    (c) a society which is, or has, a subsidiary;

    (d) required to prepare accounts under the Insurance Accounts Directive (Miscellaneous Insurance Undertakings) Regulations 1993(a); or

    (e) a society which holds, or has, at any time since the end of the preceding year of account held a deposit within the meaning of the Banking Act 1987(b), other than a deposit in the form of withdrawable share capital.

1.4 If, in respect of the year, the club/association/society* satisfies the criteria in 1.2 and 1.3 above, the availability of the exemption from an audit of the accounts is conditional upon your causing an independent accountant's report to be prepared in respect of the accounts in accordance with section 9A(3–4) of the Act. You are responsible for deciding whether that report shall be made and for

206

appointing us as reporting accountants to make that report to the members of the club/association/society*.

1.5 If the turnover falls to £90,000 or less for the year, then, provided the other criteria set out in 1.2 and 1.3 above are met, you will not need either an audit or an independent accountant's report.

Our duties as reporting accountants

1.6 We shall plan our work on the basis that an independent accountant's report is required for the year, unless you inform us in writing that either:

(a) the club/association/society* requires an audit of the accounts; or

(b) the club/association/society* requires neither an audit nor an independent accountant's report.

1.7 Should you instruct us to carry out an audit, then that assignment will be undertaken under the terms set out in our earlier letter of engagement dated ....(date), unless a new letter is issued.

1.8 Should you inform us that the club/association/society* requires neither an audit nor an independent accountant's report, then we shall have no responsibilities to the club/association/society*, except those specifically agreed upon between us in respect of other professional services.

1.9 As reporting accountants, we have a statutory responsibility to report to the members of the club/association/society* whether in our opinion:

(a) the accounts are in agreement with those accounting records kept by the club/association/society* under section 1 of the Act;

(b) having regard only to, and on the basis of, the information contained in those accounting records, the accounts have been drawn up in a manner consistent with the accounting requirements specified in section 9A(3)(b) of the Act; and

(c) the financial criteria for the exercise of the right to forgo an audit have been met.

1.10 Should our work indicate that the club/association/society* is not entitled to exemption from an audit of the accounts, then we will inform you of this. In such circumstances, we will not issue any report and will withdraw from the engagement to prepare an independent accountant's report, and will notify you in writing of the reasons. In these circumstances, if appropriate, we will discuss with you the need to appoint us as auditors.

1.11 Our work will be carried out in accordance with the professional standards for such engagements issued by the Auditing Practices Board. It will consist of comparing the accounts with the accounting records kept by the club/association/society*, and making such limited enquiries of the officers of the club/association/society* as we may consider necessary for the purpose of our report.

1.12 As part of our normal procedures, we may request you to provide written confirmation of any information or explanations given by you orally during the course of our work.

1.13 Our work as reporting accountants will not be an audit of the accounts in accordance with auditing standards. Accordingly, we will not obtain any evidence relating to entries in the accounting records, or to the accounts or to the disclosures in the accounts. Nor will we make any assessments of the estimates and judgements made by you in the preparation of the accounts. Consequently, our work as reporting accountants will not provide any assurance that the accounting records or the accounts are free from material misstatement whether caused by fraud, irregularities or error. In addition, we have no responsibility to determine whether you have maintained proper accounting records in accordance with section 1 of the Act, and we will not address this point unless you specifically request us, in writing, to do so.

Optional paragraph where the firm prepares the accounts

Since we have not carried out an audit, nor confirmed in any way the accuracy or reasonableness of the accounting records maintained by the club/association/society*, we are unable to provide any assurance as to whether the accounts that we prepare from those records present a true and fair view.

1.14 We have a professional responsibility not to allow our name to be associated with accounts which may be misleading. Therefore, although we are not required to search for such matters, should we become aware, for any reason, that the accounts may be misleading and the matter cannot be adequately dealt with by means of qualifying our opinion (or by other appropriate modifications of the report), we will not issue any report and will withdraw from the engagement, and will notify you in writing of the reasons.

1.15 Our engagement with the club/association/society* as reporting accountants for the purpose of preparing the independent accountant's report is a statutory responsibility and is distinct and entirely separate from any obligations or responsibilities arising out of the contractual arrangements agreed between us under which we are to provide the other professional services described in our earlier letter of engagement dated .... (date).

Yours

Contents noted and agreed

Signed on behalf of the committee....................... Date ....

* *delete as appropriate*

Specimen supplementary letter for a total exemption assignment for a society registered under the Industrial and Provident Societies Act 1965

To the committee of ....

Dear ....

We are pleased to accept the appointment as the accountants for your club/association/society*.

The purpose of this letter is to set out the basis on which we are engaged as accountants. This is an additional letter of engagement which is supplemental to the full letter issued to you on ....(date).

1 Your duties as officers

1.1 As officers of the club/association/society*, you are required to prepare accounts for each financial year which give a true and fair view of the state of affairs of the club/association/society* and of the profit or loss of the club/association/society* for that period. In preparing those accounts, you are required to:

- select suitable accounting policies and then apply them consistently;
- make judgements and estimates that are reasonable and prudent; and
- prepare the accounts on the going concern basis unless it is inappropriate to presume that the club/association/society* will continue in business.

You are responsible for keeping proper accounting records which disclose, with reasonable accuracy, at any time the financial position of the club/association/society* and to enable them to ensure that the accounts comply with the Friendly and Industrial and Provident Societies Act 1968 (the Act). You are also responsible for safeguarding the assets of the club/association/society* and hence for taking reasonable steps for the prevention and detection of fraud and other irregularities.

1.2 You are also responsible for determining whether, in respect of the

210

year, the club/association/society* meets the conditions for exemption from an audit of the accounts set out in section 4A of the Act, namely:

(a) a resolution not to have an audit has been passed at a general meeting at which:
  (i) less than 20 per cent of the total votes cast were cast against the resolution; and
  (ii) less than 10 per cent of the members of the society for the time being entitled under the society's rules to vote cast their votes against the resolution;
(b) notice has not been received from the Registrar of Friendly Societies requiring an audit;
(c) the society's total turnover in the preceding year is less than £90,000; and
(d) the society's balance sheet total (gross assets) for the preceding year is not more than £1.4 million.

1.3 You are also responsible for determining whether, in respect of the year, the exemption is not available for any of the reasons set out in section 4A(3) of the Act, namely that at no time during the year was the club/association/society*:

(a) a credit union within the meaning of the Credit Unions Act 1979;
(b) registered in the register of housing associations maintained by the Housing Corporation, Housing for Wales or Scottish Homes;
(c) a society which is, or has, a subsidiary;
(d) a society which prepares accounts under the Insurance Accounts Directive (Miscellaneous Insurance Undertakings) Regulations 1993(a); or
(e) a society which holds, or has, at any time since the end of the preceding year of account held a deposit within the meaning of the Banking Act 1987(b), other than a deposit in form of withdrawable share capital.

2 Our duties as accountants

2.1 Where the club/association/society* requires neither an audit nor an independent accountant's report, then we have no statutory responsibilities to the club/association/society* at all. Our only responsibilities arise from those specifically agreed upon between us in respect of other professional services. These other services are set out in our earlier letter of engagement dated .... (date).

2.2 Should our work indicate that the club/association/society* is not entitled to exemption from an audit or an independent accountant's examination of the accounts, then we will inform you of this. In these circumstances, if appropriate, we will discuss with you the need to appoint us as auditors or reporting accountants.

2.3 Our work will not be an audit of the accounts in accordance with auditing standards. Accordingly, we will not obtain any evidence relating to entries in the accounting records, or to the accounts or to the disclosures in the accounts. Nor will we make any assessments of the estimates and judgements made by you in the preparation of the accounts. Consequently, our work will not provide any assurance that the accounting records or the accounts are free from material misstatement, whether caused by fraud, or other irregularities or error.

In addition, we have no responsibility to determine whether you have maintained proper accounting records in accordance with section 1 of the Act, and we will not address this point unless you specifically request us, in writing, to do so.

2.4 Since we have not carried out an audit, nor confirmed in any way the accuracy or reasonableness of the accounting records maintained by the club/association/society*, we are unable to provide any assurance as to whether the accounts that we prepare from those records present a true and fair view.

2.5 As part of our normal procedures when preparing the accounts, we will attach an accountants' report to them. This report will state that they have been prepared from the books and records of the club/association/society* and from information supplied by the officers. (Since we have not undertaken an audit, the report will state that we do not form an opinion or give any other form of assurance on them.)* This report should not be filed with the accounts at the Registrar of Friendly Societies.

Yours

Contents noted and agreed

Signed on behalf of the committee .... Date ....

* *delete as appropriate*

Specimen audit letter of engagement for a society registered under the Friendly Societies Act 1974

The committee of .... Limited

Dear Sirs,

We are pleased to accept the appointment as auditors of your club/association/society* and are writing to confirm the matters discussed at our meeting (with you/Mr ....) on ....

We are bound by the ethical guidelines of our professional Institute, and accept instructions to act for you on the basis that we will act in accordance with those ethical guidelines.

1 Audit

1.1 Our function as auditors under the Friendly Societies Act 1974 is to examine and report on the annual accounts of the club/association/society*. The officers are responsible for the preparation of accounts giving a true and fair view, and for the maintenance of proper accounting records and an appropriate system of internal control. You are also responsible for making available to us, as and when required, all the club's/association's/society's* accounting records and all other relevant records and related information, including minutes of all committee and members' meetings.

1.2 Our legal and professional duty is to make a report to the members stating whether in our opinion the accounts of the club/association/society* which we have audited give a true and fair view of the state of the club's/association's/society's* affairs, and of the profit or loss for the year, and whether they comply with the Friendly Societies Act 1974. In arriving at our opinion we are required by law to consider the following matters, and to report on any matters in respect of which we are not satisfied:

(a) whether proper accounting records have been kept by the club/association/society* and proper returns adequate for our audit have been received from branches not visited by us;
(b) whether the club's/association's/society's* balance sheet and profit and loss account are in agreement with the accounting records and returns;

213

(c) whether we have obtained all the information and explanations which we think necessary for the purpose of our audit.

In addition, we have a professional duty to report if the accounts do not comply in any material respect with Statements of Standard Accounting Practice or Financial Reporting Standards, unless in our opinion the non-compliance is justified in the circumstances. In determining whether or not the departure is justified we consider:

(a) whether the departure is required in order for the accounts to give a true and fair view; and
(b) whether adequate disclosure has been made concerning the departure.

Our professional responsibilities also include:

(a) including in our report a description of the officers' responsibilities for the accounts where the accounts or accompanying information do not include such description; and
(b) considering whether other information and documents contained in the audited accounts is consistent with those accounts.

1.3 Our auditing procedures will be carried out in accordance with the Statements of Auditing Standards issued by the Auditing Practices Board, and will include such tests of transactions and of the existence, ownership and valuation of assets and liabilities as we consider necessary. We will ascertain the accounting systems in order to assess their adequacy as a basis for the preparation of the accounts. We will need to obtain relevant and reliable evidence sufficient to enable us to draw reasonable conclusions therefrom.

1.4 The nature and extent of our tests will vary according to our assessment of the club's/association's/society's* accounting and internal control systems, and may cover any aspects of the business operations. We shall report to the committee any significant weaknesses in, or observations on, the club's/association's/society's* systems which come to our notice and which we think should be brought to the committee's attention. Any such report may not be provided to third parties without our prior written consent. Such consent would be granted only on the basis that such reports are not prepared for the interests of anyone other than the club/association/society* in mind and that we accept no duty or responsibility to any other party as concerns the report.

1.5 The responsibility for safeguarding the assets of the club/association/society* and for the prevention and detection of fraud, error and non-compliance with laws or regulations rests with the committee. However, we will plan our audit so that we have a reasonable expectation of detecting material misstatements in the accounts resulting from irregularities, fraud or non-compliance with law or regulations but our examination should not be relied upon to disclose all such material misstatements or frauds, errors or instances of non-compliance as may exist.

1.6 As part of our normal audit procedures, we may request you to provide formal representations concerning certain information and explanations we have received from you during the course of our audit.

1.7 In order to assist us with a review of your accounts, which constitutes part of our audit, we will request sight of any documents or statements which will be issued with the accounts. We are also entitled to attend all general meetings of the club/association/society*, and to receive notice of all such meetings.

1.8 (We appreciate that the present size of your business renders it uneconomic to create a system of internal control based on the segregation of duties for different functions within each area of the business. In the running of the business we understand that, instead, the officers are closely involved with the control of the club's/association's/society's* transactions. In planning and performing our audit work we shall take account of this supervision.)†

1.9 Once we have issued our report we have no further direct responsibility in relation to the accounts for that financial year. However, we expect that you will inform us of any material event occurring between the date of our report and that of the annual general meeting which may affect the accounts.

2 Accounting

2.1 It was agreed that we should carry out the following accounting and other services on your behalf:

(a) write up the accounting records of the club/association/society*;
(b) complete the postings to the nominal ledger; and
(c) prepare the accounts for approval by yourselves.

2.2 We understand that you have agreed that your staff will:

(a) keep the records of receipts and payments;
(b) reconcile the balances monthly with the bank statements;
(c) post and balance the purchase and sales ledgers;
(d) extract a detailed list of ledger balances; and
(e) prepare details of the annual stocktaking, suitably priced and extended in a form which will enable us to verify the prices readily by reference to suppliers' invoices.

or

provide us with a copy of the valuation produced by your independent stocktakers.

3 Direct taxation

3.1 We have agreed to prepare on your behalf form CT200, your corporation tax return, which is required under the Pay and File legislation. The form CT200, together with our corporation tax computations, will be sent to you for approval and signature before submission to the Inland Revenue.

3.2 We will advise you of the corporation tax payments that are due, and the due date of payment.

3.3 There are strict time limits and penalties relating to the above. In order to avoid these penalties, we will produce statutory accounts within the required period provided that all your records are complete and presented to us within four months of the year end and all subsequent queries are promptly and satisfactorily answered.

3.4 You have asked us to undertake all correspondence with the Inland Revenue on behalf of the club/association/society*. To avoid any problems would you please send to us any forms or correspondence received from the Inland Revenue as soon as you receive them. In particular would you please ensure that no payments are made to the Inland Revenue without our approval that the demands are correct.

Payroll and year-end returns
3.5 You have asked us to maintain your payroll records and to produce your year-end returns. In order to do this we will require from you the following information:

(a) Personal details of all employees (i.e., name, NI number, home address, etc.).
(b) All P45 forms received by you.
(c) If any casual labour is taken on you are required to operate P46 procedures. The completed P46 form should be passed to us for processing.
(d) Notification within two weeks of any employee who is sick for four or more calendar days, including weekends, bank holidays, etc. This will enable us to operate statutory sick pay for you.
(e) Notification of any employee who becomes pregnant. This will enable us to operate statutory maternity pay.
(f) Details of any money or benefits made available to employees by you or by a third party through you.
(g) Hours worked, rates of pay, bonuses, etc.
(h) Notification of employees engaged by you or leaving your employment.

and/or

P11D benefits for officers and higher paid employees

3.6 You have asked us to prepare forms P11D for approval by the officers. To ensure these forms are correctly prepared we will require details of all benefits or perks received by the officers/ higher paid employees. (*Note*: A higher paid employee is someone who received (at the current level) £8,500 pa including the taxable value of benefits/perks).

3.7 There are penalties for the late submission of forms P11D. In order to avoid these, you must ensure that we receive complete and accurate details of all benefits and expenses for the tax year (NB, not accounts year) within 14 days of the end of the tax year.

and

3.8 As detailed above we have agreed to operate your payroll/P11D* system. We can also offer you advice in the following related areas:

- year end returns P14/P60 and P35*;
- casual labour P46*;
- benefits for employees and officers*.

or

3.9 You have not asked us to become involved in your PAYE system.

217

Should you require it we can offer advice on the operation of all aspects of wages and PAYE.

3.10 We will be pleased to advise on any other taxation matters referred to us.

4 Indirect taxation – value added tax

4.1 You have asked us to undertake the completion of the club's/ association's/society's* VAT returns. You have undertaken that you/your staff will ensure that:

(a) We receive all VAT records within 14 days of the end of the VAT return period. If this deadline cannot be met then we will not be held responsible for any default surcharges arising.

(b) Valid VAT invoices are received for all payments where VAT is being reclaimed.

(c) The VAT rating of supplies is correctly dealt with, i.e., between positive and zero rates, and exempt supplies.

(d) We are notified in writing of any standard-rated own consumption, including free drinks.

(e) Any input VAT on non-business expenditure is clearly marked on supporting invoices.

(f) We are notified each quarter of any payments to or for the benefit of officers or staff for fuel used for private mileage, together with the business mileage for each such person, for each quarter.

(g) All supplies made by the business are shown in the records made available to us.

or

4.2 You/your staff will be responsible for completing and submitting VAT returns. We will not be responsible for checking the VAT treatment of supplies made, i.e., between positive and zero rates, and exempt supplies unless specifically requested in writing to make a detailed review. We will ensure that the sales figure in your accounts is reconciled to your VAT returns submitted provided you:

(a) let us have copies of all returns submitted; or

(b) if you do not have access to photocopying facilities, complete our VAT return form which we will let you have on request.

Similarly, we will not specifically check the deductibility of input

VAT and the validity of supporting invoices unless specifically requested in writing to carry out a detailed review.

or

4.3 At the time of this letter you are not VAT-registered. We will ensure that you do not register late for VAT provided both:

(a) you notify us in writing within 14 days of the end of each month of the total value of supplies you have made in that month; and

(b) you notify us immediately in writing if the value of taxable supplies that you will make in the next 30 days will exceed the annual registration limit then in force.

5 Secretarial

5.1 A club/association/society* is required to file its accounts with the Registrar of Friendly Societies by 31 July each year. In order to avoid being late, we will produce statutory accounts, suitable for filing, within the required period, provided all your records are complete and presented to us within four months of the year end, and all subsequent queries are promptly and satisfactorily answered.

5.2 We have agreed to:

(a) submit the accounts to the Registrar of Friendly Societies;

(b) complete and submit the club's/association's/society's* annual return;

(c) complete and submit any other forms required by law to be filed with the Registrar of Friendly Societies, provided that you keep us fully informed of any relevant changes or events which are required to be notified to the Registrar of Friendly Societies, within one week of the change or event.

or

5.3 You have agreed to complete all the returns required by law, for example, the annual return. We shall, of course, be pleased to advise you on these and any other secretarial matters if requested.

6 Investment business

For Category A registered firms

6.1 As an incidental part of our services to you, we may advise you on investment matters. We are authorised to carry on investment business by the Institute of Chartered Accountants in England and Wales. As such we are bound by their investment business regulations.

6.2 We may advise you about the availability, attributes and potential suitability of broad types of investments, but not about the attributes or suitability of any particular investment.

6.3 Should you require any specific investment advice, we may introduce you to an independent authorised third party (ATP). We are not authorised to advise or comment on the advice received by you from the independent ATP. You agree that we may receive and retain commission from the ATP and we will notify you of any such commission within 60 days of receipt.

or

For Category B registered firms

6.4 As an incidental part of our services to you, we may advise you on investment matters. In particular, we would be pleased to introduce you to a suitable independent authorised third party (ATP) if you wish. We are authorised to carry on investment business by the Institute of Chartered Accountants in England and Wales. As such we are bound by their investment business regulations.

6.5 We may advise you about the availability, attributes and potential suitability of broad types of investments, but not about the attributes or suitability of any particular investment.

6.6 Should you require us to assist in arranging any of your investment business with the ATP, that ATP will take full responsibility for all aspects of compliance under any regulations required by the Financial Services Act 1986. We will act solely as introducers but we may comment on any advice given by the ATP to you if you so wish. You agree that we may receive and retain commission from the ATP and will notify you of any such commission within 60 days of receipt.

6.7 Under the Institute's investment business regulations, investment business carried on for a corporate finance client in the course of corporate finance activities is subject to a system of regulation which differs in certain material respects from that for investment business generally, so that if that client agrees to be treated as a corporate finance client he will enjoy the protection afforded to a corporate finance client rather than the protection that may be appropriate for individual investors.

6.8 We are satisfied that we may properly regard you as a corporate finance client. In the course of our corporate finance services to you, we may undertake investment business on your behalf and, further, we consider that such services are likely to be provided to you.

or

For Category C2 registered firms

6.9 As an incidental part of our services to you, we may advise you on investment matters. We are authorised to carry on investment business by the Institute of Chartered Accountants in England and Wales. As such we are bound by their investment business regulations.

6.10 Should you require us to assist in arranging any of your investment business, we will base these arrangements on our knowledge of your financial and non-financial affairs. You must ensure that we are kept fully up to date with any matters which may affect these arrangements.

6.11 Should you require us to conduct specific investment business on your behalf, such as reviewing any investment portfolio or advising on a specific investment, we will send you a separate letter of engagement.

6.12 Under the Institute's investment business regulations, investment business carried on for a corporate finance client in the course of corporate finance activities is subject to a system of regulation which differs in certain material respects from that for investment business generally, so that if that client agrees to be treated as a corporate finance client he will enjoy the protection afforded to a corporate finance client rather than the protection that may be appropriate for individual investors.

6.13 We are satisfied that we may properly regard you as a corporate finance client. In the course of our corporate finance services to you, we may undertake investment business on your behalf and further we consider that such services are likely to be provided to you.

7 Client monies

7.1 We may, from time to time, hold money on your behalf. Such money will be held in trust in a client bank account, which is segregated from the firm's funds. The account will be operated, and all funds dealt with, in accordance with the client money regulations of the Institute of Chartered Accountants in England and Wales.

and

7.2 All client monies will be held in an interest-bearing account. In order to avoid an excessive amount of administration, interest will only be paid to you where the amount earned in any calendar year exceeds £25. Subject to any tax legislation, interest will be paid gross.

or

7.3 If the total sum of money held on your behalf is such that a material amount of interest would arise, or would likely arise, then the money will be placed in an interest-bearing client bank account. All interest earned on such money will be paid to you. Subject to any tax legislation, interest will be paid gross.

8 Other services

8.1 We have agreed to ...

8.2 However, there are many other areas where we can be of assistance and we shall be pleased to discuss any matters with you. These other services include:

(a) reports in support of returns or claims, e.g., insurance company certificates, government claims, etc.;
(b) advice on financial matters;
(c) management accounting, including such matters as cash flow statements, costing systems, etc. and advice on management;
(d) advice on the selection and implementation of computer systems;

(e)   investigations for special purposes, e.g., examination of specific aspects of your business; and

(f)   advice on the selection and recruitment of staff.

8.3   We enclose a copy of our booklet which explains more fully the services that we can provide.

9 Fees

9.1   Our fees, which are based upon the recommendations of the Institute of Chartered Accountants in England and Wales, will take account of the degree of skill and responsibility involved and the time necessary to complete the work.

9.2   If it is necessary to carry out work outside the responsibilities outlined in this letter it will involve additional fees. Accordingly we would like to point out that it is in your interest to ensure that your records, etc. are completed to the agreed stage.

9.3   It is our normal practice to request that clients make arrangements to pay a proportion of their fee on a monthly standing order. These standing orders will be applied to fees arising from work agreed in this letter of engagement for the current and ensuing years. Once we have been able to assess the amount of work and time involved we would be grateful if you would agree to pay an amount to us on a regular basis.

9.4   Our terms relating to payment of amounts invoiced [and not covered by standing orders]† are strictly 30 days net. Prompt payment discounts may only be taken if the payment is received by us within 14 days of the date of issue of any invoice. Interest will be charged on all overdue debts at the rate stated on the invoice, which is currently .... % (APR .... %). Settlement of fees by Mastercard and Visa is accepted.

10 Quality control

As part of our ongoing commitment to providing a quality service, our files are periodically subject to an independent quality review. Our reviewers are highly experienced and professional people and, of course, are bound by the same requirements for confidentiality as our partners and staff.

223

11 Help us to give you the right service

If at any time you would like to discuss with us how our service to you could be improved, or if you are dissatisfied with the service you are receiving, please let us know, by telephoning .... (name).

We undertake to look into any complaint carefully and promptly, and to do all we can to explain the position to you. If we have given you a less than satisfactory service, we undertake to do everything reasonable to put it right. If you are still not satisfied, you may of course take up matters with the Institute.

12 Agreement of terms

Once it has been agreed, this letter will remain effective until it is replaced. We shall be grateful if you could confirm the contents of this letter by signing the enclosed copy and returning it to us immediately.

Yours

I/We* confirm that I/we* have read and understood the contents of this letter and agree that it accurately reflects my/our* fair understanding of the services that I/we* require you to undertake.

Signed on behalf of the committee .... Dated ....

* *delete as appropriate*
† *insert items as appropriate*

Specimen supplementary letter for an independent accountant's report assignment for a society registered under the Friendly Societies Act 1974

To the officers of ....

Dear ....

We are pleased to accept this appointment as the reporting accountants for your club/association/society*.

The purpose of this letter is to set out the basis on which we are engaged as reporting accountants. This is an additional letter of engagement which is supplemental to the full letter issued to you on ....
(date).

1 Accounts examination

Your duties as officers
1.1   As officers of the club/association/society* you are required to prepare accounts for each financial year which give a true and fair view of the state of affairs of the club/association/society* and of the profit or loss of the club/association/society* for that period. In preparing those accounts, you are required to:

  • select suitable accounting policies and then apply them consistently;
  • make judgements and estimates that are reasonable and prudent; and
  • prepare the accounts on the going concern basis unless it is inappropriate to presume that the club/association/society* will continue in business.

You are responsible for keeping proper accounting records which disclose with reasonable accuracy at any time the financial position of the club/association/society* and to enable them to ensure that the accounts comply with the Friendly Societies Act 1974 (the Act). You are also responsible for safeguarding the assets of the club/association/society* and hence for taking reasonable steps for the prevention and detection of fraud and other irregularities.

1.2   You are also responsible for determining whether, in respect of the

year, the club/association/society* meets the conditions for exemption from an audit of the accounts set out in section 32A of the Act,
namely:

   (a) a resolution not to have an audit has been passed at a general
meeting at which:
- (i) less than 20 per cent of the total votes cast were cast
against the resolution; and
- (ii) less than 10 per cent of the members of the society for the
time being entitled under the society's rules to vote cast
their votes against the resolution;

   (b) notice has not been received from the Registrar of Friendly
Societies requiring an audit;

   (c) the society's total turnover in the preceding year is more than
£90,000, but not more than £350,000 (£250,000 for charities);
and

   (d) the society's balance sheet total (gross assets) for the preceding
year is not more than £1.4 million.

1.3 You are also responsible for determining whether, in respect of the
year, the exemption is not available for any of the reasons set out in
section 32A(3) of the Act, namely that at no time during the year
was the club/association/society* a society or branch which holds,
or has at any time since the end of the preceding year of account
held, a deposit within the meaning of the Banking Act 1987.

1.4 If, in respect of the year, the club/association/society* satisfies the
criteria in 1.2 and 1.3 above, the availability of the exemption from
an audit of the accounts is conditional upon your causing an
independent accountant's report to be prepared in respect of the
accounts in accordance with section 39A 3–4 of the Act. You are
responsible for deciding whether that report shall be made and for
appointing us as reporting accountants to make that report to the
members of the club/association/society*.

1.5 If the turnover falls to £90,000 or less for the year, then, provided
the other criteria set out in 1.2 and 1.3 above are met, you will not
need either an audit or an independent accountant's report.

Our duties as reporting accountants

1.6 We shall plan our work on the basis that an independent accountant's report is required for the year, unless you inform us in writing
that either:

   (a) the club/association/society* requires an audit of the
accounts; or

(b)   the club/association/society* requires neither an audit nor an independent accountant's report.

1.7   Should you instruct us to carry out an audit, then that assignment will be undertaken under the terms set out in our earlier letter of engagement dated ....(date), unless a new letter is issued.

1.8   Should you inform us that the club/association/society* requires neither an audit nor an independent accountant's report, then we shall have no responsibilities to the club/association/society*, except those specifically agreed upon between us in respect of other professional services.

1.9   As reporting accountants, we have a statutory responsibility to report to the members of the club/association/society* whether in our opinion:

(a)   the accounts are in agreement with those accounting records kept by the club/association/society* under section 29 of the Act;
(b)   having regard only to, and on the basis of, the information contained in those accounting records, the accounts have been drawn up in a manner consistent with the accounting requirements specified in section 39A(3)b of the Act; and
(c)   the financial criteria for the exercise of the right to forgo an audit have been met.

1.10 Should our work indicate that the club/association/society* is not entitled to exemption from an audit of the accounts, then we will inform you of this. In such circumstances, we will not issue any report and will withdraw from the engagement to prepare an independent accountant's report, and will notify you in writing of the reasons. In these circumstances, if appropriate, we will discuss with you the need to appoint us as auditors.

1.11 Our work will be carried out in accordance with the professional standards for such engagements issued by the Auditing Practices Board. It will consist of comparing the accounts with the accounting records kept by the club/association/society*, and making such limited enquiries of the officers of the club/association/society* as we may consider necessary for the purpose of our report.

1.12 As part of our normal procedures, we may request you to provide written confirmation of any information or explanations given by you orally during the course of our work.

1.13 Our work as reporting accountants will not be an audit of the accounts in accordance with auditing standards. Accordingly, we will not obtain any evidence relating to entries in the accounting records, or to the accounts or to the disclosures in the accounts. Nor will we make any assessments of the estimates and judgements made by you in the preparation of the accounts. Consequently, our work as reporting accountants will not provide any assurance that the accounting records or the accounts are free from material misstatement whether caused by fraud, irregularities or error. In addition, we have no responsibility to determine whether you have maintained proper accounting records in accordance with section 29 of the Act, and we will not address this point unless you specifically request us, in writing, to do so.

Optional paragraph where the firm prepares the accounts

Since we have not carried out an audit, nor confirmed in any way the accuracy or reasonableness of the accounting records maintained by the club/association/society*, we are unable to provide any assurance as to whether the accounts that we prepare from those records present a true and fair view.

1.14 We have a professional responsibility not to allow our name to be associated with accounts which may be misleading. Therefore, although we are not required to search for such matters, should we become aware, for any reason, that the accounts may be misleading and the matter cannot be adequately dealt with by means of qualifying our opinion (or by other appropriate modifications of the report), we will not issue any report and will withdraw from the engagement, and will notify you in writing of the reasons.

1.15 Our engagement with the club/association/society* as reporting accountants for the purpose of preparing the independent accountant's report is a statutory responsibility and is distinct, and entirely separate, from any obligations or responsibilities arising out of the contractual arrangements agreed between us under which we are to provide the other professional services described in our earlier letter of engagement dated .... (date).

Yours

Contents noted and agreed

Signed on behalf of the committee........................ Date ....

* *delete as appropriate*

Specimen supplementary letter for a total exemption assignment for a society registered under the Friendly Societies Act 1974

To the committee of ....

Dear ....

We are pleased to accept the appointment as the accountants for your club/association/society*.

The purpose of this letter is to set out the basis on which we are engaged as accountants. This is an additional letter of engagement which is supplemental to the full letter issued to you on .... (date).

1 Your duties as officers

1.1 As officers of the club/association/society*, you are required to prepare accounts for each financial year which give a true and fair view of the state of affairs of the club/association/society* and of the profit or loss of the club/association/society* for that period. In preparing those accounts, you are required to:

- select suitable accounting policies and then apply them consistently;
- make judgements and estimates that are reasonable and prudent; and
- prepare the accounts on the going concern basis unless it is inappropriate to presume that the club/association/society* will continue in business.

You are responsible for keeping proper accounting records which disclose with reasonable accuracy at any time the financial position of the club/association/society* and to enable them to ensure that the accounts comply with Friendly Societies Act 1974 (the Act). You are also responsible for safeguarding the assets of the club/association/society* and hence for taking reasonable steps for the prevention and detection of fraud and other irregularities.

1.2 You are also responsible for determining whether, in respect of the year, the club/association/society* meets the conditions for exemption from an audit of the accounts set out in section 32A of the Act, namely:

(a) a resolution not to have an audit has been passed at a general meeting at which:
  (i) less than 20 per cent of the total votes cast were cast against the resolution; and
  (ii) less than 10 per cent of the members of the society for the time being entitled under the society's rules to vote cast their votes against the resolution;

(b) notice has not been received from the Registrar of Friendly Societies requiring an audit;

(c) the society's total turnover in the preceding year is less than £90,000; and

(d) the society's balance sheet total (gross assets) for the preceding year is not more than £1.4 million.

1.3 You are also responsible for determining whether, in respect of the year, the exemption is not available for any of the reasons set out in section 32A(3) of the Act, namely that at no time during the year was the club/association/society* a society or branch which holds, or has at any time since the end of the preceding year of account held, a deposit within the meaning of the Banking Act 1987.

2 Our duties as accountants

2.1 Where the club/association/society* requires neither an audit nor an independent accountant's report, then we have no statutory responsibilities to the club/association/society* at all. Our only responsibilities arise from those specifically agreed upon between us in respect of other professional services. These other services are set out in our earlier letter of engagement dated .... (date).

2.2 Should our work indicate that the club/association/society* is not entitled to exemption from an audit or an independent accountant's examination of the accounts, then we will inform you of this. In these circumstances, if appropriate, we will discuss with you the need to appoint us as auditors or reporting accountants.

2.3 Our work will not be an audit of the accounts in accordance with auditing standards. Accordingly, we will not obtain any evidence relating to entries in the accounting records, or to the accounts or to the disclosures in the accounts. Nor will we make any assess- ments of the estimates and judgements made by you in the preparation of the accounts. Consequently, our work will not provide any assurance that the accounting records or the accounts are free from material misstatement, whether caused by fraud, or other irregularities or error.

In addition, we have no responsibility to determine whether you have maintained proper accounting records in accordance with section 29 of the Act, and we will not address this point unless you specifically request us, in writing, to do so.

2.4 Since we have not carried out an audit, nor confirmed in any way the accuracy or reasonableness of the accounting records maintained by the club/association/society*, we are unable to provide any assurance as to whether the accounts that we prepare from those records present a true and fair view.

2.5 As part of our normal procedures when preparing the accounts, we will attach an accountant's report to them. This report will state that they have been prepared from the books and records of the club/association/society* and from information supplied by the officers. (Since we have not undertaken an audit, the report will state that we do not form an opinion or give any other form of assurance on them.)* This report should not be filed with the accounts at the Registrar of Friendly Societies.

Yours

Contents noted and agreed

Signed on behalf of the committee .... Date ....

* *delete as appropriate*

Appendix 4 – Specialist programmes and forms

The attached programmes and forms should be used as a substitute for standard programmes and forms in the areas where a tailored, specialist programme or form is required, i.e.:

1 Planning

    (a)   Professional independence questionnaire
    (b)   Analytical review form
    (c)   Systems overview form

2 Completion

    (a)   Partner completion form
    (b)   Critical review of accounts questionnaire
    (c)   Justification of audit report form

3 Tailored programmes

    (a)   Stock (where a professional valuer is used)
    (b)   Capital, reserves and statutory records
    (c)   Profit and loss account – income

4 Permanent File

    (a)   Index
    (b)   Background information
    (c)   New client checklist

Client:		Prepared by:	Date:	**Ref:**
Year/period end:	File no.:	Reviewed by:	Date:	

Professional independence questionnaire

Regulations state that 'a Registered Auditor shall not accept appointment or continue as auditor if the firm has any interest likely to conflict with the proper conduct of the audit'. This questionnaire shall be completed annually for all clients to ensure that the regulations have been complied with.

YES   NO

1 Undue dependence on an audit client

Do the total fees for this client/group of clients exceed:

(a)   10 per cent* of gross practice income? ☐ ☐
(b)   15 per cent* of the partner's gross income? ☐ ☐

Is this client/group of clients highly prestigious? ☐ ☐

*(a) becomes 5 per cent and (b) becomes 10 per cent for listed or public interest audits.

2 Loans to or from a client; guarantees; overdue fees

(a)   Do you or any of your staff have any loans or guarantees to or from the client? ☐ ☐
(b)   Does the client have significant overdue fees? ☐ ☐

3 Goods and services: hospitality

Have you or any of your staff accepted any material goods or services on favourable terms or received undue hospitality from the society? ☐ ☐

4 Litigation

Is there any actual or threatened litigation between yourself and the client in relation to fees, audit work or other work? ☐ ☐

	YES	NO

5 Family or other personal relationships

Do you or any of your staff have any personal or
family connections with the society and its officers?   ☐ ☐

6 Ex-partners and employees

(a) Has any officer of the society been a partner
or senior employee in the practice?   ☐ ☐

(b) Is the partner or any senior employee on the
audit joining or involved in substantive
negotiations with the client?   ☐ ☐

(c) Are any employees either officers or servants
of the society?   ☐ ☐ *

7 Mutual business interest

Do you have any mutual business interests with the
client or with an officer or employee of the client?   ☐ ☐

8 Beneficial interests in shares, other investment, trusts and trusteeships

Do you or any of your staff have any financial
involvement in the society in respect of the
following:

(a) Any beneficial interest in shares or other
investments?   ☐ ☐

(b) Any beneficial interests in trusts?   ☐ ☐

(c) Any trustee investments, nominee shareholdings
or 'bare trustee' shareholdings?   ☐ ☐

9 Associated firms

Are you or your staff associated with any other
practice or organisation which has any dealings
with the society?   ☐ ☐

---

* Where a 'yes' answer is given to this question the practice is precluded from acting for the society by virtue of s8(1) Friendly and Industrial and Provident Societies Act 1968 or s37(1) of the Friendly Societies Act 1974.

YES   NO

10 Provision of other services, specialist valuations and advocacy

(a)   Are any services in relation to the management of the society performed by the firm? ☐ ☐

(b)   Where the firm prepares the society's accounting records, is there any reason why the client will not accept responsibility for the records as his own? ☐ ☐

(c)   Do the accounts include any specialist valuations carried out by the firm or an associated firm? ☐ ☐

(d)   Are you currently acting for the client as an advocate in any adversarial proceeding or situation? ☐ ☐

11 Rotation of audit engagement partner

Have you been acting as the audit engagement partner for more than seven years? ☐ ☐

12 Adequate resources

Are there any problems over adequately staffing the audit with employees with the necessary expertise? ☐ ☐

13 Proper performance

Are there any aspects of the client, or other factors, that will adversely affect the firm's ability to perform the audit properly? ☐ ☐

Conclusion

Where any of the above questions have been answered 'yes', specify what action is proposed to be taken to maintain independence, and to ensure the availability of resources and the ability to perform the audit properly.

Having regard to any safeguards identified above, in my opinion independence is maintained, we have adequate resources and the ability to perform the audit properly.

Partner .... Date ....

Consultation (to be completed where appropriate)

In my opinion the steps proposed are sufficient to maintain independence and to ensure the availability of resources and the ability to perform the audit properly.

Second Partner .... Date ....

| Client: | | Prepared by: | Date: | **Ref:** |
| Year/period end: | File no.: | Reviewed by: | Date: | |

Analytical review form

	This year final £	This year draft £	Last year £	19.... £	Ref to comments
A Bar sales					
B Cost of goods sold					
C Gross profit (A−B)					
D Fruit machine income					
E Other income*					
F Salaries & wages					
G Interest payable					
H Other expenses					
I Net profit					
J Stock					
K Debtors & prepayments					
L Short-term investments					
M Cash at bank/in hand					
N Trade creditors					
O Other short-term liabilities					
P Total current assets					
Q Total current liabilities					
Gross profit (%) (C/A ×100%)					
Fruit machine contribution (%) (D / (C+D+E) × 100%)					
Gross profit contribution (%) (C / (C+D+E) × 100%)					
Other income contribution (%)* (E / (C+D+E) × 100%)					
Net profit % (I/(A+D+E) × 100%)					
Creditors' settlement (N/B × 365)					
Stock turnover (B/J)					
Liquidity current ratio (P/Q)					
Liquidity quick ratio ((P− J)/Q)					

* If there are other material income streams, then these should be shown separately.

Client:		Prepared by:	Date:	**Ref:**
Year/period end:	File no.:	Reviewed by:	Date:	

Systems overview form

Objective: To ascertain the society's system of recording and processing transactions and to assess its adequacy as a basis for the preparation of the accounts.

1 Accounting records

Estimated transactions for whole year

unless specified tick as appropriate	Manual	Computerised	Prepared by us	Volume	Value
(a) Record of income (specify):				.........Number of entries..........	
(b) Cash receipts book				.........Number of entries..........	
(c) Purchase day book				.........Number of invoices........	
(d) Cash payments book				.........Number of entries	
(e) Purchase ledger				.........Number of accounts.......	
(f) Petty cash book				.........Number of entries..........	
(g) Fixed asset register				.........Number of assets...........	
(h) Payroll				........Number of employees.....	
(i) Nominal ledger					
(j) Management accounts				Frequency:	
(k) Financial statements					
(l) Other (specify):					

2 Sales system
(Detail below the categories of income received and how a sale is first recorded.)

3 Purchases system
(Detail below the way a liability is first recognised.)

4 Details of computer system

Conclusion   **Initials**

1 The above notes are an adequate record of the client's systems*.
  The above systems require further documentation which is
  filed on ....*   ....

2 These systems do/do not* provide a reliable basis for the
  preparation of statutory accounts (only when supplemented by
  our own accounts preparation work)*.   ....

* *delete as appropriate*   Date: ....

Client:		Prepared by:	Date:	**Ref:**
Year/period end:	File no.:	Reviewed by:	Date:	

Partner completion form

Final

Initials

1 Have all outstanding items been adequately
dealt with? · Yes/N/A* · · · · · · · · · · ·

2 Has a signed letter of representation been
received? · Yes · · · · · · · · · · ·

3 Where the letter of representation is signed
by one member of the committee on behalf
of the committee, have we seen minutes of
a meeting agreeing its contents? · · · · · · · · · · · · · · Yes/N/A* · · · · · · · · · · ·

4 Are we satisfied that the committee's
representations can be relied upon? · · · · · · · · · · · · · · · · · Yes · · · · · · · · · · ·

5 Does the file contain adequate justification
of the audit report? · Yes · · · · · · · · · · ·

6 Has a letter of comment covering all material
weaknesses in the system been sent to the client? · · · Yes/N/A* · · · · · · · · · · ·

7 Has a final post balance sheet events
review been completed? · Yes/NCN†* · · · · · · · · · · ·

8 Does the balance sheet state the name of the
officer(s) who has/have approved the accounts
on behalf of the committee, together with the
date of approval? · Yes · · · · · · · · · · ·

9 Do the working papers and the tax
computation reflect final adjustments? · · · · · · · · · · · · · · · Yes · · · · · · · · · · ·

10 Have all final journals been recorded and
processed to produce a closing trial balance
agreeing with the accounts? · Yes · · · · · · · · · · ·

11 Has the final copy of the accounts been
referenced to the file to ensure all lead and
supporting schedules reflect final adjustments? · · · · · Yes · · · · · · · · · · ·

I authorise the signing of the audit report.

Signed .... Partner   Date ....

Second partner (if applicable)

Signed .... Partner   Date ....

* *delete as appropriate*
† *NCN = not considered necessary*

Client:		Prepared by:	Date:	**Ref:**
Year/period end:	File no.:	Reviewed by:	Date:	

Critical review of accounts questionnaire

	Comments	Initials	WP ref
1 Review accounting policies to determine whether they: (a) comply with SSAPs, FRSs or, in their absence, are otherwise acceptable; (b) are consistent with those of the previous period; (c) are consistently applied to all like transactions; (d) are appropriate to the nature of the client's business; (e) are disclosed in accordance with the requirements of SSAP 2.			
2 Carry out an overall review of the information in the accounts and compare it with other available data, including final analytical review. Note significant variations and obtain explanations thereto.			
3 Consider whether the accounts adequately reflect: (a) the substance of underlying transactions and balances and not merely their form; (b) the information and explanations obtained and conclusions reached on particular aspects of the audit; (c) the proper application of the four fundamental accounting concepts. Schedule points of interest on 'audit highlights'.			
4 Consider whether the review reveals any new factors which may affect the presentation of information or disclosures in the accounts.			
5 Review the accounts for proper preparation in accordance with the Friendly and Industrial and Provident Societies Act 1968/Friendly Societies Act 1974*, SSAPs, FRSs and other disclosure requirements. State whether or not a disclosure checklist has been completed in respect of the current year. If not completed in current year, state year in which it was last completed.	Yes/No*		
6 Consider whether the information contained in the committee's report (if prepared) and any other document issued with the accounts is consistent with the accounting information in the accounts, and has not been unduly influenced by the committee's desire to present matters in a favourable or unfavourable light.			

241

Conclusion

1 I have compared the ratios of the final accounts with those of the preliminary/extensive* analytical review.

2 (a) I have obtained, recorded and corroborated explanations for significant fluctuations for principal areas of the accounts.*
   or
   (b) There were no significant fluctuations requiring explanation*.

3 The committee's report and other published information is consistent with the accounts.

I am satisfied from this critical review that the accounts appear credible and have been properly prepared in accordance with the Friendly and Industrial and Provident Societies Act 1968/Friendly Societies Act 1974*.

Prepared by _____ Date _____

Reviewed by _____ Date _____

* *delete as appropriate*

Client:		Prepared by:	Date:	**Ref:**
Year/period end:	File no.:	Reviewed by:	Date:	

Justification of audit report form

This form should be used to schedule any problems encountered during the audit which could have an impact on the audit report.

---

1 Was the audit report qualified in the previous period?   Yes/No*

  If yes, give details:

---

2 Have there been any problems with books and records?   Yes/No*

  If yes, specify:

---

3 Have you encountered problems obtaining from the officers all
information and explanations necessary for the audit?   Yes/No*

  If yes, specify:

---

4 Are there any problems with going concern?   Yes/No*

---

5 Have any other problems occurred which could have an impact on the
audit report?   Yes/No*

  If yes, specify:

Conclusion

Where there are any 'yes' answers, detail below what effect they will have on the audit report.

I am satisfied that an unqualified report is appropriate*

or

In my opinion, the attached fundamental uncertainty and/or qualification is appropriate*

Prepared by   _____   _____ Date
Reviewed by   _____   _____ Date

* *delete as appropriate*

Client:		Prepared by:	Date:	**Ref:**
Year/period end:	File no.:	Reviewed by:	Date:	

Audit programme – stock

Nature of test:	*Test required Y/N*	*Covered by accountancy Y/N*	*Results satisfactory Y/N*	*Ref/ comments*	*Signature and date*
1 (a) Agree opening balances to last year's accounts.					
(b) Obtain and check, or prepare, a lead schedule for the current year's figures.					
(c) Enquire into and make notes of reasons for any major variations from expectations.					
2 Assess whether the initial materiality and/or risk assessment should be revised in view of the audit evidence obtained to date.					
3 (a) Obtain and analyse stock reports for the period.					
(b) Scrutinise and obtain explanations for any major variances from expectations.					
4 Trace a sample of deliveries around the year end to the stock reports to ensure cut-off has been applied correctly.					
5 Reconcile total bar takings per cash book to the stock reports.					
6 Ensure that all free drinks and other allowances have been treated correctly.					
7 Consider the reasonableness of allowances given for ullage and other waste – can these be justified?					
8 Investigate any material deficits or surpluses.					

Nature of test	*Test required Y/N*	*Covered by accountancy Y/N*	*Results satisfactory Y/N*	*Ref/ comments*	*Signature and date*
9 Check a sample of prices to brewers' invoices to ensure stock is correctly priced.					
10 Check a sample of selling prices to ensure that sales have been calculated correctly.					
11 Scrutinise brewers' delivery notes, invoices and statements for evidence of free goods and/or deliveries which have not been entered by the stocktaker.					
12 Consider the gross profit percentage per the stock reports in light of the final accounts, comment on any variances (these may be due to discounts).					
13 Where the stock is taken other than on the year-end date reconcile to the year-end balance.					
14 Consider whether there are any points which need to be included in a letter of representation or letter of comment.					

Client:		Prepared by:	Date:	**Ref:**
Year/period end:	File no.:	Reviewed by:	Date:	

Audit programme – capital reserves and statutory records

Nature of test	*Test required Y/N*	*Covered by accountancy Y/N*	*Results satisfactory Y/N*	*Ref/ comments*	*Signature and date*
1 Schedule all movements in reserves.					
(a) Ensure that transfers between reserves are correctly treated and authorised.					
(b) Ensure that the treatment in the accounts is correct.					
2 Review minutes of meetings and ensure that all relevant points are noted and cross-referenced to the relevant section of the file.					
3 Prepare a reconciliation of members, cross-referencing to the accounts subscription income and the members' register.*					
4 Consider whether there are any points which need to be included in a letter of representation or letter of comment.					

* For Industrial and Provident Societies only.

| Client: | | | Prepared by: | Date: | **Ref:** |
| Year/period end: | | File no.: | Reviewed by: | Date: | |

Audit programme – profit and loss account – income

Nature of test	*Test required Y/N*	*Covered by accountancy Y/N*	*Results satisfactory Y/N*	*Ref/ comments*	*Signature and date*
1 Assess whether the initial materiality and/or risk assessment should be revised in view of the audit evidence obtained to date.					
2 Ascertain details of all types of income received by the club and the method of recording. Consider whether the records are likely to be sufficient to satisfy the requirements of the Act to maintain proper books and records.					
3 Carry out audit work on all material sources of income as follows:					
Bar takings (a) Reconcile bar takings to the stock reports for the year (see stock section).					
(b) Select a sample of till rolls and: (i) Agree daily readings to the bar takings books/ sheets.					
(ii) Ensure that explanations are received/ recorded for variations between the actual cash and till readings.					
(iii) Review the till rolls for unusual items, e.g., excessive no sales.					
(iv) Ensure the transaction numbers follow on from day to day/roll to roll.					

247

	Test required Y/N	Covered by accountancy Y/N	Results satisfactory Y/N	Ref/ comments	Signature and date
Gaming machine income					
(a) Where possible check the income recorded to the machine reading, consider whether the explanations for any variances are adequate.					
(b) Ensure the emptying procedures laid down by the club have been properly followed, e.g., make sure it is not the same people emptying the machines each week.					
(c) Carry out analytical review, considering whether the income levels appear reasonable – ensure there are adequate explanations for variances.					
Subscriptions					
(a) Obtain total membership (split between full, OAPs, ladies and any other subscription class) and calculate the level of subscription earned. Reconcile this to actual receipts.					
Bingo and tote					
(a) Select a sample and check sales to the record books, if material.					
(b) Ensure there is income recorded on all relevant nights.					
(c) Ascertain level of prizes and consider whether the relationship between income and prize money is reasonable.					
Raffles					
(a) Select a sample and check income recorded to the record of tickets sold, if material.					
Door money					
(a) Select a sample and check the receipts per the cash book to the record of sales of door tickets, if material.					

	Test required *Y/N*	Covered by accountancy *Y/N*	Results satisfactory *Y/N*	Ref/ comments	Signature and date
Pool, snooker, billiards and juke box (if material) (a) Check meter reading to record of receipts, where available, consider whether the explanations for any variances are adequate.					
(b) Ensure the emptying procedures, laid down by the club, are properly followed.					
(c) Carry out analytical review, considering whether the income levels appear reasonable – ensure there are adequate explanations for variances.					
(d) Where the machines are not owned by the club, check the receipts received from the owner and ensure income has been recorded for the full period. Make sure the VAT has been accounted for correctly.					
Other income (a) For all other material forms of income, ascertain the procedure for recording, consider its adequacy and check to supporting documentation.					
4 Check to ensure that all cash is banked regularly.					
5 Conclude on whether the records of income presented for audit are adequate to satisfy the requirements to maintain proper books and records.					

Client:		Prepared by:	Date:	**Ref:**
Year/period end:	File no.:	Reviewed by:	Date:	

Permanent audit file index

1 General information
1.1 Background information ☐
1.2 Details of bankers and professional advisers ☐
1.3 Nature of business ☐
1.4 Register of laws and regulations ☐
1.5 ☐

2 Engagement details
2.1 Letter of engagement ☐
2.2 Authorisations ☐
2.3 Special instructions from client ☐
2.4 Copy of resolution re appointment ☐
2.5 New client acceptance form ☐
2.6 ☐

3 Accounting systems
3.1 Organisation chart ☐
3.2 List of books in use ☐
3.3 Notes of systems ☐
3.4 Letters of comment (copies) ☐
3.5 Details of computerisation ☐
3.6 ☐

4 Statutory information
4.1 List of members/trustees ☐
4.2 Details of mortgages/charges ☐
4.3 Copy annual return ☐
4.4 Rules ☐
4.5 ☐

5 Taxation (if no separate tax permanent file)
5.1 Direct tax elections ☐
5.2 Indirect tax elections and certificates ☐
5.3 Market values 6 April 1965 and 31 March 1982 ☐
5.4 PAYE dispensations ☐
5.5 Relief claims (e.g., rollover, ABA) ☐
5.6 ☐

6 Assets
6.1 Details of freehold/leasehold properties ☐
6.2 Details of location of title deeds ☐

6.3 Details of plant, etc. (where no fixed asset register exists) ☐
6.4 Details of intangible assets ☐
6.5 Details of professional valuations ☐
6.6 Details of insurance values and cover ☐
6.7 ☐

7 Contracts and agreements
7.1 Details of contracts and agreements with index ☐
7.2 Details of share options ☐
7.3 Bank overdraft or loan facilities, security and covenants ☐
7.4 Details of other loans ☐
7.5 ☐

8 Correspondence and information of continuing interest
8.1 Index ☐

9 Accounts
9.1 Signed copies of full accounts ☐
9.2 Accounts disclosure checklist ☐
9.3 ☐

10 Review

Year	*File updated by*	*Reviewed by*

Client:		Prepared by:	Date:	
Year/period end:	File no.:	Reviewed by:	Date:	

Background information

Exact name of society _____

Trading name (if different) _____

Registered office   Main place of business (if different)

_____   _____

_____   _____

_____   _____

Tel. No. _____   Tel No. _____

Fax No. _____   Fax No. _____

Number of business locations _____

Registered number _____

Place of registration _____

Date of incorporation _____

VAT registration number _____   Return periods _____

Year end date _____

Associated business   Yes/No   Specify _____

                                                          _____

Names of officer/secretary	*Date of birth*	*Specific responsibilities*

Other key personnel:

_____   _____

_____   _____

_____   _____

Money laundering requirements
Specify the basis and/or documents on which you have determined that this is a bona-fide business operation:

_____

_____

_____

Client:		Prepared by:	Date:	
Year/period end:	File no.:	Reviewed by:	Date:	

New client checklist

Pre-interview

		Yes	No	N/A	Initials
1	Are we satisfied that we are independent and are likely to have adequate resources and knowledge to complete the audit?	☐	☐		
2	Are we satisfied that the acceptance of the appointment would not have an adverse effect on the reputation of the practice?	☐	☐		
3	Are we satisfied that acceptance of the engagement will not create any conflict of interest with existing clients?	☐	☐		

Points for interview

1	Have we identified which marketing source gave rise to the new client?	☐	☐	☐	
2	Name of previous accountant obtained?	☐	☐	☐	
3	Section 1 of permanent file completed?	☐	☐	☐	
4	Have we requested details/copies of the items below?				
	● Rules	☐	☐	☐	
	● Last annual return	☐	☐	☐	
	● Books and records	☐	☐	☐	
	● Organisation chart	☐	☐	☐	
	● Last set of accounts	☐	☐	☐	
	● Fixed asset register	☐	☐	☐	
	● Last set of P11Ds	☐	☐	☐	
	● Last CT200	☐	☐	☐	
	● Specific proof of identity	☐	☐		
5	Has the client signed or agreed to sign the necessary authorisations?				
	● Tax 64/8	☐	☐	☐	
	● Bank authority	☐	☐	☐	
	● Building society authority	☐	☐	☐	
	● Other (specify)	☐	☐	☐	

	Yes	No	N/A	Initials

Office procedures

1 Have we written to the previous accountants for all necessary information? ☐ ☐ ☐

2 Have we written for references/information from other sources? (Specify) ☐ ☐ ☐

3 Have we sent an engagement letter covering the following?:

- Audit ☐ ☐ ☐
- Accounts preparation ☐ ☐ ☐
- Corporate tax work ☐ ☐ ☐
- PAYE ☐ ☐ ☐
- P11Ds ☐ ☐ ☐
- VAT ☐ ☐ ☐
- Secretarial ☐ ☐ ☐
- Investment business ☐ ☐ ☐
- Client money rules ☐ ☐ ☐
- Other services (specify) ☐ ☐ ☐
- Complaints procedures ☐ ☐ ☐
- Fees ☐ ☐ ☐
- Quality control ☐ ☐ ☐

4 Have any necessary tax elections been prepared and submitted? ☐ ☐ ☐

5 Have we notified the Inland Revenue and requested a copy of the last CT200 if not otherwise available? ☐ ☐ ☐

6 Have we completed form CT41G and forwarded it to the Inland Revenue? ☐ ☐ ☐

7 Have the necessary files been opened? ☐ ☐ ☐

8 Have the client's details been entered on to the time records? ☐ ☐ ☐

Appendix 5 – Letters of representation

During the course of an assignment the accountant/auditor is likely to obtain representations which he wishes to rely upon. These may be received from the secretary and other members of the committee. Where this is the case, a letter of representation should be sent to the committee to confirm the representations made.

There are three documents in the appendix:

(a)   a letter of representation for use where an audit has taken place;
(b)   a letter of representation for use on an independent accountant's report assignment or total exemption assignment; and
(c)   a committee meeting minute adopting the contents of the letter.

Specimen letter of representation for an audit

(Practice letterhead)   (Date)

Dear Sirs

During the course of the audit of your accounts for the period ending ...., the following representations were made to us by the officers. Please read these representations carefully and if you agree with our understanding, please sign and return a copy of this letter to ourselves as confirmation of this.

Representations

1   You acknowledged as officers your responsibility for making accurate representations to ourselves and for the accounts which we have prepared for the club/association*.

2   You confirmed that all accounting records had been made available to ourselves for the purpose of our audit and that all the transactions undertaken by the club/association* had been properly reflected and recorded in the accounting records. All other records and related information, including minutes of all committee and members' meetings, had been made available to ourselves.

3   You confirmed that the club/association* had no liabilities or contingent liabilities other than those disclosed in the accounts.

4   You confirmed that there had been no events since the balance sheet date which required disclosing or which would materially affect the amounts in the accounts, other than those already disclosed or included in the accounts.

5   You confirmed that the club/association* has not contracted for nor authorised any capital expenditure other than as disclosed in the accounts.

6   You confirmed that there are no laws or regulations that are central to the club's/association's ability to conduct its business.

or

You confirmed that there has been no possible or actual instance of non-compliance with those laws and regulations which provide a legal framework within which the entity conducts its business and which are central to the entity's ability to conduct its business, namely .... (specify relevant rules and regulations†), except as explained to ourselves and as disclosed in the accounts.

7   You confirmed that in your opinion the society will continue trading as a going concern.

or

You confirmed that adequate disclosure has been made in the notes to the accounts in respect of the society's ability to continue as a going concern.

8   You confirmed the following specific representations made to us during the course of your audit, relating to .... (include here any items identified on the audit file).

Yours faithfully

We confirm that we have read and understood the contents of this letter and agree that it accurately reflects the representations made to you by the officers during the course of the audit.

.... Committee Member .... Date

.... Secretary

Signed on behalf of the committee

---

* *delete as appropriate*
† *including, for example, the Licensing Act*

Letter of representation for an independent examination or total exemption assignment

(Practice letterhead) (Date)

Dear Sirs

During the course of our assignment for the period ending ...., the following representations were made to us by the officers. Please read these representations carefully and if you agree with our understanding, please sign and return a copy of this letter to ourselves as confirmation of this.

1   You acknowledged as officers your responsibility for the accounts, which we have prepared for the club/association*/ you prepared*. All the accounting records have been made available to us for the purpose of our review and all the transactions undertaken by the club/association* have been properly reflected and recorded in the accounting records.

2   You confirmed that there have been no changes in the accounting policies other than those disclosed in the accounts. In your opinion, the accounting policies are appropriate to the club/association* and conform with generally accepted accounting principles. You confirmed that all transactions and balances have been accounted for in accordance with these accounting policies.

3   You confirmed that all assets have been included in the balance sheet.

4   You confirmed that all assets included in the balance sheet exist.

5   You confirmed that the club/association* owns all the assets included in the balance sheet, unless otherwise stated in the accounts.

6   You confirmed that the cost (or value) of all the assets in the balance sheet are fairly stated.

7   You confirmed that depreciation has been provided on all fixed assets with a limited economic life in accordance with the stated accounting policy. In your opinion, the rates of depreciation are reasonable.

8   You confirmed that all liabilities have been fully recorded in the balance sheet.

9 You confirmed that all liabilities recorded in the balance sheet are properly those of the club/association*.

10 You confirmed that all liabilities have been recorded at a fair value.

11 You confirmed that there has been no netting off of assets and liabilities.

12 You confirmed that all turnover has been fully recorded and correctly classified.

13 You confirmed the specific representations made to us during the course of the review, relating to .... (include here any items identified on the file.)

Additional paragraphs where it is an accounts preparation assignment:

14 You confirmed that the club/association* has no contingent liabilities other than those disclosed in the accounts.

15 You confirmed that there has been no event since the balance sheet date which requires disclosing or which would materially affect the amounts in the accounts, other than those already disclosed or included in the accounts.

16 You confirmed that the club/association* has not contracted for, nor authorised any capital expenditure other than as disclosed in the accounts.

Yours faithfully

We confirm that we have read and understood the contents of this letter and agree that it accurately reflects the representations made to you by the officers during the course of the assignment.

.... Committee Member .... Date

.... Secretary

Signed on behalf of the committee

* *delete as appropriate*

Specimen minute of committee meeting to approve contents of letter of representation

Minutes of the meeting of the committee held at ....
(place) on .... (date) at .... (time).

Present: ....

....

....

....

The committee read the letter of representation sent by the auditors/
independent accountant*, ... (insert name).
The contents were agreed and the chairman and secretary were
authorised to sign the letter on behalf of the committee.

There being no other business, the chairman declared the meeting
closed.

....

Chairman   Secretary

* *delete as appropriate*

Appendix 6 – Promoting bodies

The Working Men's Club and Institute Union Limited

The Working Men's Club and Institute Union is a non-political federation of over 3,000 clubs registered as Industrial and Provident or Friendly Societies.

The Union is neutral on matters of politics and religion, and is open for membership to any bona fide club. There are a number of benefits of membership, which include:

(a) advocacy and defence of clubs in any legislative and other public matters;
(b) the provision of legal and other advice for clubs;
(c) the provision of convalescent homes;
(d) indoor and outdoor competitions;
(e) admission to other union clubs under reciprocal conditions.

The Working Men's Club and Institute Union Limited can be found at:

Club Union House
251–256 Upper Street
London N1 1RY.

The Royal British Legion

Clubs which affiliate to the Royal British Legion can take advantage of many of the same facilities available to those which affiliate to the Working Men's Club and Institute Union. This will include, for example, reciprocal arrangements so that members of other clubs will be entitled to use the facilities of most clubs registered with the Royal British Legion. In order to register with the Royal British Legion the club has to satisfy certain other conditions, including all members of the club being members of the Royal British Legion. In addition, the club and its members have to agree to do everything possible to further the aims, objects, principles and policy of the Royal British Legion.

For clubs that are affiliated with the Royal British Legion in addition to completing any annual return which needs to be filed with the Registry of Friendly Societies, they also have to complete an annual application for renewal of the Royal British Legion Club licence. Further information can be obtained from the Royal British Legion at:

Royal British Legion.
48 Pall Mall
London SW1Y 5JY.

The Association of Conservative Clubs

The Association of Conservative clubs was set up to advise clubs on how to get started and provide them with assistance in running the clubs, both on legal and practical matters. They have a similar affiliation agreement to the other organisations allowing members to enter any club. They also administer a club development fund, which lends money to establish and develop club premises, along with a number of other endeavours to support such an organisation. Further details can be obtained from:

The Association of Conservative Clubs
32 Smith Square
London SW1P 3HH.

Other promoting bodies

The preceding bodies are the ones that will probably be most relevant to the users of this book, but below there is a list of other bodies dealing with other types of society registered under the Industrial and Provident Societies Act 1965 or the Friendly Societies Act 1974 which may from time to time be useful.

The Community Transport Association

Providing advice, information, training, etc. to transport firms. This can be found at:

The Community Transport Association
Highbank
Holton Street
Hyde
Cheshire SK14 2NY.

The Co-operative Union

This Union unifies a large number of retail societies and also other co-operative organisations in areas such as national policy representation and collective protection. It also provides members with a number of important professional services. The Union can be found at:

The Co-operative Union
Holy Oake House
Hanover Street
Manchester
M60 0AS.

ICOM (The National Federation of Worker Co-operatives)

In addition to providing the model rules for all types of co-operative community enterprises, it also provides advice on structure, helping organisations to obtain charitable status, etc. ICOM can be found at:

Bassalli House
20 Central Road
Leeds LS1 6DE.

The National Federation of Community Organisations

The purpose of the coalition is to increase recognition and support for community groups, and for the national organisations which support and service such groups. The address is:

The National Federation of Community Organisations
8–9 Upper Street
London N1 0PQ.

The National Federation of Women's Institutes

The purpose of the Institute is to provide a democratic, social and educational organisation for women, providing the opportunity of working and learning together to improve the quality of life in the community, particularly in rural areas, and to enable them to develop their own skills and talents. The address is:

The National Federation of Women's Institutes
104 New Kings Road
London SW6 4LY.

The National Society of Allotment and Leisure Gardeners Limited

The society provides help in both legal and practical areas. The address is:

The National Society of Allotment and Leisure Gardeners Limited
O'Dell House
Hunters Road
Corby
Northants NN17 1JE.

The Scottish Agricultural Organisation Limited

The purpose of SAO is to strengthen the profitability of farming and other rural industries in Scotland by supporting and developing co-operation and co-operatively organised businesses. The address is:

The Scottish Agricultural Organisation Limited
Rural Centre
West Maines
Ingliston
Mid Lothian EH28 8NZ.

Village Retail Services Association

This organisation has been set up to support local village shops. The address is:

Village Retail Services Association
Halstock
Yeovil
Somerset BA22 9QY.

264

Index

The following abbreviations have been used: F, I & P Act 68 (Friendly and Industrial and Provident Societies Act 1968); FSA 74 (Friendly Societies Act 1974); IPSA 65 (Industrial and Provident Societies Act 1965).